Be A Better Reader

EIGHTH EDITION

NILA BANTON SMITH

PEARSON

Pronunciation Key

Symbol	Key Word	Respelling	Symbol	Key Word	Respelling
a	act	(akt)	u	book	(buk)
ah	star	(stahr)		put	(put)
ai	dare	(dair)	uh	cup	(kuhp)
aw	also	(AWL soh)	ə	a *as in*	
ay	flavor	(FLAY vər)		along	(ə LAWNG)
e	end	(end)		e *as in*	
ee	eat	(eet)		moment	(MOH mənt)
er	learn	(lern)		i *as in*	
	sir	(ser)		modify	(MAHD ə fy)
	fur	(fer)		o *as in*	
i	hit	(hit)		protect	(prə TEKT)
eye	idea	(eye DEE ə)		u *as in*	
y	like	(lyk)		circus	(SER kəs)
ir	deer	(dir)	ch	chill	(chil)
	fear	(fir)	g	go	(goh)
oh	open	(OH pen)	j	joke	(johk)
oi	foil	(foil)		bridge	(brij)
	boy	(boi)	k	kite	(kyt)
or	horn	(horn)		cart	(kahrt)
ou	out	(out)	ng	bring	(bring)
	flower	(FLOU ər)	s	sum	(suhm)
oo	hoot	(hoot)		cent	(sent)
	rule	(rool)	sh	sharp	(shahrp)
yoo	few	(fyoo)	th	thin	(thin)
	use	(yooz)	*th*	then	(*then*)
			z	zebra	(ZEE brə)
				pose	(pohz)
			zh	treasure	(TREZH ər)

Acknowledgments: Grateful acknowledgment is made to the following for copyrighted material: **Associated University Presses:** "The House on the Border" by Aziz Nesin from *Contemporary Turkish Literature*. Reprinted by permission of Associated University Presses. **Alfred A. Knopf:** "Mother to Son" by Langston Hughes, edited by Arnold Rampersad with David Roessel, Associate Editor from *The Collected Poems of Langston Hughes*. Copyright © 1994 by The Estate of Langston Hughes. Reprinted by permission of Alfred A. Knopf, a division of Random House, Inc. **James Lim:** "Grandfather" by James Lim from *Grandfather*. Reprinted by permission of the author. **Random House:** From "I Know Why the Caged Bird Sings" by Maya Angelou from *I Know Why the Caged Bird Sings*. Copyright © 1969 and renewed 1997 by Maya Angelou. Reprinted by permission of Random House, Inc. **University of New Mexico Press:** From "The Way to Rainy Mountain" by N. Scott Momaday from *The Way to Rainy Mountain*. Copyright © 1969 by The University of New Mexico Press. Reprinted by permission of The University of New Mexico Press. **Viking Penguin, a division of Penguin Group (USA) Inc.:** "The Turtle—Chapter 3" by John Steinbeck from *The Grapes of Wrath*. Copyright © 1939, renewed copyright © 1967 by John Steinbeck. Reprinted by permission of Viking Penguin, a division of Penguin Group (USA) Inc. **Writer's House, LLC:** From "I See the Promised Land" by Martin Luther King, Jr. from *A Testament Of Hope: The Essential Writings Of Martin Luther King, Jr.* Copyright © 1968 Martin Luther King Jr.; copyright © renewed 1996 Coretta Scott King. Reprinted by arrangement with The Heirs to the Estate of Martin Luther King, Jr. c/o Writer's House as agent for the proprietor New York, NY. Note: Every effort had been made to locate the copyright owner of material reproduced in this component. Omissions brought to our attention will be corrected in subsequent editions.

Photo Credits: Cover images, clockwise from top left: © Pearson, Charmaine Whitman/Pearson, © Getty Images, © Kristina_KB/Shutterstock, © Getty Images, © JuiceDrops, © JuiceDrops, © Iztok Noc/Shutterstock, © Lynne Furrer/Shutterstock, © Brand X Pictures; Cover background: © JuiceDrops; Lesson and unit opener: © Stockbyte; p. 46: © COLOR-PIC/Animals Animals—All rights reserved; p. 83 (left): © Bert Hardy/Hulton Archive/Getty Images; p. 103: © AP Images; p. 118: NOAA; p. 119: © Miguel Angelo Silva/Shutterstock; p. 125: © CORBIS; p. 161: © Mark Lennihan/AP Images.

Staff Credits: Joshua Adams, Melania Benzinger, Karen Blonigen, Laura Chadwick, Andreea Cimoca, Katie Colón, Nancy Condon, Barbara Drewlo, Kerry Dunn, Marti Erding, Sara Freund, Daren Hastings, Ruby Hogen-Chin, Mariann Johanneck, Julie Johnston, Mary Kaye Kuzma, Mary Lukkonen, Carol Nelson, Carrie O'Connor, Marie Schaefle, Julie Theisen, Chris Tures, Mike Vineski, Charmaine Whitman, Sue Will

Copyright © 2009 by Pearson Education, Inc. or its affiliate(s). All rights reserved. Printed in the United States of America. This publication is protected by copyright, and permission should be obtained from the publisher prior to any prohibited reproduction, storage in a retrieval system, or transmission in any form or by any means, electronic, mechanical, photocopying, recording, or likewise. For information regarding permission(s), write to: Pearson School Rights and Permissions Department, One Lake Street, Upper Saddle River, New Jersey 07458.

Pearson® is a trademark, in the U.S. and/or in other countries, of Pearson Education, Inc. or its affiliate(s).

1-800-992-0244
www.pearsonschool.com

ISBN-13: 978-0-7854-6662-8
ISBN-10: 0-7854-6662-2

1 2 3 4 5 6 7 8 9 10   12 11 10 09 08

Contents

Unit One — Growth and Change 6

Lesson

1 **Character** 6
LITERATURE SELECTION
from *The Way to Rainy Mountain*

2 **Interpreting a Table** 11
SOCIAL STUDIES SELECTION
"Independence Comes to Latin America"

3 **Understanding Sequence** 17
SCIENCE SELECTION
"DNA and Cell Division"

4 **Understanding Mathematical Terms** 22
MATHEMATICS SELECTION
"Mathematics as a Language"

Lesson

5 **Using Context Clues** 28

6 **Main Idea and Supporting Details** 30

7 **Questioning as a Reading Strategy** 32

8 **Analogies** 34

9 **Reading a Bank Statement** 36

Unit Two — Destiny 38

Lesson

10 **Plot** 38
LITERATURE SELECTION
"August Heat"

11 **Reading a Map** 44
SOCIAL STUDIES SELECTION
"Africa's Climates"

12 **Outlining** 51
SCIENCE SELECTION
"Ecosystem Essentials"

13 **Understanding Geometric Terms** 56
MATHEMATICS SELECTION
"Basic Geometric Terms"

Lesson

14 **Taking Notes and Summarizing** 62

15 **Suffixes** 64

16 **Prefixes** 66

17 **Base Words and Roots** 67

18 **Reading a Credit Card Statement** 68

Unit Three — Observations 70

Lesson

19 **Setting** 70
LITERATURE SELECTION
from *I Know Why the Caged Bird Sings*

20 **Analyzing** 77
SOCIAL STUDIES SELECTION
"Our Global Economy"

21 **Main Idea and Supporting Details** 82
SCIENCE SELECTION
"Quicksand"

22 **Using a Calculator** 87
MATHEMATICS SELECTION
"Getting the Most Out of a Calculator"

Lesson

23 **Multiple-Meaning Words** 92

24 **Recognizing Denotation and Connotation** 94

25 **Recognizing Propaganda** 95

26 **Reading a Bus Schedule** 96

Contents
continued

Unit Four **Perseverance** 98

Lesson

27 **Theme** 98
LITERATURE SELECTION
"The Turtle"

28 **Analyzing a Primary Source** 102
SOCIAL STUDIES SELECTION
"I See the Promised Land"

29 **Reading a Diagram** 108
SCIENCE SELECTION
"How a Camera Works"

30 **Word Problems** 113
MATHEMATICS SELECTION
"Solving Word Problems"

Lesson

31 **Transitional Words and Phrases** 117

32 **Improving Reading Rate** 118

33 **Distinguishing Fact From Opinion** 121

34 **Completing an Employment** 122
Application

Unit Five **Transitions** 124

Lesson

35 **Figures of Speech** 124
LITERATURE SELECTION
"The Road Not Taken," "Grandfather,"
and "Mother to Son"

36 **Cause and Effect** 128
SOCIAL STUDIES SELECTION
"After Independence"

37 **Steps in a Process** 133
SCIENCE SELECTION
"From Star to Supernova"

38 **Understanding Logic** 138
MATHEMATICS SELECTION
"Reading Conditional Statements"

Lesson

39 **Reading Dialect** 142

40 **Analogies** 144

41 **Reading a Road Map** 146

Unit Six **Perspectives** 148

Lesson

42 **Mood and Tone** 148
LITERATURE SELECTION
"The House on the Border"

43 **Making Inferences** 155
SOCIAL STUDIES SELECTION
"The 'Other China'"

44 **Organizing Data** 160
SCIENCE SELECTION
"Specialists of the Canine World"

45 **Understanding Theorems** 165
MATHEMATICS SELECTION
"Step by Step: The Binomial Theorem"

Lesson

46 **Comparing and Contrasting** 170

47 **Fallacies in Reasoning** 172

48 **Etymology** 173

49 **Comparing Car Ads** 174

How to Use *Be A Better Reader*

For more than thirty years, **Be A Better Reader** has helped students improve their reading skills. **Be A Better Reader** teaches the comprehension and study skills that you need to read and enjoy all types of materials—from library books to the different textbooks that you will encounter in school.

To get the most from **Be A Better Reader**, you should know how the lessons are organized. As you read the following explanations, it will be helpful to look at some of the lessons.

In each of the first four lessons of a unit, you will apply an important skill to a reading selection in literature, social studies, science, or mathematics. Each of these lessons includes the following nine sections.

▶ BACKGROUND INFORMATION

This section gives you interesting information about the selection you are about to read. It will help you understand the ideas that you need in order to learn new skills.

▶ SKILL FOCUS

This section teaches you a specific skill. You should read the Skill Focus carefully, paying special attention to words that are printed in boldface type. The Skill Focus tells you about a skill that you will use when you read the selection.

▶ CONTEXT CLUES OR WORD CLUES

This section teaches you how to recognize and use different types of context and word clues. These clues will help you with the meanings of the underlined words in the selection.

▶ STRATEGY TIP

This section gives you suggestions about what to look for as you read. The suggestions will help you understand the selection.

▶ SELECTIONS

There are four kinds of selections in **Be A Better Reader**. A selection in a literature lesson is similar to a selection in a literature anthology, library book, newspaper, or magazine. A social studies selection is like a chapter in a social studies textbook or an encyclopedia. It often includes maps or tables. A science selection, like a science textbook, includes special words and sometimes diagrams. A mathematics selection will help you acquire skill in reading mathematics textbooks.

▶ COMPREHENSION QUESTIONS

Answers to the questions in this section can be found in the selection itself. You will sometimes have to reread parts of the selection to complete this activity.

▶ CRITICAL THINKING ACTIVITY

The critical thinking activity includes questions whose answers are not directly stated in the selection. For these questions, you must combine the information in the selection with what you already know in order to infer the answers.

▶ SKILL FOCUS ACTIVITY

In this activity, you will use the skill that you learned in the Skill Focus section at the beginning of the lesson to answer questions about the selection. If you have difficulty completing this activity, reread the Skill Focus section.

▶ READING-WRITING CONNECTION

In this writing activity, you will have a chance to use the information in the selection you read about, by writing about it. Here is your chance to share your ideas about the selection.

Additional Lessons

The remaining lessons in each unit give you practice with such skills as using a dictionary, an encyclopedia, and other reference materials; using phonics and syllabication in recognizing new words; locating and organizing information; and adjusting your reading rate. Other reading skills that are necessary in everyday life, such as reading a bus schedule, are also covered.

Each time you learn a new skill in **Be A Better Reader**, look for opportunities to use the skill in your other reading at school and at home. Your reading ability will improve the more you practice reading!

unit one
Growth and Change

LESSON 1
Skill: Character

BACKGROUND INFORMATION
In this excerpt from his autobiography, *The Way to Rainy Mountain*, N. Scott Momaday, a Kiowa, recalls his fond and vivid memories of his grandmother, who has died. Momaday's grandmother had witnessed many changes in the Kiowa way of life. As American Indians were forced to move to reservations, many of their customs were lost or needed to be altered.

SKILL FOCUS: Character
When developing a **character**, an author can make several choices. One choice is whether to make the character **static** or **dynamic**. A static character remains the same from beginning to end. A dynamic character undergoes a change due to events.

Another important choice is how to reveal a character's personality. An author can do the following:

- give background about the character
- reveal what the character says
- show how the character behaves
- tell what others say and think about the character
- share his or her thoughts about the character

▶ Read the passage below about the Kiowa people. Answer the questions to tell about the characters.

They were a mountain people, a mysterious tribe of hunters. In the late seventeenth century they began a long migration. Along the way the Kiowa were befriended by the Crows, who gave them the culture and religion of the Plains. They acquired horses, and their ancient nomadic spirit was suddenly free of the ground. They acquired Tai-me, the sacred Sun Dance doll, from that moment the object and symbol of their worship, and so shared in the divinity of the sun. Not least, they acquired the sense of destiny, therefore courage and pride.

1. What does the Kiowas' background suggest about their personality?
   _____
   _____

2. Are the Kiowa a static or dynamic people?
   _____
   _____

CONTEXT CLUES: Synonyms
Sometimes an author will clarify the meaning of an unfamiliar word by using a **synonym**—a word or phrase that has the same or a similar meaning—as a context clue. Read the following sentences to find the meaning of *migration*.

In the late seventeenth century they began a long <u>migration</u> *to the south and east. It was a journey toward the dawn, and it led to a golden age.*

In the sentence above, *journey* is similar in meaning to *migration*.

▶ Read the sentence below. Circle the phrase that is a synonym for the underlined word.

They never understood the grim, <u>unrelenting</u> *advance of the U.S. cavalry, a cavalry that had a policy of never giving up.*

In this selection, the words *reverence, postures,* and *intensity* are underlined. Look for synonym context clues to help you understand their meanings.

> **Strategy Tip**
>
> As you read this excerpt from *The Way to Rainy Mountain*, see whether Momaday's main character changes over the course of her life. What conclusions can you draw about the character's personality?

6 LESSON 1 Character

READING A LITERATURE SELECTION

from The Way to Rainy Mountain
N. Scott Momaday

A single knoll rises out of the Plains in Oklahoma, north and west of the Wichita Range. For my people, the Kiowas, it is an old landmark, and they gave it the name Rainy Mountain. The hardest weather in the world is there. Winter brings blizzards, hot tornadic winds arise in the spring, and in summer the prairie is an anvil's edge.... Loneliness is an aspect of the land. All things in the Plains are isolated; there is no confusion of objects in the eye, but one hill or one tree or one man. To look upon that landscape in the early morning, with the sun at your back, is to lose the sense of proportion. Your imagination comes to life, and this, you think, is where Creation was begun.

I returned to Rainy Mountain in July. My grandmother had died in the spring, and I wanted to be at her grave. She had lived to be very old and at last infirm. Her only living daughter was with her when she died, and I was told that in death her face was that of a child.

I like to think of her as a child. When she was born, the Kiowas were living the last great moment of their history. For more than a hundred years they had controlled the open range from the Smoky Hill River to the Red, from the headwaters of the Canadian to the fork of the Arkansas and Cimarron. In alliance with the Comanches, they had ruled the whole of the southern Plains. War was their sacred business, and they were among the finest horsemen the world has ever known. But warfare for the Kiowas was preeminently a matter of disposition rather than of survival, and they never understood the grim, unrelenting advance of the U.S. cavalry. When at last, divided and ill-provisioned, they were driven onto the Staked Plains in the cold rains of autumn, they fell into panic. In Palo Duro Canyon

they abandoned their crucial stores to pillage and had nothing then but their lives. In order to save themselves, they surrendered to the soldiers at Fort Sill and were imprisoned in the old stone corral that now stands as a military museum. My grandmother was spared the humiliation of those high gray walls by eight or ten years, but she must have known from birth the affliction of defeat, the dark brooding of old warriors.

Her name was Aho, and she belonged to the last culture to evolve in North America. Her forebears came down from the high country in western Montana nearly three centuries ago. They were a mountain people, a mysterious tribe of hunters whose language has never been positively classified in any major group. In the late seventeenth century they began a long migration to the south and east. It was a journey toward the dawn, and it led to a golden age. Along the way the Kiowas were befriended by the Crows, who gave them the culture and religion of the Plains. They acquired horses, and their ancient nomadic spirit was suddenly free of the ground. They acquired Tai-me, the sacred Sun Dance doll, from that moment the object and symbol of their worship, and so shared in the divinity of the sun. Not least, they acquired the sense of destiny, therefore courage and pride. When they entered upon the southern Plains they had been transformed. No longer were they slaves to the simple necessity of survival; they were a lordly and dangerous society of fighters and thieves, hunters and priests of the sun. According to their origin myth, they entered the world through a hollow log. From one point of view, their migration was the fruit of an old prophecy, for indeed they emerged from a sunless world. . . .

✔ My grandmother had a <u>reverence</u> for the sun, a holy regard that now is all but gone out of mankind. There was a wariness in her, and an ancient awe. She was a Christian in her later years, but she had come a long way about, and she never forgot her birthright. As a child she had been to the Sun Dances; she had taken part in those annual rites, and by them she had learned the restoration of her people in the presence of Tai-me. She was about seven when the last Kiowa Sun Dance was held in 1887 on the Washita River above Rainy Mountain Creek. The buffalo were gone. In order to consummate the ancient sacrifice—to impale the head of a buffalo bull upon the medicine tree—a delegation of old men journeyed into Texas, there to beg and barter for an animal from the Goodnight herd. She was ten when the Kiowas came together for the last time as a living Sun Dance culture. They could find no buffalo; they had to hang an old hide from the sacred tree. Before the dance could begin, a company of soldiers rode out from Fort Sill under orders to disperse the tribe. Forbidden without cause the essential act of their faith, having seen the wild herds slaughtered and left to rot upon the ground, the Kiowas backed away forever from the medicine tree. That was July 20, 1890, at the great bend of the Washita. My grandmother was there. Without bitterness, and for as long as she lived, she bore a vision of deicide.

✘ Now that I can have her only in memory, I see my grandmother in the several <u>postures</u> that were peculiar to her: standing at the wood stove on a winter morning and turning meat in a great iron skillet; sitting at the south window, bent above her beadwork, and afterwards, when her vision failed, looking down for a long time into the fold of her hands; going out upon a cane, very slowly as she did when the weight of age came upon her; praying. I remember her most often at prayer. She made long, rambling prayers out of suffering and hope, having seen many things. I was never sure that I had the right to hear, so exclusive were they of all mere custom and company. The last time I saw her she prayed standing by the side of her bed at night. . . . I do not speak Kiowa, and I never understood her prayers, but there was something inherently sad in the sound, some merest hesitation upon the syllables of sorrow. She began in a high and descending pitch, exhausting her breath to silence; then again and again—and always the same <u>intensity</u> of effort, of something that is, and is not, like urgency in the human voice. Transported so in the dancing light among the shadows of her room, she seemed beyond the reach of time. But that was illusion; I think I knew then that I should not see her again.

COMPREHENSION

1. Name three details from the first two sentences that Momaday uses to describe Rainy Mountain.

2. Why has Momaday returned to Rainy Mountain?

3. Why were the Kiowas no longer the rulers of the southern Plains?

4. How had the Kiowas changed during their migration in the seventeenth century?

5. What were some of the "postures" that were peculiar to Momaday's grandmother?

6. Draw a line to match the following words with their correct meanings.

reverence	**a.** urgency
postures	**b.** regard and awe
intensity	**c.** standing, sitting, or bent over

CRITICAL THINKING

1. Rainy Mountain has a value that a visitor might not appreciate at first.
   a. What physical conditions of the place make it seem uninviting?

   b. Why, then, is the place so important to Momaday?

2. Explain the cause of the "dark brooding of old warriors" that Momaday's grandmother knew as a child.

3. Explain why Momaday refers to the end of the Kiowas' migration as the beginning of "a golden age"?

LESSON 1 Character **9**

4. What can you infer about Momaday's grandmother from the various "postures" that he remembers?

_____
_____

SKILL FOCUS: CHARACTER

1. Read the following passages about Momaday's grandmother. On the line after each passage, tell what the passage reveals about her. Then identify which of the techniques from the Skill Focus on page 6 that Momaday uses.

   a. "Her only living daughter was with her when she died, and I was told that in death her face was that of a child."

   _____

   Technique: _____

   b. "Transported so in the dancing light among the shadows of her room, she seemed beyond the reach of time."

   _____

   Technique: _____

2. Reread the passage with the ✔ next to it. How might the event described in that passage have changed or influenced the grandmother's personality?

   _____
   _____

3. Reread the passage with the ✘ next to it. What conclusions can you draw about Momaday's grandmother from her actions and words?

   _____
   _____

4. Is Momaday's grandmother a static or a dynamic character? Explain your answer.

   _____
   _____
   _____

Reading-Writing Connection
On a separate sheet of paper, write a paragraph describing a close friend or family member who is no longer a part of your daily life. Include details that would help the person come alive in someone's mind.

LESSON 2

Skill: Interpreting a Table

BACKGROUND INFORMATION

"Independence Comes to Latin America" explores what helped bring about independence in Latin American countries. Centuries ago, a handful of European countries ruled most of the land in the Caribbean and the Americas. The United States, itself, was once a colony of Great Britain and, in order to gain its independence, fought against Great Britain in the Revolutionary War. The desire for independence has shaped the history of many nations, including those in Latin America.

SKILL FOCUS: Interpreting a Table

A **table** organizes information into rows and columns. Headings usually appear along the top and left side of the table. These headings make it easy to see what kinds of facts the table contains. If some facts need to be abbreviated to save space, the table usually has a key that explains abbreviations. Some tables also provide additional information in footnotes. Footnotes are notes at the bottom of a table that further explain something in the table.

▶ Study the table below. Answer the questions.

Comparing Six States of the United States of America		
State	**Year It Became a State**	**State Capital**
Alabama	1819	Montgomery
Alaska	1959	Juneau
Arizona	1912	Phoenix
Arkansas	1836	Little Rock
California	1850	Sacramento
Colorado	1876	Denver

1. What is the title of the table?

_____

2. What are the headings?

_____

3. What information can you find in the table?

_____

CONTEXT CLUES: Usage

In your reading, you may come across a word you know that is used in an unusual way. Consider the following example of unusual **usage**.

*Both of these revolutions had **embraced** liberty and equality as ideas.*

Sometimes knowing what a word means in other contexts can be helpful. For example, you probably know that *embrace* means "to hold someone close, in affection." In the sentence above, *embraced* has a similar meaning—"hold close to your heart ideas that are important to you."

▶ Read the sentence below. First, write a definition for the underlined word as it would most frequently be used. Then write what the word means in the sentence.

*The world had just seen two powerful revolutions, both of which **sparked** revolts in other places.*

1. _____

_____

2. _____

_____

In this selection, the words *studded*, *furthering*, and *secure* are underlined. Think how you use these words to figure out their meanings in the sentences.

Strategy Tip

As you read "Independence Comes to Latin America," use the information in the table together with the information in the paragraphs.

LESSON 2 Interpreting a Table **11**

READING A SOCIAL STUDIES SELECTION

Independence Comes to Latin America

From about 1500 to 1800, Latin America was a region divided among several European nations. Spain governed the greatest number of colonies in Central America, South America, and the Caribbean. Portugal ruled Brazil. Great Britain, France, and the Netherlands held small colonies.

In general, the Latin American colonies were home to large farming estates. Harvests of sugar and other tropical crops brought great wealth to both the landowners and the governing countries. Gold and silver mines underline studded the colonies. Enslaved native populations did most of the physical labor. The colonists were also importing an increasing number of enslaved Africans.

Colonial governments were run by white people, who held the highest positions in society and in commerce. European-born whites were at the top, followed by the native-born whites, or **creoles** (CREE ohlz). Creoles found advancement difficult because the best jobs usually went to European-born whites. Beneath the creoles were two other groups: **mestizos** (me STEE zohs) and **mulattoes** (muh LAH tohz). The mestizos were of white and native heritage. The mulattoes were of white and African heritage. Mestizos and mulattoes often lived in colonial towns and had some education. They found little opportunity for advancement, however. Often they were the targets of racial discrimination. Enslaved colonists, of course, had no standing at all.

News of Change Sparks Revolt

By 1800, however, the scene was set for dramatic change. The world had just seen two powerful revolutions. One revolution had created the United States. The other revolution had changed France's government from a **monarchy** to a **republic**. Both revolutions had embraced liberty and equality as ideals.

These revolutions gave many Latin Americans reason to hope. The first Latin American nation to achieve independence was Haiti in 1804. A revolt of Haiti's free mulattoes and enslaved Africans began during the French Revolution. The rebel army took control, but was put down by Napoleon's troops. Then the rebels rose up again to defeat the French.

✔ Napoleon's rise to power—especially his capture of Spain—distracted several European nations from their colonial pursuits. This resulted in furthering some Central American independence movements. A series of revolts in Mexico ended when Spain regained its king. The Mexican upper class, however, took advantage of a Spanish rebellion in 1820 to declare independence. General Agustín Iturbide led that movement and subsequently proclaimed himself emperor. He was later overthrown, and Mexico became a republic in 1823. By then, five Spanish colonies that had been part of Iturbide's empire had consolidated. This union, the United Provinces of Central America, lasted for less than a decade before its members became truly independent.

The Revolution Moves South

News of Napoleon's capture of Spain emboldened independence movements in South America, too. Paraguay achieved independence quickly in 1811. Argentine rebels took control of their government and established an independent nation in 1816. The nation was called the United Provinces of South America. Less than a decade later, all the colonies in Central and South America that were once held by Spain and Portugal had gained their independence.

In many cases, independence was the result of bloody struggle and civil war. Rebel leaders such as Bernardo O'Higgins and José de San Martín became legendary in those struggles. The chief leader of the movement in South America, however, was Simón Bolívar. Bolívar was a Venezuelan soldier who trained rebel armies and led a series of revolts. He became known as "The Liberator" and the "George Washington of South America." Bolívar became president of the new nations of Great Colombia and Peru, whose independence he helped secure. Bolívar tried to create a strong union of South American nations—strong enough to stand against Spain,

Independent Countries of Latin America

Country/Colonial Power	Year of Independence	Comments
Antigua and Barbuda (B)	1981	———
Argentina (S)	1816	First name as an independent nation was the United Provinces of South America and later the United Provinces of the Río de la Plata
Bahamas (B)	1973	Granted self-government in 1964
Barbados (B)	1966	———
Belize (B)	1981	Britain's last colony on the mainland of the Americas
Bolivia (S)	1825	Separated from Peru in 1825; named for Simón Bolívar
Brazil (P)	1822	———
Chile (S)	1818	Independence proclaimed by Bernardo O'Higgins in 1818
Colombia (S)	1819	———
Costa Rica (S)	1838	***
Cuba (S)	1898	Spanish-American War ended Spanish colonialism in the Americas
Dominica (B)	1978	———
Dominican Republic (S)	1924	Formerly known as Santo Domingo; first constitutionally elected government installed in 1924
Ecuador (S)	1830	+++
El Salvador (S)	1839	***
Grenada (B)	1974	Smallest independent nation in the Western Hemisphere
Guatemala (S)	1839	***
Guyana (B)	1966	Formerly known as British Guiana
Haiti (F)	1804	First Latin American colony to gain independence, resulting from revolt led by Toussaint L'Ouverture, a former slave
Honduras (S)	1838	***
Jamaica (B)	1962	———
Mexico (S)	1824	Republic established after series of revolts and brief rule by Emperor Agustín I
Nicaragua (S)	1838	***
Panama (S)	1903	+++
Paraguay (S)	1811	———
Peru (S)	1824	———
St. Kitts and Nevis (B)	1983	Granted self-government in 1967
St. Lucia (B)	1979	Ceded by France in 1814; granted self-government in 1967
St. Vincent and the Grenadines (B)	1979	———
Suriname (N)	1975	Acquired from Britain in 1667 in exchange for New Amsterdam (New York) and known before its independence as Dutch Guiana
Trinidad and Tobago (B)	1962	———
Uruguay (S)	1825	———
Venezuela (S)	1830	+++

(B) = Great Britain   (F) = France   (N) = the Netherlands   (P) = Portugal   (S) = Spain

*** = Broke from Spain in 1821; date given for independence is date of secession from the United Provinces of Central America

+++ = First achieved independence in 1821–1822 as part of Great Colombia; date given for independence is date of secession from Great Colombia

LESSON 2   Interpreting a Table   **13**

should Spain attempt to retake its former colonies. He also tried to encourage political ties between these new nations and the United States. **Factionalism**, however, kept the new nations from finding common ground. Nations that had cooperated at first began to grow apart. Hopes for a union failed. Within ten years of Bolívar's death in 1830, there were 17 independent Latin American countries.

Twentieth-Century Independence

After 1839, no other European colonies gained independence for almost 60 years. Cuba became an independent nation in 1898 as a result of the Spanish-American War. That war also made the United States a colonial power in Latin America. As part of the settlement of the war, Spain gave control of Puerto Rico to the United States.

✔ In 1917, the United States purchased the Danish West Indies, which became known as the U.S. Virgin Islands. Only four colonial powers still controlled parts of Latin America. Those powers were Great Britain, France, the Netherlands, and the United States. Several British colonies gained their independence between 1960 and 1985 through diplomacy rather than warfare.

Today Great Britain still governs Anguilla, Bermuda, the Cayman Islands, the Falkland Islands, Montserrat, the Turks and Caicos Islands, and the British Virgin Islands. France controls Guadeloupe, Martinique, and French Guiana. French Guiana is the only dependency on the Latin American mainland. Aruba and the Netherlands Antilles remain part of the Netherlands. The United States still exercises some authority over Puerto Rico and the U.S. Virgin Islands. In most cases, these **dependencies** have a fair amount of self-government and perhaps will gain total independence in the future.

COMPREHENSION

1. Which European nations governed colonies in Latin America from 1500 to 1800?

2. What racial similarity do creoles, mestizos, and mulattoes share? What are the racial differences among them?

3. What news from abroad inspired discontented Latin Americans to consider breaking away from their governing countries?

4. What was the United Provinces of Central America?

5. What did Simón Bolívar, Bernardo O'Higgins, and José de San Martín have in common?

6. How did the United States first become a colonial power in Latin America?

14 LESSON 2 Interpreting a Table

7. Which European nations continue to govern colonies in Latin America today?

_____

_____

_____

8. Write the letter of the correct meaning on the line next to each word.

_____ studded   **a.** causing to move ahead

_____ secure   **b.** were scattered over

_____ furthering   **c.** to make safe or certain

CRITICAL THINKING

1. Explain why you think the Latin American colonies began to depend upon the importation of enslaved Africans.

_____

_____

2. Suppose you are living in a Latin American colony and are hearing about the revolutions in the United States and France.

    a. If you were a mestizo or a mulatto, why might independence appeal to you?

_____

_____

    b. If you were a creole, why might independence appeal to you?

_____

_____

3. Identify each of the following statements as fact or opinion by writing _F_ or _O_ on the line provided.

_____ **a.** Were it not for the American Revolution, independence would not have come to Latin America.

_____ **b.** Agustín Iturbide proclaimed himself Mexican emperor in the early 1820s.

_____ **c.** It is better to gain independence through diplomacy rather than warfare.

4. Name at least two details from the selection that support this idea: Simón Bolívar did much to shape the history of Latin America.

_____

_____

5. Explain the difference between Spain's standing as a colonial power in Latin America by 1825 and its standing by the beginning of the twentieth century.

_____

_____

6. Reread the final paragraph of the selection. What do you think is the chief economic activity in most of the remaining Latin American dependencies? Explain.

_____

_____

LESSON 2   Interpreting a Table   **15**

SKILL FOCUS: INTERPRETING A TABLE

1. What four categories of information does the table on page 13 provide?
   _____
   _____

2. All of the following facts are true. Put an ✘ next to each fact that appears in the table on page 13.

   a. _____ Suriname once was a British possession.

   b. _____ José de San Martín was a Latin American freedom fighter.

   c. _____ Brazil became an independent nation in 1822.

   d. _____ The United States held colonial power in Latin America.

   e. _____ The nation of Great Colombia consisted of the present-day nations of Ecuador, Panama, and Venezuela.

   f. _____ There once were three "Guianas"—one British, one Dutch, and one French.

3. Review the facts that you marked with an ✘ above. Try to find each one in the selection. Circle the letters of the facts that appear *only* in the table.
   a   b   c   d   e   f

4. Using information from the table on page 13 only, underline the names of the following present-day nations that were *not* once Spanish colonies.

   a. Argentina   d. Haiti   g. Suriname

   b. Trinidad and Tobago   e. Costa Rica   h. Belize

   c. Dominican Republic   f. Uruguay   i. Honduras

5. Compare the table on page 13 with the two paragraphs marked with a ✔.

   a. Which five Spanish colonies were part of Iturbide's empire before they became truly independent?
   _____

   b. Which British colonies became independent between 1960 and 1985?
   _____

Reading-Writing Connection

Many countries that have gained independence in the past few decades have done so peacefully, through diplomacy. Think of a conflict that you might experience with another person. On a separate sheet of paper, write a skit in which you and the other person use reason and compromise to resolve the conflict peacefully.

16 LESSON 2 Interpreting a Table

LESSON 3

Skill: Understanding Sequence

BACKGROUND INFORMATION

"DNA and Cell Division" is about the stages animal cells go through and how scientists came across the concepts of genes and heredity. One of the goals of the U.S. Human Genome Project, which began in 1990, is to map the human genome to discover the genes that cause disease. Scientists already know that changes in single genes cause muscular dystrophy and Huntington's disease. When more than one cell is involved, the causes of disease become far more complicated.

SKILL FOCUS: Understanding Sequence

Scientists recognize the importance of **sequence**, or order. The logical sequencing of information makes it possible for a scientist, a mathematician, or even a writer to present facts in a clear and understandable way.

There are three kinds of sequence.

1. **Chronological sequence**, or "time order," presents events in the order in which they take place.

2. **Spatial sequence** presents details depending on where they are located in relationship to each other, for example, from top to bottom or from left to right.

3. **Order of importance sequence** presents information in order of importance, for example, from least importance to greatest importance.

▶ Look at the table below and decide which kind of sequence is being used in each column. Fill in the sequence in the last column.

CONTEXT CLUES: Definition

You can learn the meaning of new words if their **definitions** appear in the same or the next sentence of a selection. Read the sentences below. Look for context clues that provide a definition for the underlined words.

*The term cell cycle describes the continuous process by which cells prepare for division and then divide into new cells, called **daughter cells**.*

If you didn't know what the term *daughter cells* means, you could find clues in the sentence. In the sentence the term *daughter cells* is defined by the phrase "new cells."

▶ Read the sentence below. On the lines, write the definition for the underlined word as found in the sentence.

*The stage of the cell cycle during which the cell grows and copies its chromosomes is called **interphase**.*

_____

_____

In this selection the words *cells*, *mitosis*, and *cytoplasm* are underlined. As you read, look for their definitions within the text to learn their meanings.

> **Strategy Tip**
>
> As you read "DNA and Cell Division," ask yourself, "Why does the writer use this type of sequence to present information?"

Topic	Examples in sequence	Kind of sequence
Layers of the Atmosphere	troposphere, stratosphere, mesosphere	
Animal Speeds	zebra (40 mph), lion (50 mph), cheetah (70 mph)	
From Tadpole to Frog	egg, tadpole, frog	

LESSON 3 Understanding Sequence **17**

DNA and Cell Division

If you look at a picture of yourself as a toddler, you will see that your body has changed dramatically since then. Your height and weight have increased as you have become older because the number of cells that make up your body has increased. Every part of you has been growing.

THE CELL CYCLE

Even as you read these words, the cells in your body are growing. Materials that flow into each cell cause it to increase in size. When a cell reaches its size limit—the point at which it can no longer transport materials throughout itself—it divides, forming two new cells. The term *cell cycle* describes the continuous process by which cells prepare for division and then divide into new cells, called **daughter cells**.

Interphase

The stage of the cell cycle during which the cell grows and copies its **chromosomes** (KROM mi sohmz) is called **interphase** (IN ter fayz). It is the longest stage of the cell cycle. Each cell houses chromosomes that are made up of **DNA**, or deoxyribonucleic acid. DNA holds the genetic information that determines the makeup of an organism. DNA has a shape like a coiled ladder, called a "double helix." The double helix consists of units called **nucleotides** (NOO klee oh teyedz), which combine sugar and phosphate with one of four bases: adenine (A), thiamine (T), cytosine (C), and guanine (G). These bases always link together in the same way: adenine with thiamine (A–T or T–A) and cytosine with guanine (C–G or G–C). See Figure 1.

When a cell prepares to reproduce, the ladder of DNA divides into two strands. The nucleotides on each strand attract matching, free-floating nucleotides inside the cell. As a result, a new double-stranded DNA, identical to the original DNA, forms.

Near the end of interphase, the division of DNA has produced two "offspring" of each chromosome. Now the cell is ready to divide.

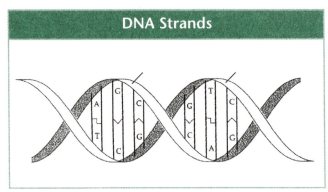

FIGURE 1. This diagram shows two DNA strands.

Mitosis

The second stage of the cell cycle, mitosis (my TOH sis), occurs when a cell divides, passing on copies of its DNA to its daughter cells. Mitosis has four stages. See Figure 2 on page 19.

In **prophase** (PROH fayz), an organelle (a part of a cell with a specific function) called a centriole helps separate the duplicated chromosomes. As mitosis begins, two pairs of centrioles in the cytoplasm (complex jelly-like material outside a cell nucleus) move apart. Fine threads of protein called spindle fibers appear between them to help ensure normal cell division. By the end of prophase, the centriole pairs have moved to opposite ends of the cell. The spindle fibers have aligned to create a football-shaped structure.

In **metaphase** (ME tə fayz), the chromosome pairs line up across the center of the cell. Each pair is attached to a spindle fiber.

During **anaphase** (AN ə fayz), each pair of chromosomes separates to form two single chromosomes. One chromosome from each pair is pulled by the spindle fibers to opposite ends of the cell, and two sets of single chromosomes are formed.

In **telophase** (TEL ə fayz), a protective nuclear membrane forms around each set of chromosomes. The spindle fibers disappear.

Mitosis ends when the cell membrane begins to pinch the cell in two, causing the cytoplasm to divide, producing two identical daughter cells.

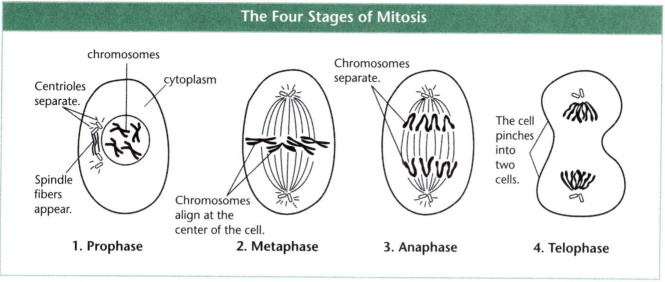

FIGURE 2. This diagram shows the four stages of mitosis.

✔ HOW WE KNOW

In 1665, English scientist Robert Hooke gave the name "cells" to the structures he saw as he studied a slice of cork under a microscope. Not until the 1800s, however, would the work of German scientists Matthias Schleiden (1838) and Theodor Schwann (in 1839) help prove that cells are the building blocks of all living things.

A few years later, Austrian monk Gregor Mendel conducted a series of experiments with garden peas and discovered the **laws of heredity**. He published his findings in 1866. In the early 1900s, several scientists working independently linked Mendel's studies of heredity with the process of cell division. In 1915, American scientist Thomas Hunt Morgan proposed the chromosome theory—that genes establish heredity and that specific genes appear in specific positions on chromosome "maps."

The major remaining enigma involved how genes do their work. In the early 1940s, American scientists George Beadle and Edward Tatum supplied part of the answer: They discovered a link between genes and enzymes. Then in 1944, a scientific team at the Rockefeller Institute proved that genetic information is transferred from **parent cells** to daughter cells by DNA.

Scientists understood by now that DNA consists of sugar, phosphate, and the bases adenine, cytosine, guanine, and thiamine—but in what arrangement? The answer came in 1953, when James Watson and Francis Crick presented the Watson-Crick model for DNA, or the double helix model. Experiments by Arthur Kronberg proved that their double helix model was indeed correct.

Since that time, scientists have manufactured DNA and begun to decipher DNA's **genetic code**. It is hoped that future research will not only add to the scientific understanding of DNA and cell division, but will also provide keys to identifying and treating a wide range of genetic disorders.

COMPREHENSION

1. What does the term *cell cycle* mean?
   _____
   _____

2. During which stage of the cell cycle are chromosomes duplicated?
   _____
   _____

LESSON 3 Understanding Sequence

3. When a ladder of DNA splits, how do the two resulting strands behave in a similar way?

_____

_____

4. What are the four phases of mitosis?

_____

_____

5. What important discovery did Gregor Mendel make as a result of his experiments with peas?

_____

_____

6. When and by whom was the double helix model for DNA presented?

_____

_____

7. Complete each sentence by filling in the correct word from below.

cells cytoplasm mitosis

a. _____ is the stage in which a cell divides, passing on copies of its DNA to its daughter cells.

b. Mitosis ends when the _____ is divided and two identical daughter cells are produced.

c. The building blocks of all living things are

_____.

CRITICAL THINKING

1. In what sense is cell division both the cause and the effect of cell growth?

_____

_____

2. Explain why *double helix* is an accurate description of the DNA model.

_____

_____

3. Conclude why the way bases in nucleotides link together helps ensure the accurate duplication of chromosomes.

_____

_____

4. Why is the formation of nuclear membranes during telophase an important part of mitosis?

_____

_____

5. How might an understanding of the cell cycle help scientists identify and treat genetic disorders?

_____

_____

20 LESSON 3 Understanding Sequence

SKILL FOCUS: UNDERSTANDING SEQUENCE

1. What type of sequence is used in the two main parts of the selection? Explain.
   _____
   _____

2. Put an ✘ next to the fact in each pair that comes first in the correct sequence.

   a. ____ The DNA ladder within a cell divides.

      ____ Free-floating nucleotides are attracted to nucleotides on each DNA strand.

   b. ____ The laws of heredity were established.

      ____ Cells were proven to be the building blocks of all life.

3. Write the following terms for stages of cell growth and division in their correct sequence: *anaphase, interphase, metaphase, prophase, telophase.*
   _____
   _____

4. Reread the section with the ✘ next to its heading. What three sequential steps are mentioned in this section?
   _____
   _____

5. Reread the section with the ✔ next to its heading. Then number each of the following statements, from longest ago (1) to most recent (8), to show the correct chronological sequence.

   ____ Mendel experiments with garden peas.

   ____ Kronberg confirms the Watson-Crick model.

   ____ Hooke uses the term *cells* to describe microscopic structures.

   ____ Rockefeller Institute scientists prove that DNA is responsible for the transfer of genetic information.

   ____ Morgan proposes the chromosome theory.

   ____ Schleiden and Schwann help establish that cells are the building blocks of all life.

   ____ Beadle and Tatum discover a link between genes and enzymes.

   ____ Watson and Crick present the double helix model for the structure of DNA.

Reading-Writing Connection

Look through some recent newspapers or magazines to find out about genetic research. On a separate sheet of paper, list the topics you find. Then write a few sentences explaining which topic you think is the most important. Explain why.

LESSON 3 Understanding Sequence **21**

LESSON 4

Skill: Understanding Mathematical Terms

BACKGROUND INFORMATION

"Mathematics as a Language" is about how math has its own language. Have you ever tried to learn a language other than your own? Have you ever tried to communicate with someone who speaks another language? If so, you have probably realized the difficulty of expressing ideas when a language barrier exists. The language of numbers is usually considered a universal language, but it has terms that are vital to understanding the concepts.

SKILL FOCUS: Understanding Mathematical Terms

What does it mean to be *real*, to be *positive*, to be *dense*? You may be familiar with these terms on an everyday basis. However, in math the meaning can be very different. These words are examples of **mathematical terms**, words that have special meaning when used in a mathematical context. For example, the *envelopes* that you use to mail a letter are nothing at all like the *envelopes* that you find when studying mathematical surfaces and curves.

▶ Read each word in the chart below. Fill in the chart with each word's common, everyday meaning and its mathematical meaning.

Word	Common Meaning	Mathematical Meaning
positive		
negative		
equal		

Word Clues

The terms *expression* and *equation* are used very often in mathematics, particularly in algebra. It is important to understand the difference between these terms so that you aren't confused as you study mathematics.

An **expression** is a mathematical phrase that uses numbers, letters, and operation symbols. For example, the expression $a + 3$ may be used to convey any one of the following.

- a plus 3
- a increased by 3
- the sum of a and 3

An **equation** is a sentence that states that two expressions are equal. For example, $a + 3 = 9$ is an equation. Below are the basic differences between an expression and an equation.

1. An equation contains an equal sign.

2. An equation tells you something about the relationship between the two expressions.

3. Some equations can be solved.

4. Expressions can never be solved.

Strategy Tip

As you read "Mathematics as a Language," remember that many words have more than one meaning. Make sure that you understand the mathematical definitions.

22   LESSON 4   Understanding Mathematical Terms

(READING A MATHEMATICS SELECTION)

Mathematics as a Language

Mathematics is a language, like English or Spanish or Japanese; that is, every word, sign, and symbol in the language has a meaning. The key to understanding the language of mathematics is to learn the meanings of these words, signs, and symbols.

With the strong emphasis on mathematics in this technological age, it is important to acquire the special skills needed to read in this field. Why does mathematics demand special reading skills? For one thing, math vocabulary can be challenging. Some otherwise familiar words may have special meanings in mathematics. For example, the common meanings of the words *radical*, *field*, *real*, and *positive* may be quite familiar to you. Their mathematical meanings, however, are completely different from their common meanings. Other words, such as *collinear*, *monomial*, and *circumference*, are also important to mathematics and have exclusively mathematical meanings.

Reading mathematics can also pose a challenge because both words and **symbols** (signs that represent mathematical terms) are used to convey information. Reading in most other subject areas involves only words. In mathematics, however, explanations and instructions may be given in words, and other information may be given in symbols. In fact, math expressions, such as those shown below, often involve reading symbols alone.

$$a + b \div c \qquad \angle ABC$$

In this lesson, you will practice reading both familiar and unfamiliar words as well as symbols. Review the words and symbols that you already know. Study the unfamiliar ones as you might study words in a foreign language. Look critically at each word or symbol, think carefully about its meaning, and then reinforce your understanding with continued practice.

Mathematical Words

Many mathematical words have meanings that are similar to the common meanings of the words, as in the following examples.

Word	Mathematical Meaning
member	element in a set
set	collection of elements
dense	crowded or tightly packed together

Mathematics also uses many words whose meanings in mathematics differ from their common meanings. Because the mathematical meanings are specialized, you cannot rely on your knowledge of the common meanings to figure them out. Also many dictionaries often do not include mathematical meanings, so you need to consult your mathematics textbooks for these definitions.

The following table shows both the common and the mathematical meanings of several words that you will encounter frequently in your mathematical reading.

Word	Common Meaning	Mathematical Meaning
angle	point of view; perspective	shape formed by two rays with a common point
positive	optimistic; confident	having a value greater than zero
rational	involving reason and logic	a number that can be expressed as an integer or by a ratio of two integers
property	something owned; a characteristic trait, quality, or attribute	a rule that is true for a set of numbers
operation	a surgical procedure for remedying an injury or disease	the process of carrying out a rule on a set of numbers; addition, subtraction, multiplication, division

LESSON 4   Understanding Mathematical Terms   **23**

Symbol	Meaning	Illustration
=	equals	$8 + 8 = 10 + 6$
≠	does not equal	$2 + 0 \neq 0$
≈	is approximately equal to	$\pi \approx 3.14$
>	is greater than	$4 + 3 > 5$
<	is less than	$3 + 2 < 6$
$a < x < b$	x is between a and b	$4 < 7 < 9$
+	addition; sum	$a + b$
−	subtraction; difference	$a - b$
•	multiplication; product	$a \cdot b$
/	division; quotient	a / b

Mathematical Symbols

Mathematicians make wide use of symbols. A few of the frequently used symbols are listed in the table above.

Do you recognize each of the symbols in the table? Do you fully understand their meanings? Would you know how to use each one if you came across it in your textbook? Learn the meanings of any symbols that are unfamiliar to you so that you can identify their meanings as you read them. For example, you must be able to understand that $10 + x < 27$ means "the sum of 10 and x is less than 27."

Expressions and Formulas

A skill related to reading symbols—and just as important—is knowing how to interpret numbers together with other kinds of symbols. In many areas of mathematics, most notably in algebra, you will often encounter mathematical **expressions** and **equations**. An expression is a combination of symbols, numbers, and letters. An equation is a statement showing that two expressions are equal. For example, consider the equation below.

$$\frac{a + b}{5} = 10$$

It means that the sum of a and b divided by 5 is equal to 10.

Knowing how to read **formulas** is crucial to mathematics comprehension. Formulas are rules that show the relationships between quantities. For example, consider the formula for the area of a trapezoid.

$$A = \tfrac{1}{2} h(b_1 + b_2)$$

In this formula, there are four **variables**, or letters used to represent unknown numbers. A stands for the area of the trapezoid (that is, the space within the lines that form the trapezoid), h stands for the height of the trapezoid, and b_1 and b_2 identify the two bases, as shown.

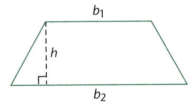

You can use this formula to find any one of the variables if you know the values of the other three.

Whenever you read a mathematical formula, find out what the letters represent so that you can first express their meanings in your own words and then translate them into numbers.

Now you see why reading in mathematics is different from reading in other subject areas. You must sometimes attribute specialized meanings to familiar words. You must read letters and substitute meanings for them. You must read numbers and formulas, combining them with symbols of various kinds and bringing meaning to them all. Learning to read and understand not only math words but also many symbols, expressions, equations, and formulas is essential to your success in working with mathematics.

COMPREHENSION

1. According to the selection, what two characteristics of mathematical language create the need for special reading skills?

   _____

   _____

   _____

   _____

2. What is the meaning of each of the following symbols?

   a. > _____

   b. ≠ _____

   c. + _____

   d. / _____

   e. ≈ _____

3. What is a mathematical expression?

   _____

   _____

   _____

4. In what area of mathematics do you most work with mathematical expressions and equations?

   _____

   _____

   _____

5. According to the conclusion of the selection, what is the one main factor that makes reading in mathematics different from most other kinds of reading?

   _____

   _____

   _____

CRITICAL THINKING

1. Reread the second paragraph of the selection.

   a. Explain why you think the writer describes our times as a "technological age."

   _____

   _____

   _____

   b. Explain what mathematics has to do with the fact that this is a "technological age."

   _____

   _____

   _____

2. Why might it be more difficult to figure out the mathematical meanings of words such as *monomial* and *collinear* than that of words such as *field* or *positive*?

   _____

   _____

   _____

LESSON 4 Understanding Mathematical Terms **25**

3. The use of symbols makes reading mathematics more challenging than other kinds of reading. Why, then, do you think that symbols are used so often in math?

4. Assign number values to a and b. Then find c in the equation $a + b = c$.

5. Review the formula for finding the area of a trapezoid. If the height of a trapezoid is 4 inches and the bases are 5 inches and 12 inches, what is the area?

6. Compare what the mathematical definitions of *intersect, member,* and *set* have in common.

7. Translate the following equation into a verbal sentence. Then solve the equation.

$$3x + 5 = 20$$

8. Read the mathematical expression below.

$$4y \div 3$$

a. Can it be solved? Explain your answer.

b. Using the mathematical expression above, write an equation.

26 LESSON 4 Understanding Mathematical Terms

SKILL FOCUS: UNDERSTANDING MATHEMATICAL TERMS

1. Describe the meaning of the underlined word in each of the following sentences by writing *mathematical* or *nonmathematical* on the line provided.

   _____ a. We practiced for the soccer game in the <u>field</u> near the shopping center.

   _____ b. If you multiply a negative number by another negative number, the product will be a <u>positive</u> number.

   _____ c. If I don't measure the <u>circumference</u> of this tabletop, I might wind up not buying enough trim to go all the way around it.

   _____ d. You are not being <u>rational</u>; stop and think things through.

   _____ e. The writer of this letter to the editor expresses some <u>radical</u> ideas.

   _____ f. Would a floor lamp look good in that <u>angle</u> between the sofa and the chair?

2. All of the following words appear in the selection. For each one, write its meaning as a mathematical term. Then write a sentence that shows its nonmathematical use.

   a. *area*

   Mathematical term: _____

   Sentence with nonmathematical meaning: _____

   _____

   b. *difference*

   Mathematical term: _____

   Sentence with nonmathematical meaning: _____

   _____

   c. *expression*

   Mathematical term: _____

   Sentence with nonmathematical meaning: _____

   _____

   d. *symbol*

   Mathematical term: _____

   Sentence with nonmathematical meaning: _____

   _____

Reading-Writing Connection

Mathematics is not the only field of study with specialized terms. On a separate sheet of paper, make a list of words that have a special meaning in some other subject area, such as in geography or in music. Define the meaning of each term in that subject area. If the word has a more general, everyday meaning, list that as well.

LESSON 4 Understanding Mathematical Terms **27**

LESSON 5

Skill: Using Context Clues

When you come across an unfamiliar word while reading, you have two choices: You can look it up in a dictionary, or you can determine its meaning by using context clues. **Context clues** are hints about the meaning of an unfamiliar word that appear in nearby words, phrases, or sentences. Some common types of context clues include a **definition** or **restatement, examples, comparison, contrast, cause and effect**. Sometimes, however, you must **infer meaning**.

Definition or Restatement

Sometimes a difficult word is simply defined or restated in a sentence. Context clues of this type are often signaled by a form of the verb *to be* and words and phrases such as *or*, *that is*, and *in other words*.

> *Nobody knows what effect a <u>miasma</u>, or <u>encompassing fog</u>, of greenhouse gases will have on Earth.*

Examples

At other times, a writer can reveal the meaning of a word by giving examples. Words and phrases like *such as*, *like*, and *for example*, and sometimes dashes signal examples.

> *The burning of <u>fossil fuels—coal, oil, and natural gas</u>—causes the emission of carbon dioxide, which contributes to the warming of Earth's atmosphere.*

Comparison and Contrast

An unfamiliar word might be compared or contrasted with a familiar word. Words often used to signal comparisons include *like* and *as*. Words often used to signal contrasts include *unlike, but, not, although*, and *on the other hand*.

> *We risk <u>dangerous</u> changes to our environment if we do* not *reduce greenhouse gases to remain on a <u>benign</u> environmental course.*

Cause and Effect

You can also determine a word's meaning if the writer uses it in a cause-and-effect relationship. This type of context clue helps you figure out the meaning of one word from its effect on another. Cause-and-effect relationships are often signaled by words and phrases such as *because, since, therefore*, and *as a result*.

> *Because energy-conserving technologies are <u>underutilized</u>, we have <u>not</u> reduced emissions <u>as much as we could</u>.*

Inferring Meaning

Sometimes, however, a writer does not provide direct information that you can use to figure out the meanings of words that are unfamiliar to you. When context clues are less obvious, you can sometimes *infer* the meaning of an unfamiliar word based on the words around it or in nearby sentences. Search the context to see what information is given. Then try to make the connection between the information and the unfamiliar word.

> *Some people have suggested <u>containing</u> the sites where fossil fuels are burned. On the other hand, many believe that such <u>capping</u> of greenhouse gas emissions will be hugely expensive and ultimately unnecessary.*

Read the passage on page 29 about the problem of global warming. Use context clues to figure out the meaning of each underlined word. Write its meaning in the space provided. Then identify the type of context clues you used.

28   LESSON 5   Using Context Clues

Global Warming

As the sun's energy is absorbed by the Earth, it is converted into heat. The heat is trapped by water vapor and then increases, augmented by carbon dioxide. However, because the amount of carbon dioxide in the atmosphere builds, the effect of trapped heat is exacerbated. If global warming is not mitigated, scientists say, the Earth will continue to warm and oceans will rise, causing potentially life-threatening changes. Coastal areas will be inundated by floods of water that are released as polar ice melts. Furthermore, deserts will spread, and previously fertile areas will turn arid. Many lobbyists for steel, oil, and automobile industries disavow these theories, claiming that they are overstated or are mere inventions. These detractors point out that stabilizing emissions will be extremely expensive and will be possible only in industrialized countries. These countries, thus, will be penalized for their advances in industry. Scientists continue to argue, however, that waiting for unequivocal, absolute proof of global warming may put the planet in danger of ruin.

1. augmented: _____

   Type of context clue: _____

2. exacerbated: _____

   Type of context clue: _____

3. mitigated: _____

   Type of context clue: _____

4. inundated: _____

   Type of context clue: _____

5. arid: _____

   Type of context clue: _____

6. disavow: _____

   Type of context clue: _____

7. overstated: _____

   Type of context clue: _____

8. detractors: _____

   Type of context clue: _____

9. penalized: _____

   Type of context clue: _____

10. unequivocal: _____

    Type of context clue: _____

LESSON 5 Using Context Clues

LESSON 6

Skill: Main Idea and Supporting Details

When you read a paragraph that is long or complex, you can determine the most important information by looking for the main idea and the supporting details. The **main idea** expresses the subject of the paragraph. The **supporting details** are examples, opinions, or facts that support the main idea. Finding the main idea and supporting details in a paragraph will help you understand the paragraph and extract the information that will be most useful to you.

Some details in a paragraph are more important than others. **Major details** help develop or complete the thought expressed by the main idea, while details that are not important to the main idea are called **minor details**. They may help make the main idea more interesting, but the main idea does not depend on them.

A. The following paragraph describes an important development in the treatment of disease. Look for the main idea and supporting details as you read.

The first successful vaccination was developed in the 1790s by Edward Jenner. At that time, smallpox epidemics broke out frequently. The disease produced a high fever, killing thousands. Many survivors were left maimed and disfigured by the skin eruptions that the disease caused. Jenner noticed that milkmaids (women who worked with dairy cows) did not get smallpox, even during epidemics. On further investigation, he found that most of these women had contracted from the cattle a disease called cowpox, which is similar to smallpox, but much milder. He concluded that contracting cowpox had somehow protected the women from getting smallpox. In a daring experiment, Jenner took fluid from a cowpox lesion (an open sore on the skin) and scratched it into the arm of a boy. The boy developed a very mild case of cowpox; but when he was exposed to smallpox, he remained healthy. Jenner had invented the vaccination. In fact, although he did not know exactly how the vaccination worked, he had laid the foundation for the science of immunology.

The main idea is stated in the first sentence: *The first successful vaccination was developed in the 1790s by Edward Jenner.* The first sentence of a paragraph often, but not always, expresses the main idea. In this paragraph, the major supporting details tell the story of how Jenner developed the vaccination. Here are the first three details.

1. Jenner noticed that milkmaids (women who worked with dairy cows) did not get smallpox, even during epidemics.

2. On further investigation, he found that most of these women had contracted a disease from the cattle called cowpox, which is similar to smallpox, but much milder.

3. He concluded that contracting cowpox had somehow protected the women from getting smallpox.

List the other two details.

4. _____

5. _____

30 LESSON 6 Main Idea and Supporting Details

B. Each paragraph below describes how later scientists built upon Jenner's foundation. Read the paragraphs carefully. Then below each one, write the main idea and three major supporting details.

Nearly 70 years later, a French chemist named Louis Pasteur discovered the scientific principle that explained why vaccination worked. As Pasteur studied bacteria, he learned that these microbes reproduce like other living organisms and that they are responsible for such diverse effects as fermentation and disease. Pasteur's work with disease-causing bacteria, especially anthrax, led him to an important discovery. By injecting animals with a weakened form of the microbe, he found that he could inoculate, or protect, them against the disease. The inoculation caused the animal to develop antibodies that fought the anthrax bacteria. Furthermore, the antibodies remained in the animal and were able to fight off later exposures to the disease. One of Pasteur's greatest accomplishments, a vaccine against rabies, was based on these findings.

Main Idea:

_____

Major Supporting Details:

1. _____

2. _____

3. _____

Pasteur's work with harmful bacteria led to discoveries that resulted in safer surgical practices. Before the late 1800s, surgeons thought it unnecessary to clean their instruments or wash their hands before surgery. As a result, these surgeons would infect and often kill patients with the bacteria that remained on their hands and instruments. It is estimated that sepsis, or bacterial infection, killed as many as half the women who gave birth in hospitals and a large percentage of patients who needed operations. After studying Pasteur's findings on germs and disease, British surgeon Joseph Lister developed the practice of antisepsis, using carbolic acid as a cleansing agent and heat to sterilize surgical instruments. As a result, surgery saved more lives than it took, and hospitals became places where people were likely to recover rather than die.

Main Idea:

_____

Major Supporting Details:

1. _____

2. _____

3. _____

LESSON 6 Main Idea and Supporting Details **31**

LESSON 7
Skill: Questioning as a Reading Strategy

> Asking yourself **questions** as you read is an excellent strategy for making sure that you comprehend what you read. It also helps you connect what you are reading to what you already know about the topic. Questioning can lead you to other sources of information, such as experts on the subject or other books about the topic.

Read the following selection, noting the underlined sections and the questions in the margin. Then answer the questions that follow.

Migration

For many centuries, humans have puzzled over the ability of animals to migrate over long distances, often over unfamiliar territory. For example, homing pigeons return to breeding places from thousands of miles away. <u>Salmon find their way back to the rivers of Canada and Alaska where they were born after having spent most of their lives 3,500 miles away on the coast of North Korea. Pets have found their way home over hundreds of miles of unfamiliar landscape</u>.

1. How do they do that?

After years of observation and research, scientists have some clues about how animals are able to accomplish these amazing feats.

Many animals are able to use landmarks, such as mountains, rivers, coasts, and plant life, to recognize a route that they have traveled before. They can even use the wind to locate a familiar climate! <u>Animals sense the passage of time in their travels by the angle of the sun above the horizon, by the pattern of daylight and night, and by their own inner biological clocks that tell them when to rest and eat</u>.

2. How does this ability help the animals find their way?

<u>Scientists have studied bird migration extensively</u>. Birds navigate by landmarks, sunlight, and the patterns of the stars. Some birds—pigeons, sparrows, and bobolinks, for example—have magnetic material in their bodies that helps them locate the magnetic fields around Earth. The angle at which the magnetic waves appear above Earth helps them track their progress as they travel. Other creatures that have this magnetic sensitivity include yellowfin tuna, honeybees, and even some bacteria. <u>Sharks' sensitivity to electrical fields in the water helps them find their way around</u>.

3. What discoveries have the scientists made as a result of their study?

4. How could I find out more about how this ability works?

Animals' other acute senses assist their ability to navigate. Birds can hear the sounds of wind on mountains and oceans many miles away. Salmon can remember the smell of the streams in which they were born and spent their early days. Other animals, including lost pets, often use their sense of smell to find their way home. <u>Scientists believe that animals use a combination of sight, hearing, smell, and reaction to temperature and weather to help them navigate as they migrate in search of food, shelter, and breeding grounds</u>.

5. How do the senses help animals navigate as they migrate?

32 LESSON 7 Questioning as a Reading Strategy

1. Read question 1 in the margin. Then answer it by using information found in the selection.

   _____

   _____

   _____

2. Answer question 2 in the margin by thinking about the information given in the selection.

   _____

   _____

   _____

3. Answer question 3 in the margin by using information you find in the selection.

   _____

   _____

   _____

4. Name three sources that you might use to answer question 4 in the margin.

   _____

   _____

   _____

5. Answer question 5 in the margin by using information found in this selection.

   _____

   _____

   _____

6. Write two questions you asked yourself while reading the selection and tell how you found the answers. If the answers are not provided in the selection, indicate which sources of information you might use.

   a. _____

   _____

   _____

   b. _____

   _____

   _____

LESSON 7 Questioning as a Reading Strategy **33**

LESSON 8

Skill: Analogies

> An **analogy** is a comparison that shows the same relationship between two pairs of words.

To complete an analogy by choosing a missing word, follow these two steps. Determine the **relationship** between the first pair of words. The types of relationships that can be expressed in analogies include the following.

Type of Relationship	Example
word to antonym	big : small
word to synonym	small : little
cause to effect	stumble : fall
part to whole	seed : apple
item to category	mouse : rodent
action to item	beat : drum

To complete the second pair of words, choose a word that establishes the same relationship. Make sure that the second word pair matches the first word pair grammatically, such as noun to noun or adjective to adjective.

For example, the words *tragic* and *comic* are both adjectives; they are antonyms, or opposites. To choose a word to complete this analogy with *wild*, you would look for a word that is an adjective and also an antonym for *wild*, such as *tame*.

You can express an analogy in two ways. One way is with words.

Tragic is to *comic* as *wild* is to *tame*; or, something that is *tragic* is the opposite of something that is *comic*.

The other way is to use colons for the words *is to* (:) and *as* (::).

tragic : comic :: wild : tame

Read and complete each of the following analogies by writing the correct word from the choices given. Then identify the type of relationship expressed in each analogy.

1. ape : mammal :: snake : _____   reptile   fangs   insect

    Relationship _____

2. cut : scissors :: write : _____   letter   envelope   pen

    Relationship _____

3. nose : face :: knuckle : _____   arm   hand   head

    Relationship _____

4. hatred : love :: cowardice : _____   fear   admiration   courage

    Relationship _____

34   LESSON 8   Analogies

5. fire : burned :: medicine : _____   healed   pain   bitter

Relationship _____

6. chapters : novel :: stanzas : _____   play   poem   story

Relationship _____

7. outrageous : appalling :: acceptable : _____   happy   satisfactory   compromise

Relationship _____

8. sleigh : vehicle :: cottage : _____   household   dwelling   woods

Relationship _____

9. flooding : destruction :: fertilization : _____   green   lawn   growth

Relationship _____

10. rake : leaves :: shovel : _____   snow   grass   hoe

Relationship _____

11. irritable : irascible :: concise : _____   obscure   brief   ambiguous

Relationship _____

12. raise : lower :: contract : _____   agreement   touch   expand

Relationship _____

13. goose : flock :: bee : _____   sting   hive   swarm

Relationship _____

14. cold : freezing :: heat : _____   sweat   boiling   temperature

Relationship _____

15. flying : jet :: driving : _____   truck   vehicle   license

Relationship _____

16. comedy : laughter :: tragedy : _____   drama   sorrow   sad

Relationship _____

17. doctor : physician :: lawyer : _____   legal   attorney   courtroom

Relationship _____

18. grief : felicity :: vulgarity : _____   refinement   joy   affection

Relationship _____

19. ballet : dance :: ballad : _____   tango   singer   song

Relationship _____

20. Tokyo : Japan :: London : _____   bridge   England   city

Relationship _____

LESSON 8 Analogies **35**

LESSON 9

Skill: Reading a Bank Statement

If you have a checking account, you will receive a **bank statement**, or record of your banking activities, from your bank each month. The statement shows the two main kinds of banking activities that occurred during the month: **deposits**, or how much money has gone into your account, and **withdrawals**, or how much money has been paid out of the account.

You probably will make most deposits and withdrawals by check. Sometimes, however, you may transfer funds by phone, use a bank card at an automated teller machine (ATM), or use a debit card (DC) instead of a check. These activities will also appear on your monthly statement. The statement will also show your **balance**, or the amount of money remaining in your account, and sometimes the bank's **fees** or **service charge**. It is important to keep an accurate record of your checking account. If your records are correct, the checkbook balance and the balance on the bank statement should match.

Study the bank statement below.

COUNTY BANK & TRUST COMPANY

1221 West Jefferson Street
Glenview, Illinois 60025

ANITA MORALES
614-B SPRUCE DRIVE
GLENVIEW, IL 60026

STATEMENT PERIOD: 5/15/07–6/14/07
ACCOUNT NUMBER: 1733805
TELEPHONE ASSISTANCE: (312) 555-7825

BEGINNING BALANCE: $671.54
DEPOSITS/CREDITS: $2,460.00
WITHDRAWALS/FEES: $1,236.62
ENDING BALANCE: $1,894.92

DATE	DESCRIPTION	DEPOSITS	WITHDRAWALS	BALANCE
5/15	CBT ATM CASH WITHDRAWAL		50.00	621.54
5/21	CHECK PAID — 246		61.81	559.73
5/21	DC TRANS/FOOD BAZAAR		23.35	536.38
5/21	SERVICE CHARGE		8.00	528.38
5/22	CHECK PAID — 245		40.00	488.38
5/22	DEPOSIT	1,230.00		1,718.38
5/24	CBT ATM CASH WITHDRAWAL		60.00	1,658.38
5/28	CHECK PAID — 247		57.92	1,600.46
6/1	DC TRANS/FOOD BAZAAR		44.43	1,556.03
6/4	CHECK PAID — 248		525.00	1,031.03
6/8	DEPOSIT	50.00		1,081.03
6/8	CBT ATM CASH WITHDRAWAL		50.00	1,031.03
6/11	CHECK PAID — 249		143.39	887.64
6/12	CHECK PAID — 251		26.50	861.14
6/12	CHECK PAID — 250		113.72	747.42
6/14	DEPOSIT	1,180.00		1,927.42
6/14	DC TRANS/CUTS ABOVE		32.50	1,894.92

A. On the line after each sentence, write whether the statement is *true* or *false*.

1. The ending balance as of this statement date is $1,236.62 _____

2. Three ATM withdrawals were made during this period. _____

3. A debit card was used to pay for three purchases. _____

4. After check 247 was paid, the balance in the account was $1,927.42. _____

5. Check 245 for $40.00 was paid on May 18. _____

B. Fill in the circle next to the correct answer to each question.

1. What period of time does this bank statement cover?
   - ○ May 12, 2007–June 5, 2007
   - ○ May and June of 2007
   - ○ May 15, 2007–June 14, 2007
   - ○ June 5, 2007–June 14, 2007

2. On what date was there a balance of $1,718.38?
   - ○ May 22
   - ○ June 12
   - ○ May 24
   - ○ May 15

3. What was the amount of check 246?
   - ○ $61.81
   - ○ $23.35
   - ○ $559.73
   - ○ $143.39

4. What kind of transaction caused a withdrawal of $44.43?
   - ○ check
   - ○ ATM withdrawal
   - ○ deposit
   - ○ debit card

5. What is the number 1733805?
   - ○ the account number for the person who received the statement
   - ○ the telephone number to call with queries about this statement
   - ○ the account holder's Social Security number
   - ○ the check number

6. On which date did the bank not only pay on a check but also process a debit card transaction?
   - ○ June 8
   - ○ May 21
   - ○ May 15
   - ○ May 12

7. Which check was not paid during this statement period?
   - ○ 244
   - ○ 245
   - ○ 249
   - ○ 250

8. Why does check 245 appear on this statement after check 246?
   - ○ Check 245 was voided after it was written.
   - ○ Check 245 came in later than check 246 and so was paid later.
   - ○ An error was made in processing the checks.
   - ○ Check 245 was for less money.

LESSON 9 Reading a Bank Statement **37**

unit two
Destiny

LESSON 10
Skill: Plot

BACKGROUND INFORMATION

In "August Heat," the author explains a strange chain of events, asking the reader to decide: "Is it only coincidence, or is it fate?" Some people believe in coincidence—that things occur by chance, accidentally. Others believe in fate—that things occur for a purpose, that they are destined.

SKILL FOCUS: Plot

Writing that tells a story has a certain structure, or **plot**. Most plots contain the following elements.

1. **Conflict** The author creates a struggle, or conflict, that drives the story. The conflict may be internal or external.

2. **Rising Action** As one or more characters try to deal with the conflict, the tension or suspense in the story builds. This is called the rising action.

3. **Climax** At some point, the tension or suspense builds up to its strongest point. Often what happens in the climax comes as a surprise.

4. **Falling Action** Here the reader often sees how the conflict has changed the characters.

5. **Resolution** Most stories end with information about how the main conflict is resolved.

▶ Using the chart below, write about the conflict, the rising action, the climax, the falling action, and the resolution of the well-known tale, "The Three Little Pigs."

1. Conflict: _____

2. Rising Action: _____

3. Climax: _____

4. Falling Action: _____

5. Resolution: _____

CONTEXT CLUES: Antonyms

When you read a word in context that you don't know, an antonym in nearby phrases or sentences can help you figure out its meaning. **Antonym** context clues are words that are opposites, as in the following example.

I'm not bankrupt; my business is __prosperous__ enough.

If you don't know the meaning of the word *prosperous*, the words *not bankrupt* can help you. *Prosperous* and *bankrupt* are antonyms, words that are opposite in meaning.

▶ Read the sentence below. Circle the word that is an antonym of the underlined word.

So __busy__ was I with my work that I left my lunch untouched—I had no time to be lazy.

In "August Heat," the words *oppressively*, *oasis*, and *resumed* are underlined. As you read, look for antonym context clues to help you understand their meanings.

```
              3. Climax
                 /\
                /  \
2. Rising Action   4. Falling Action
              /      \
             /        \
1. Conflict            5. Resolution
```

> **Strategy Tip**
>
> Knowing the elements of the plot can help you understand why certain things in a story happen at certain times. Identify the five elements of the plot as you read "August Heat."

38 LESSON 10 Plot

READING A LITERATURE SELECTION

August Heat

W. F. Harvey

Phenistone Road, Clapham, August 20th, 19__. I have had what I believe to be the most remarkable day in my life, and while the events are still fresh in my mind, I wish to put them down on paper as clearly as possible.

Let me say at the outset that my name is James Clarence Withencroft.

I am 40 years old, in perfect health, never having known a day's illness.

By profession I am an artist, not a very successful one, but I earn enough money by my black-and-white work to satisfy my necessary wants.

My only near relative, a sister, died five years ago, so that I am independent.

I breakfasted this morning at nine, and after glancing through the morning paper I lighted my pipe and proceeded to let my mind wander in the hope that I might chance upon some subject for my pencil.

The room, though door and windows were open, was <u>oppressively</u> hot, and I had just made up my mind that the coolest and most comfortable place in the neighborhood would be the deep end of the public swimming pool, when the idea came.

I began to draw. So intent was I on my work that I left my lunch untouched, only stopping work when the clock of St. Jude's struck four.

The final result, for a hurried sketch, was, I felt sure, the best thing I had done.

It showed a criminal in the courtroom immediately after the judge had pronounced sentence. The man was fat—enormously fat. The flesh hung in rolls about his chin; it creased his huge, stumpy neck. He was clean shaven (perhaps I should say a few days before he must have been clean shaven) and almost bald. He stood in the courtroom, his short, clumsy fingers clasping the rail, looking straight in front of him. The feeling that his expression conveyed was not so much one of horror as of utter, absolute collapse.

There seemed nothing in the man strong enough to sustain that mountain of flesh.

I rolled up the sketch, and without quite knowing why, placed it in my pocket. Then with the rare sense of happiness which the knowledge of a good thing well done gives, I left the house.

I believe that I set out with the idea of calling upon Trenton, for I remember walking along Lytton Street and turning to the right along Gilchrist Road at the bottom of the hill where the men were at work on the new streetcar lines.

From there onwards I have only the vaguest recollections of where I went. The one thing of which I was fully conscious was the awful heat, that came up from the dusty asphalt pavement as an almost solid wave. I longed for the thunder promised by the great banks of copper-colored cloud that hung low over the western sky.

I must have walked five or six miles, when a small boy roused me from my reverie by asking the time.

It was 20 minutes to seven.

When he left me I began to take stock of my bearings. I found myself standing before a gate that led into a yard bordered by a strip of thirsty earth, where there were flowers, purple stock and scarlet geranium. Above the entrance was a board with the inscription—

CHS. ATKINSON TOMBSTONES
WORKER IN ENGLISH AND
ITALIAN MARBLES

From the yard itself came a cheery whistle, the noise of hammer blows, and the cold sound of steel meeting stone.

A sudden impulse made me enter.

A man was sitting with his back toward me, busy at work on a slab of curiously veined marble. He turned around as he heard my steps and stopped short.

It was the man I had been drawing, whose portrait lay in my pocket.

He sat there, huge and fat, the sweat pouring from his scalp, which he wiped with a red silk handkerchief. But though the face was the same, the expression was absolutely different.

LESSON 10   Plot   **39**

He greeted me smiling, as if we were old friends, and shook my hand.

I apologized for my intrusion.

"Everything is hot and glary outside," I said. "This seems an <u>oasis</u> in the wilderness."

"I don't know about the oasis," he replied, "but it certainly is hot, as hot as the devil. Take a seat, sir!"

He pointed to the end of the gravestone on which he was at work, and I sat down.

"That's a beautiful piece of stone you've got hold of," I said.

He shook his head. "In a way it is," he answered; "the surface here is as fine as anything you could wish, but there's a big flaw at the back, though I don't expect you'd ever notice it. I could never make a really good job of a bit of marble like that. It would be all right in the summer like this; it wouldn't mind the blasted heat. But wait till the winter comes. There's nothing quite like frost to find out the weak points in stone."

"Then what's it for?" I asked.

The man burst out laughing.

"You'd hardly believe me if I was to tell you it's for an exhibition, but it's the truth. Artists have exhibitions: so do grocers and butchers; we have them too. All the latest little things in headstones, you know."

He went on to talk of marbles, which sort best withstood wind and rain, and which were easiest to work; then of his garden and a new sort of carnation he had bought. At the end of every other minute he would drop his tools, wipe his shining head, and curse the heat.

I said little, for I felt uneasy. There was something unnatural, uncanny, in meeting this man.

I tried at first to persuade myself that I had seen him before, that his face, unknown to me, had found a place in some out-of-the-way corner of my memory, but I knew that I was doing little more than trying to fool myself.

Mr. Atkinson finished his work, spat on the ground, and got up with a sigh of relief.

"There! What do you think of that?" he said, with an air of evident pride.

The inscription which I read for the first time was this—

SACRED TO THE MEMORY OF
JAMES CLARENCE WITHENCROFT
BORN JAN. 18TH, 1860.
HE PASSED AWAY VERY SUDDENLY
ON AUGUST 20TH, 19—

"In the midst of life we are in death."

For some time I sat in silence. Then a cold shudder ran down my spine. I asked him where he had seen the name.

"Oh, I didn't see it anywhere," replied Mr. Atkinson. "I wanted some name, and I put down the first that came into my head. Why do you want to know?"

"It's a strange coincidence, but it happens to be mine."

He gave a long, low whistle.

"And the dates?"

"I can only answer for one of them, and that's correct."

"It's a strange thing!" he said.

But he knew less than I did. I told him of my morning's work. I took the sketch from my pocket and showed it to him. As he looked, the expression of his face altered until it became more and more like that of the man I had drawn.

"And it was only the day before yesterday," he said, "that I told Maria there were no such things as ghosts!"

Neither of us had seen a ghost, but I knew what he meant.

"You probably heard my name," I said.

"And you must have seen me somewhere and have forgotten it! Were you at Clacton-on-Sea last July?"

I had never been to Clacton in my life. We were silent for some time. We were both looking at the same thing, the two dates on the gravestone, and one was right.

"Come inside and have some supper," said Mr. Atkinson.

His wife is a cheerful little woman, with the flaky red cheeks of the country-bred. Her husband introduced me as a friend of his who was an artist. The result was unfortunate, for after the sardines and watercress had been removed, she brought me out a Doré Bible, and I had to sit and express my admiration for nearly half an hour.

I went outside, and found Atkinson sitting on the gravestone smoking.

We <u>resumed</u> the conversation at the point we had left off.

"You must excuse my asking," I said, "but do you know of anything you've done for which you could be put on trial?"

He shook his head.

"I'm not a bankrupt, the business is prosperous enough. Three years ago I gave turkeys to some of the police at Christmas, but that's all I can think of. And they were small ones, too," he added as an afterthought.

He got up, fetched a can from the porch, and began to water the flowers. "Twice a day regular in the hot weather," he said, "and then the heat sometimes gets the better of the delicate ones. And ferns, good Lord! They could never stand it. Where do you live?"

I told him my address. It would take an hour's quick walk to get back home.

"It's like this," he said. "We'll look at the matter straight. If you go back home tonight, you take your chances of accidents. A cart may run over you, and there's always banana skins and orange peels, to say nothing of fallen ladders."

He spoke of the improbable with a seriousness that would have been laughable six hours before. But I did not laugh.

"The best thing we can do," he continued, "is for you to stay here till 12 o'clock. We'll go upstairs and smoke; it may be cooler inside."

To my surprise I agreed.

We were sitting in a long, low room beneath the roof. Atkinson has sent his wife to bed. He himself is busy sharpening some tools at a little oilstone, smoking one of my cigars the while.

The air seems charged with thunder. I am writing this at a shaky table before the open window. The leg is cracked, and Atkinson, who seems a handy man with his tools, is going to mend it as soon as he has finished putting an edge on his chisel.

It is after 11 now. I shall be gone in less than an hour. But the heat is stifling.

It is enough to send a man mad.

LESSON 10 Plot

COMPREHENSION

1. a. Which character tells this story?

_____

_____

b. What personal background information does the narrator share as the story opens?

_____

_____

2. What is the subject of the sketch of which he is so proud?

_____

_____

_____

3. a. Why is Withencroft surprised when Atkinson turns to greet him?

_____

_____

b. Why is Withencroft surprised again when he sees what Atkinson has been doing?

_____

_____

4. What do Withencroft and Atkinson do together as the evening progresses?

_____

_____

_____

5. Complete the sentence by filling in the correct word from below.

oppressively oasis resumed

a. The family from Alaska considered the

warm, sandy beach a(n) _____ from the cold winter.

b. After a short break, the painter

_____ her work on the painting.

c. People rose up against the _____ harsh laws of the dictator.

CRITICAL THINKING

1. Identify each of the following statements by writing *fact* or *opinion* on the line provided.

_____ **a.** The sketch was the best that Withencroft ever had done.

_____ **b.** Atkinson worked with English and Italian marble.

_____ **c.** Meeting Atkinson was an unnatural, uncanny experience.

2. Explain why you think Withencroft tells us his personal history before sharing his story.

_____

_____

3. Discuss why the inscription at the bottom of the tombstone is meaningful.

_____

_____

42 LESSON 10 Plot

4. Contrast how Withencroft and Atkinson react to the unusual circumstances in which they find themselves.

5. At the end of the story, why does Withencroft say that the heat is enough to drive a man insane?

6. What do you think will happen to Withencroft, and why?

SKILL FOCUS: PLOT

1. A story may have more than one conflict in it, but one main conflict usually drives the story. Write one sentence that describes the main conflict.

2. Reread the passage with the ✔ next to it. This description appears before the story's tension begins to build. Why, then, is it important to the later part of the plot?

3. Describe what happens in the rising action of this story.

4. Where is the climax in "August Heat"? Explain.

Reading-Writing Connection

Think about someone you met by chance, but later felt that you were destined to know. On a separate sheet of paper, write a short story about the circumstances of the meeting and how that person changed your life in some way. Remember to include the five elements of plot in your story. If this has not happened to you in your life, use your imagination to write the story.

LESSON 11

Skill: Reading a Map

BACKGROUND INFORMATION

In "Africa's Climates," you will read about the various climate regions found on the continent of Africa. Geographers divide the world into climate regions. Climate regions are areas that have different climates, such as the Mediterranean climate (which is warm and dry in summer and mild and moist in winter) and the tropical rain forest climate (which is hot and rainy). Unlike weather, which can change from day to day, climate is the average weather of an area over a long period of time.

SKILL FOCUS: Reading a Map

A map often provides more than a picture of a geographic area. A map can show specific facts in a way that is easier to read than if they were written in a paragraph or a list form.

One very common type of map is a **climate map**. A climate map shows the general conditions of temperature and precipitation that characterize an area. Very often, climate maps use colors and patterns to show the various climate regions in a particular area. A map key will indicate which color or pattern stands for which climate region.

▶ The map below is a climate map of Australia. Study the map to answer the questions.

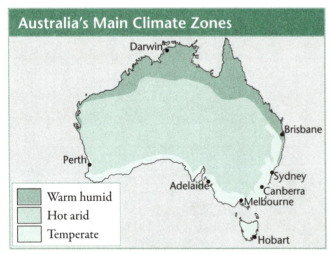

Australia's Main Climate Zones

1. Which climate is most common on the continent of Australia?

   _____

2. In what climate zone is Canberra located?

   _____

CONTEXT CLUES: Inferring and Defining

When you come across an unfamiliar word in your reading, you may have to **infer** its meaning or you may find a **definition** context clue to help you determine its meaning.

Read the sentence below, and look for context clues for the underlined words. A different kind of context clue is given for each underlined word.

   The treetops are so __dense__ that they form a __canopy__, or "umbrella," that blocks sunlight from reaching the ground.

You can infer that *dense* means "thick," since the dense, or thick, treetops block the sun from reaching the ground. An approximate definition of *canopy* appears in the same sentence, because a canopy is defined as an "umbrella."

▶ Read the sentence below. Circle the words in the sentence that helped you figure out the meaning of the underlined word.

   The climate in Africa is further __modified__ by the impact of ocean currents—for example, the cooling Benguela Current, which flows north from the Cape of Good Hope toward the Congo, and the warming Mozambique Current, which passes through the channel between the island of Madagascar and the southeast coast of Africa.

In this selection, the words *terrain*, *astride*, and *stable* are underlined. As you read, look for definition clues as well as other clues that will help you infer meanings for these words.

Strategy Tip

As you read each section of "Africa's Climates," look at the climate map on page 47 to help locate information presented in the text.

44   LESSON 11   Reading a Map

READING A SOCIAL STUDIES SELECTION

AFRICA'S CLIMATES

Africa is the second-largest continent on Earth; and because of its size and placement, Africa has a wide variety of climates. Straddling the equator, Africa stretches 4,970 miles (7,998 kilometers) from its northernmost point, Cape Blanc in Tunisia, to its southernmost tip, Cape Agulhas in South Africa. At its widest point (measured from Cape Verde, Senegal, in the west to Ras Hafun, Somalia, in the east), Africa is about 4,700 miles (7,565 kilometers) wide. Africa is about three times the size of Europe and covers one-fifth of the total land surface of Earth.

The highest point on the continent is Mt. Kilimanjaro in Tanzania. Rising as high as 19,340 feet (5,896 meters), Mt. Kilimanjaro's peaks wear a constant cap of snow. On the other extreme is the lowest part of Africa: the Qattara Depression, in Egypt, which lies 436 feet (133 meters) below sea level.

Except for the north coast and the Atlas Mountains in the northwest part of the continent, the terrain of Africa consists of vast, rolling plateaus marked by a number of large, saucer-shaped basins.

Different Climate Zones

From north to south, the continent is cut almost equally in half by the equator, so that most of Africa lies within the tropical regions. Because of the "bulge" formed by West Africa, the greater part of Africa's territory lies north of the equator. The continent's position astride the equator heavily influences its climates.

Temperatures are high for most of the year in the northern and southern tropical zones. In high altitudes in parts of the interior, however, temperatures are much cooler because of the height of the mountains. This is especially true in the mountains of East Africa and parts of central and southern Africa. The climate in Africa is further modified by the impact of ocean currents—for example, the cooling Benguela Current, which flows north from the Cape of Good Hope toward the Congo, and the warming Mozambique Current,

which passes through the channel between the island of Madagascar and the southeast coast of Africa. In addition, the climate is affected by the absence of mountain chains, which elsewhere serve as climatic barriers.

Africa has six primary **climate zones**: tropical rain forest climate, tropical wet-and-dry climate, steppe climate, desert climate, Mediterranean climate, and vertical climate.

Tropical Rain Forest Climate

✔ The central portion of the continent and the east coast of the island nation of Madagascar have a **tropical rain forest climate**. Tropical rain forests are always hot and rainy. Evergreens, oil palms, and many different species of tropical hardwood trees tower above the forest floor. The treetops are so dense that they form a canopy, or "umbrella," that blocks sunlight from reaching the ground. The ground is covered with a thick blanket of shrubs, ferns, mosses, and a variety of other plants.

In Madagascar, the average annual temperature is about 80 degrees Fahrenheit, and the average annual rainfall is about 70 inches (178 centimeters).

Tropical Wet-and-Dry Climate

The single largest climate zone in Africa is found in the savanna. The savanna covers almost half of Africa, extending toward the equator from the semiarid regions. The savanna has a **tropical wet-and-dry climate**. This means that temperatures remain warm all year long. Rain falls during the rainy season of summer, but the winter season is dry. The total annual rainfall for this zone varies from about 20 inches (50 centimeters) to more than 60 inches (152 centimeters).

The landscape shows equal variety. For example, some parts of the savanna have many trees; other parts are almost treeless. The grassland zone, with its annual rainfall of 20 to 35 inches (50 to 89 centimeters), is covered with low grasses, shrubs, and a scattering of small deciduous trees. The savanna is home to most of Africa's large animals. Elephants,

LESSON 11 Reading a Map **45**

The African continent contains a great variety of wildlife. The Serengeti Plain in Tanzania is home to baboons, zebras, giraffes, and lions.

giraffes, zebras, and antelope all roam the savanna and gather at waterholes throughout the region.

Landlocked in south-central Africa, Zambia is one of the countries in the savanna region. Zambia's countryside is mostly high plateau consisting of bush and savanna. Five rivers cross the land, and the Muchinga Mountains divide the eastern half of the country. Zambia's climate is tropical with three seasons: May through August is the cool, dry season; September through November is the hot, dry season; and December through April is the rainy season.

As you may know, temperatures near the equator tend to be warm. However, temperatures are always cooler in the highlands than at sea level. Therefore, parts of tropical Africa, such as Zambia, are cooler than you might expect because they lie at high elevations.

Steppe Climate

Away from the equator to the north and south, the savanna grades into the drier **steppe climate**. Africa's steppes are similar to much of the Great Plains in the United States. Summers are quite hot and winters can be rather cool. The average annual rainfall in this zone varies between 10 to 20 inches (25 to 50 centimeters) and is concentrated in one season. The so-called "thornbush zone" in the steppe region has an annual rainfall of 12 to 20 inches (30 to 50 centimeters). Here the land is covered with thin grass and a scattering of succulent (water-retaining) or semisucculent trees.

Desert Climate

North and south of the savanna lie deserts, similar to the desert in the southwestern United States. Africa has a proportionately larger desert than any other continent in the world except for Australia. Each of the African desert areas—the Sahara in the north, the Horn in the east, and the Kalahari and Namib in the southwest—receives less than 10 inches (25 centimeters) of rainfall annually.

Days in a **desert climate** are extremely hot, but nights are often extremely chilly, for there are no clouds to keep the day's heat from escaping. In the Sahara Desert, for example, the daily and seasonal extremes of temperature are very great. The average temperature during the summer rises above 90 degrees Fahrenheit (32 degrees Celsius), but during the cold season, the temperature at night often drops below freezing. While the Sahara receives almost no rain, parts of the Kalahari may receive as much as 10 inches (25 centimeters) per year.

Mediterranean Climate

A few small areas along Africa's northern and southern coasts have what is called a **Mediterranean climate**. This zone is small in the United States, as well, and it is associated primarily with California. Mediterranean winters are cool and rainy, while summers are warm and dry. Dense shrubs, some grasses, and scattered trees all grow in this pleasant climate. In the highlands of eastern Africa, particularly in Uganda and Kenya, rainfall is well distributed throughout the year, and the temperatures are stable.

Vertical Climate

The few mountainous regions of Africa have a **vertical climate**. In this climate, the temperature and amount of rainfall varies with the altitude, or height, of the mountains. The mountain regions of Ethiopia and Tanzania in East Africa and the interior of Madagascar are examples of vertical climates.

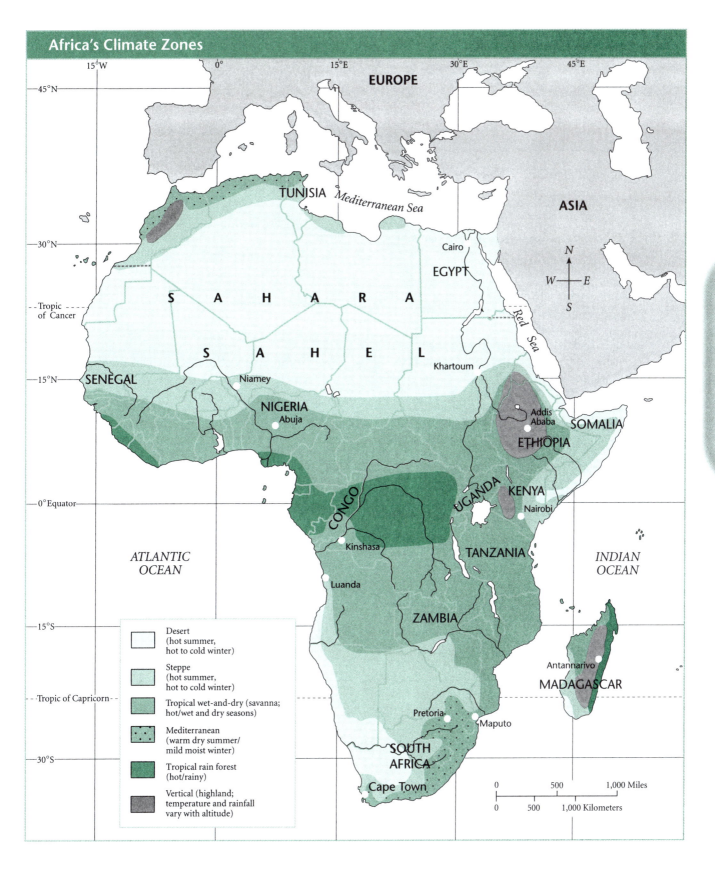

LESSON 11 Reading a Map 47

COMPREHENSION

1. Which landmarks are given to designate Africa's location extremes?

   a. north _____

   b. south _____

   c. west _____

   d. east _____

2. Why are temperatures often cool in parts of Africa's interior?

   _____

   _____

3. How do the Benguela Current and the Mozambique Current differ in their effects upon Africa's climate?

   _____

   _____

4. **a.** How many primary climate zones does Africa have?

   _____

   _____

   b. Name the climate zones.

   _____

   _____

5. What is meant by a Mediterranean climate?

   _____

   _____

6. What part of the United States is like the steppes of Africa?

   _____

   _____

7. In the desert climate, why can the nights be much chillier than the days?

   _____

   _____

8. Draw a line to match the following words with their correct meanings.

stable	**a.** a land's physical features
astride	**b.** placed on both sides of
terrain	**c.** having little or no variation

CRITICAL THINKING

1. Explain why Africa has so many climates.

   _____

   _____

2. Describe how the presence of mountains affects a climate.

   _____

   _____

3. Reread the section with a ✔ next to its heading.

   a. How might the heat of the tropical rain forest climate be related to the presence of a canopy?

   _____

   _____

48 LESSON 11 Reading a Map

b. Scientists speculate that many plants with powerful medicinal benefits have yet to be discovered in the world's rain forests. What characteristic of this climate zone tends to support that idea?

_____

_____

4. How do conditions in the savanna support the idea that much variation may exist within a single climate zone?

_____

_____

5. Below the equator, the seasons are reversed, with winter coming in the middle of the year and summer beginning at year's end. How does this fact help prove that Zambia, which lies below the equator, is an example of a tropical wet-and-dry climate?

_____

_____

6. Imagine packing for a trip to Africa in June. How would your choice of clothing for a stay in Zambia be different from your choice of clothing for a stay in eastern Madagascar?

_____

_____

SKILL FOCUS: READING A MAP

1. Look at the climate map on page 47. Then evaluate each statement by writing *true* or *false* on the line provided.

_____ **a.** To enjoy a Mediterranean climate in Africa, you must go either to the very north or the very south of that continent.

_____ **b.** A wide band of steppe climate lies along Africa's Atlantic coast.

_____ **c.** Every one of Africa's countries includes at least two climate zones.

_____ **d.** The easternmost point in continental Africa, in Somalia, lies in the desert climate zone.

_____ **e.** The tropical rain forest and tropical wet-and-dry climates lie next to each other.

_____ **f.** The climate of Madagascar varies greatly.

_____ **g.** No areas with a desert climate lie along the African seacoast.

_____ **h.** Most of Africa lies within the tropical regions, between the Tropic of Cancer and the Tropic of Capricorn.

2. Locate the equator on the map on page 47.

a. Which climate zone dominates Africa above the equator?

_____

LESSON 11 Reading a Map **49**

b. As the equator passes through Africa, through which climate zone does it pass for the greatest distance?

_____

c. Which climate zone dominates Africa below the equator?

_____

3. If you were traveling through the island nation of Madagascar, from west to east, through which climate zones would you pass?

_____

_____

4. Using the map on page 47, describe the climate of each of the following cities.

   a. Cairo, Egypt

   _____

   _____

   b. Abuja, Nigeria

   _____

   _____

   c. Cape Town, South Africa

   _____

   _____

   d. Addis Ababa, Ethiopia

   _____

   _____

   e. Niamey, Nigeria

   _____

   _____

Reading-Writing Connection

Do some research to find out what climate zones are found in your state. Create a climate map that shows these climates. Then on a separate sheet of paper, write a paragraph or two explaining how the climate affects life in your state.

LESSON 12

Skill: Outlining

BACKGROUND INFORMATION

In "Ecosystem Essentials," you will learn about various ecosystems and how people fit into them. Many outdoor areas are ecosystems. A neighborhood park is an ecosystem. A small creek is an ecosystem. Even a backyard can be considered an ecosystem. Basically, an ecosystem is a group of living things that interact with each other and with their nonliving environment. People can be part of ecosystems, as can plants, animals, water, and soil.

SKILL FOCUS: Outlining

If you have ever tried to understand a passage filled with information, you know that it is easier to do if you organize the information in a logical way. One way to organize information is by **outlining**.

In an outline, you use main headings and subheadings to arrange important information. The main headings are labeled with Roman numerals (I, II, III); the subheadings for supporting details are labeled with capital letters (A, B, C). Below each subheading, you may include minor details, each labeled with an Arabic numeral (1, 2, 3).

Here is an example of part of an outline.

I. Main idea

  A. Supporting detail

  B. Supporting detail

    1. Minor detail

    2. Minor detail

To create correct outline form, follow these steps.

1. Look for the main idea of each section. Restate the main idea in a phrase for each heading.

2. Look for supporting details for each main idea. Restate them as subheadings.

3. Begin each heading and subheading with a capital letter.

4. Indent each minor detail.

5. If you include minor details, list more than one for each heading.

▶ Read the paragraph below. Fill in the outline.

Some relationships within ecosystems are actually helpful to one or both organisms involved. Commensalism is a relationship in which one organism benefits and the other organism in the partnership is unaffected. In mutualism, both organisms benefit.

I. Main idea: _____

  A. Supporting detail: _____

  B. Supporting detail: _____

CONTEXT CLUES: Definition

Definitions in your reading can provide the meanings of unfamiliar words. In scientific articles, unfamiliar words may be defined or restated in the sentence in which they first appear.

Read the following sentence. Look for a definition to help explain the underlined word.

If you look very closely, you can see that it is an entire <u>ecosystem</u>—a group of organisms interacting with one another and with the nonliving environment.

If you don't know the meaning of *ecosystem*, read on. The rest of the sentence defines the word.

▶ Read the sentence below. Circle the words that define the underlined word.

All organisms that are not producers are <u>consumers</u>, organisms that obtain energy by eating other organisms.

In this selection, the words *competition, predation,* and *producers* are underlined. As you read, look for definitions within the text to learn their meanings.

> **Strategy Tip**
>
> As you read "Ecosystem Essentials," notice the article's main headings. Look for the main ideas and supporting details in each section.

LESSON 12 Outlining **51**

READING A SCIENCE SELECTION

Ecosystem Essentials

A park might look like just a patch of grass with a tree or two, a few shrubs, or perhaps some wildflowers, and a small stream running through it. If you look very closely, though, you can see that it is an entire **ecosystem**—a group of organisms interacting with one another and with the nonliving environment.

The living part of any ecosystem is a community. A forest community may include deer, rabbits, insects, trees, wildflowers, and mushrooms. A pond community may be made up of fish, frogs, herons, insects, and plants. Each population of a community includes all the members of a particular species that live in the same area. One population of a forest community might be all the oak trees that grow there. Another population could be all the termites that live in the trees.

Interactions in Ecosystems

Populations within an ecosystem constantly interact and are acted upon by outside forces.

Each organism in a community must obtain resources—food, water, and other things that it needs to survive. When the amounts of these resources are limited, competition occurs. Competition is a relationship in which living things struggle with each other to obtain resources. A mature, established tree, for example, may compete with its own seedlings for light and for minerals in the soil.

Another type of limiting relationship in an ecosystem is predation (pri DAY shən). Predation occurs when one organism, the predator, kills and eats another, the prey. The double line graph in Figure 1 illustrates the connection between populations of predators and prey.

Some relationships within ecosystems are actually helpful to one or both organisms involved. **Commensalism** (kə MEN sə LI zəm) is a relationship in which one organism benefits and the other organism in the partnership is unaffected. In **mutualism** (MYOO chə wə LI zəm), both organisms benefit. Figure 2 shows the various types of relationships that exist in communities in an ecosystem.

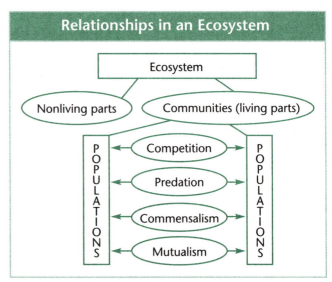

FIGURE 2. This chart shows the relationships between populations in an ecosystem.

Not all the changes that occur in ecosystems result from interaction among their organisms. Floods, droughts, and bitter winters are examples of external factors that can alter an ecosystem. Plant and animal diseases can enter a community and change the size and balance of its populations. Human activity, such as deforestation, hunting, and pollution, has an impact on ecosystems as well.

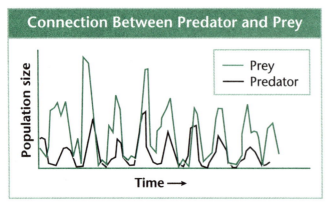

FIGURE 1. This graph shows how the relationship between predators and prey affects population.

Energy Flow in Ecosystems

For populations to survive, energy must constantly flow through ecosystems. The primary source of energy for all organisms is the sun. Energy from the sun enters the ecosystem and is trapped by <u>producers</u>, organisms that use the sun's energy to make their own food. The food is made through photosynthesis (FOH to SIN thə sis), the process plants use to make complex molecules from simple ones.

Producers use some of their food to carry out their life processes, and then they store the rest. The stored food makes the producer a source of energy for organisms that feed on the producer. Plants, some protists, and blue-green algae are examples of producers.

All organisms that are not producers are **consumers**, organisms that obtain energy by eating other organisms. Some consumers eat only producers, and others eat only consumers. Still other consumers—most humans, for example—eat both consumers and producers.

A **decomposer**, which feeds on dead organic matter, is another type of organism in an ecosystem. Decomposers obtain energy by breaking down dead organisms. Decomposers, such as mushrooms, return some nutrients to the ecosystem during their feeding process. The nutrients are used by producers in carrying out such life processes as photosynthesis.

Energy moves through an ecosystem by the feeding relationships of its organisms. A **food chain** is a model that shows some of an ecosystem's feeding relationships. Here is an example of a food chain.

SUN → GRASS → MOUSE → SNAKE → HAWK

An ecosystem contains many different, overlapping food chains. A **food web** is a model that shows the connections among food chains. In the example of a food web in Figure 3, rabbits and mice eat a producer, grass. Snakes and hawks feed on rabbits and mice; however, a snake can be eaten by a hawk.

It is important to remember that a food chain shows how energy is transferred through an ecosystem. Energy enters the ecosystem through producers, and some of the energy is passed along to the consumers that eat the producers. However, a great amount of the energy is lost to the ecosystem in the form of heat.

An **energy pyramid** is a model that shows how energy is transferred and lost in a food chain. Look at Figure 4. You can see that energy is transferred from the grass to the mouse to the snake to the hawk. Note that the shape of the pyramid shows that each level contains less energy than the level below. There is more energy to support life at the beginning of a food chain than at the end.

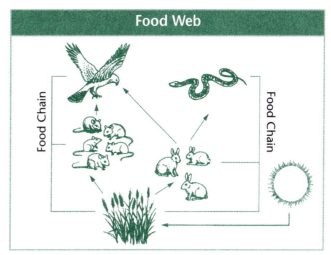

FIGURE 3. This food web shows a particular food chain in an ecosystem.

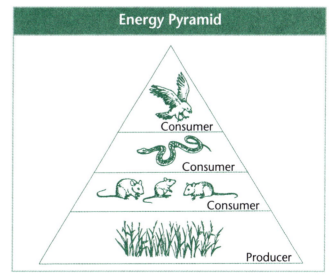

FIGURE 4. This energy pyramid shows the transfer of energy in an ecosystem.

COMPREHENSION

1. What is the main idea of the section titled "Interactions in Ecosystems"?

   _____

   _____

2. What is the difference between commensalism and mutualism?

   _____

   _____

3. When does competition occur in a community?

   _____

   _____

4. What is the main idea of the section titled "Energy Flow in Ecosystems"?

   _____

   _____

5. What is the primary source of energy for all organisms?

   _____

   _____

6. Complete each sentence by filling in the correct word from below.

      producers   predation   competition

   a. When one organism kills and eats another, it is an example of _____.

   b. _____ use the energy from the sun to make their own food.

   c. A relationship in which living things struggle with each other to obtain resources is called _____.

CRITICAL THINKING

1. Look at Figure 1 on page 52. Explain what happens when the population of prey increases.

   _____

2. What effect might an oil spill have on an aquatic ecosystem?

   _____

3. Conclude what would happen in an ecosystem if the population of predators, such as hawks or snakes, was eliminated.

   _____

4. When the hummingbird drinks nectar from a flower, it obtains nutrients it needs to live. As the bird moves from flower to flower, it transfers pollen. This is an example of

   a. competition.

   b. predation.

   c. mutualism.

   d. commensalism.

54 LESSON 12 Outlining

SKILL FOCUS: OUTLINING

1. Complete the following outline for the first section of the selection.

   I. Interactions in Ecosystems

       A. _____

           1. _____

           2. _____

       B. _____

           1. _____

           2. _____

       C. _____

           1. _____

           2. _____

2. Create an outline for the second section of the selection.

   II. Energy Flow in Ecosystems

       A. _____

           1. _____

           2. _____

           3. _____

       B. _____

           1. _____

           2. _____

3. Suppose you were asked to write a brief report on a kind of ecosystem that interests you. After doing some research and jotting down notes, create an outline that will help you write the report. Complete the outline on a separate sheet of paper.

_____

_____

_____

_____

Reading-Writing Connection

On a separate sheet of paper, use your notes and outline to write a brief report on the ecosystem of your choice. Include a diagram if you wish.

LESSON 13

Skill: Understanding Geometric Terms

BACKGROUND INFORMATION

"Basic Geometric Terms" is about words used in the subject of geometry, which is the study of relationships among points, lines, angles, and shapes. The discovery of geometry is often attributed to the ancient Greeks (600 B.C.–A.D. 450), but earlier civilizations also knew about geometry.

For example, the ancient Babylonians and the ancient Egyptians had formulas for finding area and volume. The Babylonians also understood the relationship between the circumference of a circle and its diameter (π), and the relationship among the sides of a right triangle (the Pythagorean theorem).

The Greeks, however, were the first to formalize the study of geometry and write proofs. This work became the basis for Euclidean geometry, the geometry you study in high school.

SKILL FOCUS: Understanding Geometric Terms

Terms and **symbols** are important in solving **geometry** problems. Terms and symbols tell you very specific things about a figure. Therefore when you read a word that names a shape, you think of what you know about that shape.

If you had a problem dealing with a square, you would probably picture four equal sides and four right angles. What else do you know about squares? You may know that the diagonals are equal and perpendicular, and that they form isosceles triangles. You may or may not need this information to solve a given problem.

Figures also help you to solve geometry problems. If a figure is not drawn for you, you can draw one yourself. Mark the points, lines, and angles on the picture to show the properties involved.

▶ Read the geometry terms below. Picture the shape in your mind. Then write a sentence to describe it. For example, a circle is a closed shape with no angles and curved sides.

1. triangle _____

_____

2. square _____

_____

3. angle _____

_____

WORD CLUES

Many words in geometry describe specific properties of shapes. Knowing the meanings of these words will assist you in forming the mental pictures of the various shapes. Remember that many of these words contain word parts that come from Latin or Greek. In the word *triangle*, *tri-* is a prefix meaning "three"; in *quadrilateral*, *quadri-* is a prefix meaning "four"; in *diagonal*, *dia-* is a prefix meaning "across"; and in *equilateral*, *equ-* is a Latin root meaning "equal."

> **Strategy Tip**
>
> "Basic Geometric Terms" describes the properties of some shapes. As you read the description of a shape, look at the picture and find the part of the figure that is being described.

56 LESSON 13 Understanding Geometric Terms

(READING A MATHEMATICS SELECTION)

Basic Geometric Terms

More than numbers, geometry uses words, symbols, and pictures to describe relationships within or between figures. To study geometry, you must know how to go from words to pictures or from pictures to words. The following chart contains a list of commonly used symbols and words, their meanings, and their marks on a figure.

Word/Symbol	Meaning	Illustration
‖	is parallel to	 $\overline{AB} \parallel \overline{XY}$
⊥	is perpendicular to, forms a right angle	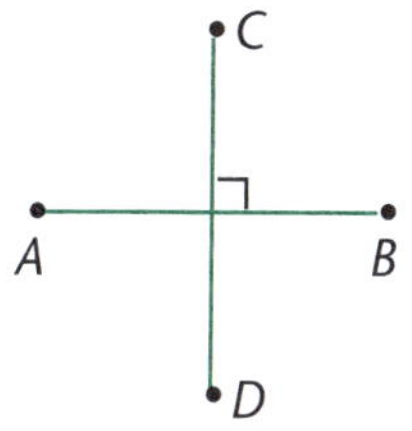 $\overline{AB} \perp \overline{CD}$
≅	is **congruent** to, has the same size and shape	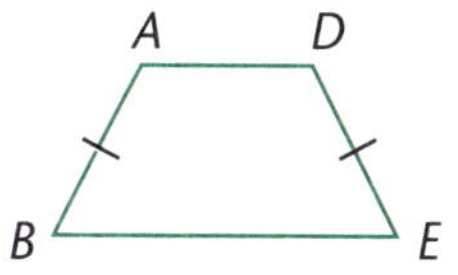 $\overline{AB} \cong \overline{DE}$ 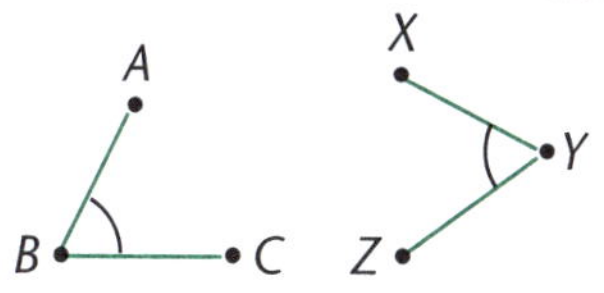 $\quad$ $\angle ABC \cong \angle XYZ$
≇	is not congruent to	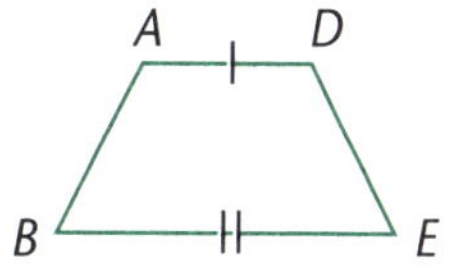 $\overline{AD} \not\cong \overline{BE}$
midpoint	point exactly halfway between two points	 $\overline{RM} = \overline{MS}$
bisects	cuts a line or angle into two congruent lines or angles	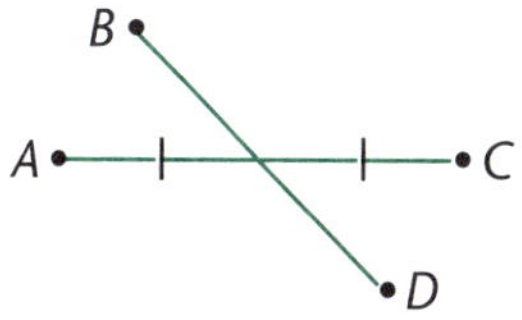 $\overline{BD}$ bisects $\overline{AC}$ 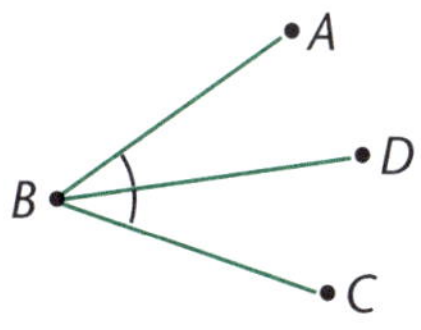 $\quad$ $\overline{BD}$ bisects $\angle ABC$

MATHEMATICS

LESSON 13 Understanding Geometric Terms **57**

The names of figures also give you information about the figures. You can use the definition of a figure to draw conclusions about a given figure.

Quadrilaterals and Parallelograms

All four-sided figures are quadrilaterals (kwah drə LAT ə rəlz). The specific names of quadrilaterals give you more information about the properties of the figures. One category of quadrilateral is the parallelogram (par ə LEL ə gram). As the name implies, a parallelogram has parallel lines. The definition of a parallelogram is a "quadrilateral with two pairs of parallel lines." However, a parallelogram has other properties that can be proven by the definition: Opposite sides are congruent; opposite angles are congruent; and the diagonals bisect each other. When you read the word *parallelogram*, you can, therefore, picture a figure that looks like the one below.

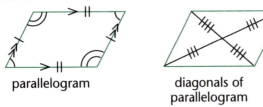

parallelogram   diagonals of parallelogram

A rectangle is a parallelogram with one 90° angle. From this definition, you know that a rectangle has all the properties of a parallelogram and at least one right angle. By using the definition of a parallelogram, you can expand your image of a rectangle to include four right angles and congruent diagonals.

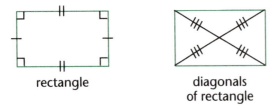

rectangle   diagonals of rectangle

A rhombus (RAHM bəs) is a parallelogram with four equal sides, with its diagonals **perpendicular** to each other.

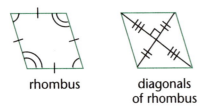

rhombus   diagonals of rhombus

The last of the parallelograms is the square, which has all the properties of both a rectangle and a rhombus. Therefore, a square has four congruent sides and four 90° angles, and its diagonals are congruent and bisect each other at right angles.

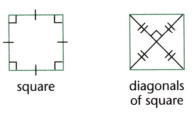

square   diagonals of square

Triangles

Triangles are three-sided figures, and in all triangles, the sum of the measures of the angles is 180°. Some triangles have special names that give you more information about the figure, such as *isosceles, equilateral,* and *right*.

An isosceles (eye SAHS ə leez) triangle has two congruent sides and two congruent angles. In an isosceles triangle, the base is the side between the congruent sides, and the vertex is the angle opposite the base. An equilateral (ee kwi LAT ə rəl) triangle has three congruent sides and three congruent angles. A right triangle has one right angle.

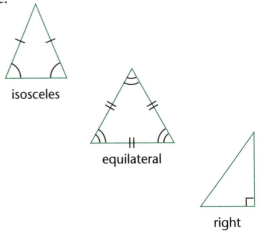

isosceles

equilateral

right

As you study geometry, you will see that it requires you to draw conclusions from "given" information. You must be able to support your conclusions, using rules or definitions that you learn. The phrase "because that is what the picture looks like" is never enough to support a conclusion; you need to be able to read the words and symbols in order to get the necessary information about a figure.

When you look at the following picture, all you know for certain is that it is a quadrilateral. You must read the "given" description that follows to gain more information. As you read the description, it might help you to trace the figure.

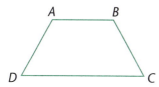

Description: In quadrilateral *ABCD*, $\overline{AB} \parallel \overline{CD}$, and $\overline{AD} \cong \overline{BC}$. Point *M* is the midpoint of $\overline{DC}$, and $\overline{MC} \cong \overline{AB}$. △*ADM* is an isosceles triangle with vertex *A*.

When all the relationships given in the description are marked, the figure looks like the following.

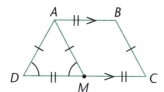

When you draw a figure yourself, you may have to redraw it once you have read and understood all the given information. For example, the following figure is drawn twice. The first picture shows the figure you might draw before you have read all the information. The second represents the redrawn version that accurately reflects all the information given in the description.

Description: In △*RST*, $\overline{RS} \perp \overline{ST}$ and ∠*STR* ≅ ∠*TRS*.

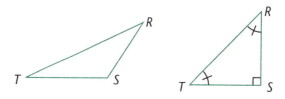

When you study figures in geometry, carefully read the words that describe them. Also be sure to pay close attention to the symbols, keeping in mind that the symbols contain as much information as the words.

COMPREHENSION

1. Write each of the following symbols in words.

   a. $\overline{CD} \perp \overline{GH}$

   _____

   _____

   b. △*XYZ* ≅ △*DEF*

   _____

   _____

   c. $\overline{MN} \parallel \overline{FG}$

   _____

   _____

   d. ∠*ABC* ≇ ∠*PRQ*

   _____

   _____

2. What is a midpoint?

   _____

   _____

3. Circle the letter of the description that correctly defines a square.

   a. a figure with two sets of parallel lines
   b. a four-sided figure with equal sides
   c. a parallelogram with four equal sides
   d. a parallelogram with four equal sides and four 90° angles

4. What is an isosceles triangle?

   _____

   _____

LESSON 13 Understanding Geometric Terms

CRITICAL THINKING

1. For each picture, write the relationship shown.

   a.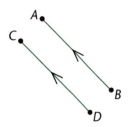

   _____

   _____

   b.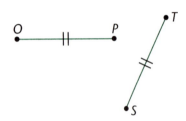

   _____

   _____

   c.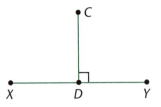

   _____

   _____

   d.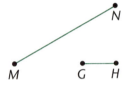

   _____

   _____

2. Use the marks on each figure to name the figure as specifically as possible.

   a.

   _____

   b.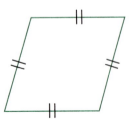

   _____

   c.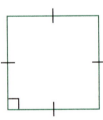

   _____

   d.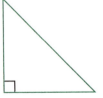

   _____

60 LESSON 13 Understanding Geometric Terms

SKILL FOCUS: UNDERSTANDING GEOMETRIC TERMS

1. Read the description of each figure carefully and mark the figure to show all the information given in the description.

   a. In △ABC, D is a point on $\overline{BC}$.
      $\overline{AD}$ bisects ∠BAC.
      ∠ABC ≅ ∠ACB

   b. Quadrilateral QRST is a parallelogram.
      M is the midpoint of $\overline{QR}$.
      $\overline{MR} \cong \overline{RS}$
      $\overline{QT} \perp \overline{TS}$

2. Draw the figure in each description below.

   a. In quadrilateral MNOP, $\overline{MN} \parallel \overline{OP}$.
      $\overline{NO} \perp \overline{OP}$
      ∠MPO < 90°

   b. In quadrilateral ABCD, $\overline{AB} \cong \overline{CD}$.
      Diagonals $\overline{AC} \perp \overline{BD}$.

Reading-Writing Connection

How might knowing the properties of a square or a rectangle help a builder or an architect design a house? On a separate sheet of paper, write a paragraph or two explaining your idea and then draw a picture to illustrate it.

LESSON 14

Skill: Taking Notes and Summarizing

Whether you are studying for a test, doing research for a report, or just trying to remember what you read, you will find some reading skills especially helpful. Two of the most helpful skills for recalling factual material often work together: **taking notes** and **summarizing.**

Taking notes means jotting down the details in a passage that you need. For example, if you are reading to find the answer to a specific question, you will focus only on the details that help answer your question. You need not use complete sentences in your notes; write just enough for each note to make sense.

While taking notes helps you remember the specific details in a passage, summarizing helps you remember main ideas and the relationship among some of the supporting details. It requires an almost opposite kind of thinking. When you summarize, you use very specific details to make more general statements. You can summarize material from the notes you took on a specific passage. For example, look at how the writer summarizes the passage below from her notes.

In the following example, look for the details that a student noted and the summary she created. Think, too, about the details that she did not bother to include in her notes and the statements made in her summary.

European explorers searched Latin America for gold, and they were often successful in their quest. Along the way, however, they also found other kinds of treasure. One such treasure was more colorful than gold, for American Indians had learned to make dyes that far surpassed anything that the Europeans had. American Indians in Peru, for example, had developed more than 100 different dyes, so strong and bright that their centuries-old cloth in museum displays today still dazzles the eye with its richness. The first native dye to become popular with Europeans was brazilin, which produced a reddish-purple hue. It proved so popular, in fact, that the land where the trees grew from which brazilin was made earned the name *tierra de brasil*—or, as we know it today, Brazil. Brazilin soon was eclipsed by cochineal, a scarlet dye processed from the bodies of an insect native to Mexico. Cochineal was marketed all over Europe and colored the "redcoats" of the English army, among other things.

Notes
- *native dyes—strong and bright—a form of riches for Europeans in Latin America*
- *brazilin (from trees; reddish-purple) first to become popular with Europeans*
- *then cochineal (from insects; scarlet) used widely throughout Europe*

Summary
    European explorers in Latin America found wealth by marketing the strong, bright dyes that American Indians made. Brazilin, a reddish-purple hue produced from a certain kind of tree, became very popular in Europe and gave the country of Brazil its name. Cochineal, a scarlet color made from a Mexican insect, found an even greater market in Europe.

62 LESSON 14 Taking Notes and Summarizing

The following passage describes two other Latin American products that also had a strong effect on Europe. On the lines provided, take some notes on the passage. Then summarize the passage.

In the nineteenth century, two natural products from Latin America made yet another powerful impact upon European industry. As the Industrial Revolution progressed, Europeans were finding that Asian hemp, the type of rope they had been using most often, was not tough enough for their latest needs. Sisal from Latin America made a much stronger and smoother rope. Soon both agricultural and manufacturing industries were switching to sisal. Europeans found many uses for South American rubber, as well. American Indians had used rubber to waterproof cloaks, footgear, and bottles, and to make rubber balls, but Europeans had considered rubber only a novelty.

In 1839, however, American inventor Charles Goodyear discovered the process of vulcanization (a process that American Indians actually had used for centuries). Vulcanization involves heating rubber and mixing it with sulfur to strengthen it and remove its stickiness. Vulcanized rubber was soon used throughout Europe and the United States to make water-resistant clothes, equipment (prized especially by explorers and pioneers), and machine parts. Later it insulated electrical wires and made bicycle tires practical. Since their introduction to Europe, both sisal and rubber have played an important role in industries in other parts of the world, as well.

Notes

1. _____

2. _____

3. _____

4. _____

5. _____

Summary

_____

_____

_____

_____

_____

_____

_____

_____

LESSON 14 Taking Notes and Summarizing

LESSON 15

Skill: Suffixes

A **suffix** is a word part that is added at the end of a word to change its meaning.
The addition of a suffix can also change a word from one part of speech to another.

    thank (verb) + **ful** (suffix) = **thankful** (adjective)

When a word ends in *e* and the suffix begins with a vowel, you drop the final *e*
before adding the suffix. Usually, you make no spelling change if the suffix begins
with a consonant.

    sterile (adjective meaning "free of germs") + **ize** (suffix meaning "to make") = **sterilize** (verb)

Some suffixes and their meanings are given below.

Suffixes That Make Nouns	
-dom	state or condition of
-ee	person receiving an action
-ist	person who does or believes
-ity	state or condition of
-ry	practice of
Suffixes That Make Adjectives	
-al	like, suited to
-ian	person or thing belonging to a group
-ive	tending to, toward
Suffixes That Make Verbs	
-ify	to make or cause to have or be like
-ize	to make or cause to be

A. Change each of the words below and on page 65 by adding the suffix that changes it to a new part of speech with a new meaning. Then write the new word on the line provided.
The first one is done for you.

	Word	Change To	New Word
1.	art	noun meaning "doer of art"	artist
2.	employ	noun meaning "one who receives employment"	
3.	fort	verb meaning "to make like a fort"	
4.	wise	noun meaning "state of being wise"	
5.	reptile	adjective meaning "belonging to the group called reptiles"	

64 LESSON 15 Suffixes

6.	insane	noun meaning "condition of being mentally unstable"	_____
7.	music	adjective meaning "skilled in the art of combining vocal or instrumental sounds"	_____
8.	dentist	noun meaning "the practice of being a dentist"	_____
9.	standard	verb meaning "to make standard"	_____
10.	disrupt	adjective meaning "tending to throw into confusion"	_____
11.	journal	noun meaning "one who writes for newspapers or journals"	_____

B. Use the words above to complete the following sentences. Use each word only once.

1. The practice of _____ requires that dentists be people who are skillful at using tools.

2. A prize-winning _____ reports on the national political scene in her new column in our local newspaper.

3. Before the trial, the lawyer entered a plea of _____ and claimed his client was not sane enough to stand trial.

4. Vitamins help to _____ your body against disease.

5. At her new job, Anisha was named _____ of the month because of her hard work and cooperative attitude.

6. Knowledge can be acquired early, but _____ grows slowly over a person's lifetime.

7. Dinosaurs had many _____ traits, such as laying eggs instead of having live births as mammals do.

8. The _____ experimented with different colors and forms throughout his career.

9. An automobile manufacturer sets up a standard or model for what a car will be like so

   that he can _____ each automobile that he produces.

10. The parents did their best to nurture the _____ ability of their gifted child, who started playing the violin at the age of five.

11. Theodore was _____ in class because he wandered around, spoke up loudly, and interrupted the teacher.

LESSON 15 Suffixes **65**

LESSON 16

Skill: Prefixes

A **prefix** is a word part that is added to the beginning of a word to change its meaning. Some prefixes and their meanings are given below.

Prefix	Meaning	Prefix	Meaning
ante-	before	intra-	to the inside
anti-	against	pro-	in place of
en-	to cause to be	retro-	back, backward
ex-	away from	semi-	half
dia-	across	syn-	together with
inter-	among, between	trans-	beyond

A. Read each word or word part below and the meaning that follows it. Then write the correct prefix before each word.

1. _____ national — occurring between countries

2. _____ noun — word used in place of a noun

3. _____ rage — to make extremely angry

4. _____ war — against all armed conflicts

5. _____ dated — occurred before a certain date

6. _____ chronize — to make things match in time

7. _____ circle — half of a circle

8. _____ hale — send breath away from the body

B. Select one of the words above to complete each of the following sentences.

1. The _____ protest occurred because so many people were opposed to the war.

2. The children sat in a _____ on the floor, facing the librarian who read them a story.

3. On a very cold day, you will probably _____ many frosty breaths into the air.

4. If we want to be sure to meet exactly on time, we must _____ our watches before we leave.

5. The Olympic Games are _____ athletic competitions designed to bring together people of different nations.

6. The exploration of eastern Canada by the Vikings _____ the discoveries of Columbus by about 500 years.

7. When you write, be careful that the _____ you use matches the noun that it replaces.

8. The judgments of the umpire in a baseball game are sure to _____ at least some of the fans.

LESSON 17
Skill: Base Words and Roots

A **base word** is a word to which prefixes and suffixes can be added. A base word is complete in meaning and can stand alone. For example, *war* is a base word. You can add the prefix *anti-* to make *antiwar* or the suffix *-ing* to make *warring*.

A **root** is a combining form that takes prefixes and suffixes, but it cannot be used alone. Many roots came into the English language from Latin and Greek. Below are some frequently used Latin and Greek roots and their meanings.

Latin Roots		Greek Roots	
aqua	water	*anthrop*	human
capit	head	*arch*	ancient
cogn	know	*chrom*	color
cred	believe	*dem*	people
fact	do or make	*hydr*	water
fid	belief, faith	*log*	word, study
lect	read	*micro*	small
loqu	talk, speech	*neo*	new
omni	all	*poly*	many
verb	word	*psych*	mind

A. Write the meaning of each root below. Then write a word that contains that root, and the word's meaning. The first one is done for you.

Root	Meaning	Word	Meaning
1. psych	mind	psychology	study of the mind
2. cred			
3. verb			
4. hydr			
5. dem			

B. Circle the letter of the word or phrase that most closely matches the meaning of the underlined word.

1. the study of <u>anthropology</u>   **a.** human culture   **b.** law   **c.** mathematics   **d.** plants

2. diving with an <u>aquanaut</u>   **a.** boat   **b.** underwater explorer   **c.** oxygen pack   **d.** plane

3. the shape of a <u>polygon</u>   **a.** triangle   **b.** circle   **c.** line   **d.** many-sided figure

4. the teeth of an <u>omnivore</u>   **a.** all animals   **b.** animals that eat animal food

     c. animals that eat all foods   **d.** animals that eat vegetable food

LESSON 18

Skill: Reading a Credit Card Statement

Many kinds of businesses, such as banks, department stores, and gas stations, allow you, the customer, to buy on credit by issuing you a **credit card**. Using a credit card means agreeing to the terms that the issuer sets. One of those terms is your **credit limit**, the maximum amount that you can charge to the card. Another term, the **finance charge**, is the amount of interest the issuer adds to the unpaid balance.

Each month you will receive a **statement** from the issuer of the credit card. The statement provides information about your use of the card for that statement period and about any payments you have made during that period. It also explains how the amount that you owe has been calculated. For example, if you have used a bank's credit card to borrow cash, the interest you are being charged to repay that may be different from the interest you are being charged to repay other purchases.

Study the credit card statement below. Then answer the questions that follow.

EAGLE BANK
Credit Card Statement

CARD MEMBER
Marissa Gould
1052 Westland Way, Apt. 2C
Los Angeles, CA 90012-3013

Account Number: 5010 2190 4874 5555

New Balance	Minimum Payment Due	Due Date	Amount Enclosed
$840.79	$26.00	11/01/07	$75.00

MAKE CHECKS PAYABLE TO EAGLE BANK
To avoid additional finance charges, pay the new balance by the due date.

DATE	REFERENCE NUMBER	DESCRIPTION	AMOUNT
9/03	24555378223460951089069	LIBERTY MUSIC ENCINO CA	33.74
9/12	7521193823811377430155	MACK'S RIBS MALIBU CA	13.35
9/15	89443636342016845670095	COMP. NET SERVICE LOS ANG CA	19.95
9/19	33067263960093847263056	TOP TOPS 800-555-6541 TX	59.03
9/25	7521938238113774301512	MACK'S RIBS MALIBU CA	14.12
9/27	40730739573068274008788	PAYMENT—THANK YOU	−60.00

ACCOUNT SUMMARY

Statement Closing Date:	10/02/07	Previous Balance:	$752.78
Credit Limit:	$3,500.00	Purchases/Fees:	$140.19
Cash Advance Limit:	$1,800.00	Cash Advances:	$0.00
Available Credit:	$2,659.21	Finance Charges:	$7.82
		Payments/Credits:	$60.00
		New Balance:	$840.79

Balance Rate Applied To	Daily Periodic Rate	Corresponding Annual Percentage Rate	Finance Charge
Purchases/Other Charges			
$752.78	.035%	12.6 %	$7.82
Cash Advances			
$0.00	.053%	19.27%	$0.00

SEND PAYMENTS TO:
Eagle Bank Services
P. O. Box 84391
Pasadena, CA 91116-4391

SEND INQUIRIES TO:
Eagle Bank Services
P. O. Box 85002
Pasadena, CA 91116-5002

TO REPORT LOST OR STOLEN CARDS OR FOR CUSTOMER SERVICE CALL 1-800-555-2171

A. Use the credit card statement on page 68 to fill in the circle next to the correct answer to each question below.

1. What is the closing date of this statement?
   - ○ November 1, 2007
   - ○ October 2, 2007
   - ○ November 2, 2007
   - ○ October 1, 2007

2. How many purchases did the card member charge during this statement period?
   - ○ five
   - ○ seven
   - ○ six
   - ○ eight

3. How much finance charge is being applied to the unpaid balance?
   - ○ $26.00
   - ○ $14.12
   - ○ $12.65
   - ○ $7.82

4. How much did the card member pay on this account the previous month?
   - ○ $26.00
   - ○ $75.00
   - ○ $60.00
   - ○ $140.19

5. If the card member wants to avoid paying any finance charges, how much should she pay this month?
   - ○ $752.78
   - ○ $840.79
   - ○ $75.00
   - ○ $1,800.00

6. If the card member wanted to purchase up to her credit limit, how much above her present balance could she charge?
   - ○ $2,659.21
   - ○ $752.78
   - ○ $3,500.00
   - ○ $840.79

B. Use the credit card statement on page 68 to complete each sentence below.

1. This credit card was issued by _____ to _____.

2. The card member's account number is _____.

3. The minimum payment due is _____, but the card member is paying

   _____ this month.

4. The card member charged a purchase of $33.74 at _____.

5. The card member could get a total cash advance of _____.

6. The code that identifies each business at which a purchase was made is called the _____.

7. You can assume that the card member subscribes to an Internet provider and

   pays _____ for that service each month.

8. During this statement period, the card member twice charged purchases

   at _____ for a total of _____.

9. If the card member wanted to make a $400.00 purchase, she probably would be wiser

   to charge it than to pay cash that she had gotten through a cash advance because _____

   _____.

10. You can tell that the purchase from Top Tops was a catalog order because _____

    _____.

LESSON 18   Reading a Credit Card Statement   **69**

unit three
Observations

LESSON 19
Skill: Setting

BACKGROUND INFORMATION
In *I Know Why the Caged Bird Sings*, the first in a series of her autobiographical books, Maya Angelou describes her early days in Stamps, Arkansas. Much of the writing of this award-winning poet and novelist stresses themes like courage, perseverance, and achievement. Maya Angelou's works often depict strong female role models. Born in St. Louis, Missouri, Angelou spent much of her childhood with her grandmother in rural Arkansas.

SKILL FOCUS: Setting
Setting is the time and place of a written work. The time may include the historical era, the year, the season, or the time of day. The place may be a country, a community, a building—even a room in a home or school.

When you think about setting, consider these questions.

- Where and when does the story take place?
- What details give clues to the setting?
- How does the setting affect the story?

▶ Read the paragraph below. Then, in the center oval on the Idea Web in the next column, write the setting being described. In the surrounding ovals, write the details that bring the setting to life. You can add extra ovals if you need to.

The Store was my favorite place to be. Alone and empty in the mornings, it looked like an unopened present from a stranger. Opening the front doors was pulling the ribbon off the unexpected gift. The light would come in softly (we faced north), easing over the shelves of mackerel, salmon, tobacco, thread. It fell flat on the big vat of lard and by noontime during the summer the grease had softened to a thick soup.

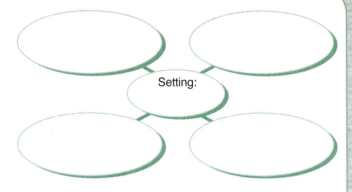

Setting:

CONTEXT CLUES: Inferring Meanings
Sometimes when you see an unfamiliar word in a story, you must **infer** its meaning. To do this, you use information from other parts of the sentence and what you already know to determine what the word means. Read the following and look for clues to infer the meaning of the underlined word.

. . . <u>troubadours</u> on their ceaseless crawlings through the South . . . sang their sad songs of The Brazos while they played juice harps and cigar-box guitars.

You can infer from other words in the sentence that the word *troubadours* has to do with traveling musicians who sing and play instruments.

▶ Read the sentence below. Circle the words that help you infer the underlined word's meaning.

They took out a certain round, harmless bone and rubbed salt, <u>coarse</u> brown salt that looked like fine gravel, into the flesh.

In this selection, the words *affluent*, *prophesied*, and *inordinate* are underlined. Look for words or phrases that help you infer the meanings of these words.

> **Strategy Tip**
>
> As you read, look for details that tell you when and where this autobiographical account is set.

70   LESSON 19   Setting

from I Know Why the Caged Bird Sings
Maya Angelou

When I was three and Bailey four, we had arrived in the musty little town, wearing tags on our wrists which instructed—"To Whom It May Concern"— that we were Marguerite and Bailey Johnson, Jr., from Long Beach, California, en route to Stamps, Arkansas, c/o Mrs. Annie Henderson.

Our parents had decided to put an end to their calamitous marriage, and Father shipped us home to his mother. A porter had been charged with our welfare—he got off the train the next day in Arizona—and our tickets were pinned to my brother's inside coat pocket.

I don't remember much of the trip, but after we reached the segregated southern part of the journey, things must have looked up. Negro passengers, who always traveled with loaded lunch boxes, felt sorry for "the poor little motherless darlings" and plied us with cold fried chicken and potato salad.

Years later I discovered that the United States had been crossed thousands of times by frightened Black children traveling alone to their newly affluent parents in Northern cities, or back to grandmothers in Southern towns when the urban North reneged on its economic promises.

The town reacted to us as its inhabitants had reacted to all things new before our coming. It regarded us a while without curiosity but with caution, and after we were seen to be harmless (and children), it closed in around us as a real mother embraces a stranger's child. Warmly, but not too familiarly.

We lived with our grandmother and uncle in the rear of the Store (it was always spoken of with a capital *s*), which she had owned some twenty-five years.

Early in the century, Momma (we soon stopped calling her Grandmother) sold lunches to the

sawmen in the lumberyard (east Stamps) and the seedmen at the cotton gin (west Stamps). Her crisp meat pies and cool lemonade, when joined to her miraculous ability to be in two places at the same time, assured her business success. From being a mobile lunch counter, she set up a stand between the two points of fiscal interest and supplied the workers' needs for a few years. Then she had the Store built in the heart of the Negro area. Over the years it became the lay center of activities in town. On Saturdays, barbers sat their customers in the shade on the porch of the Store, and troubadours on their ceaseless crawlings through the South leaned across its benches and sang their sad songs of The Brazos while they played juice harps and cigar-box guitars.

The formal name of the Store was the Wm. Johnson General Merchandise Store. Customers could find food staples, a good variety of colored thread, mash for hogs, corn for chickens, coal oil for lamps, light bulbs for the wealthy, shoestrings, hair dressing, balloons, and flower seeds. Anything not visible had only to be ordered.

Until we became familiar enough to belong to the Store and it to us, we were locked up in a fun House of Things where the attendant had gone home for life.

≈

Each year I watched the field across from the Store turn caterpillar green, then gradually frosty white. I knew exactly how long it would be before the big wagons would pull into the front yard and load on the cotton pickers at daybreak to carry them to the remains of slavery's plantations.

During the picking season my grandmother would get out of bed at four o'clock (she never used an alarm clock) and creak down to her knees and chant in a sleep-filled voice, "Our Father, thank you for letting me see this New Day. Thank you that you didn't allow the bed I lay on last night to be my cooling board, nor my blanket my winding sheet. Guide my feet this day along the straight and narrow, and help me to put a bridle on my tongue. Bless this house, and everybody in it. Thank you, in the name of your Son, Jesus Christ. Amen."

Before she had quite arisen, she called our names and issued orders, and pushed her large feet into homemade slippers and across the bare lye-washed wooden floor to light the coal-oil lamp.

The lamplight in the Store gave a soft make-believe feeling to our world which made me want to whisper and walk about on tiptoe. The odors of onions and oranges and kerosene had been mixing all night and wouldn't be disturbed until the wooded slat was removed from the door and the early morning air forced its way in with the bodies of people who had walked miles to reach the pickup place.

"Sister, I'll have two cans of sardines."

"I'm gonna work so fast today, I'm gonna make you look like you standing still."

"Lemme have a hunk uh cheese and some sody crackers."

"Just gimme a coupla them fat peanut paddies." That would be from a picker who was taking his lunch. The greasy brown paper sack was stuck behind the bib of his overalls. He'd use the candy as a snack before the noon sun called the workers to rest.

In those tender mornings the Store was full of laughing, joking, boasting and bragging. One man was going to pick two hundred pounds of cotton, and another three hundred. Even the children were promising to bring home fo' bits and six bits.

The champion picker of the day before was the hero of the dawn. If he <u>prophesied</u> that the cotton in today's field was going to be sparse and stick to the bolls like glue, every listener would grunt a hearty agreement.

The sound of the empty cotton sacks dragging over the floor and the murmurs of waking people were sliced by the cash register as we rang up the five-cent sales.

If the morning sounds and smells were touched with the supernatural, the late afternoon had all the features of the normal Arkansas life. In the dying sunlight the people dragged, rather than their empty cotton sacks.

Brought back to the Store, the pickers would step out of the backs of trucks and fold down, dirt-disappointed, to the ground. No matter how much they had picked, it wasn't enough. Their wages wouldn't even get them out of debt to my grandmother, not to mention the staggering bill that waited on them at the white commissary downtown.

The sounds of the new morning had been replaced with grumbles about cheating houses, weighted scales, snakes, skimpy cotton and dusty rows. In later years I was to confront the stereotyped picture of gay songsinging cotton pickers with such <u>inordinate</u> rage that I was told even by fellow Blacks that my paranoia was embarrassing. But I had seen the fingers cut by the mean little cotton bolls, and I had witnessed the backs and shoulders and arms and legs resisting any further demands.

Some of the workers would leave their sacks at the Store to be picked up the following morning, but a few had to take them home for repairs. I winced to picture them sewing the coarse material under a coal-oil lamp with fingers stiffening from the day's work. In too few hours they would have to walk back to Sister Henderson's Store, get vittles and load, again, onto the trucks. Then they would face another day of trying to earn enough for the whole year with the heavy knowledge that they were going to end the season as they started it: without the money or credit necessary to sustain a family for three months. In cotton-picking time the late afternoons revealed the harshness of Black Southern life, which in the early morning had been softened by nature's blessing of grogginess, forgetfulness, and the soft lamplight.

✔ Weighing the half-pounds of flour, excluding the scoop, and depositing them dust-free into the thin paper sacks held a simple kind of adventure for me. I developed an eye for measuring how full a silver-looking ladle of flour, mash, meal, sugar or corn had to be to push the scale indicator over to eight ounces or one pound. When I was absolutely accurate our appreciative customers used to admire: "Sister Henderson sure got some smart grandchildrens." If I was off in the Store's favor, the eagle-eyed women would say, "Put some more in that sack, child. Don't you try to make your profit offa me."

✔ Then I would quietly but persistently punish myself. For every bad judgment, the fine was no silver-wrapped Kisses, the sweet chocolate drops that I loved more than anything in the world, except Bailey. And maybe canned pineapples. My obsession with pineapples nearly drove me mad. I dreamt of the days when I would be grown and able to buy a whole carton for myself alone.

Although the syrupy golden rings sat in their exotic cans on our shelves year round, we only tasted them during Christmas. Momma used the juice to make almost-black fruit cakes. Then she lined heavy soot-encrusted iron skillets with the pineapple rings for rich upside-down cakes. Bailey and I received one slice each, and I carried mine around for hours, shredding off the fruit until nothing was left except the perfume on my fingers. I'd like to think that my desire for pineapples was so sacred that I wouldn't allow myself to steal a can (which was possible) and eat it alone out in the garden, but I'm certain that I must have weighed the possibility of the scent exposing me and didn't have the nerve to attempt it.

Until I was thirteen and left Arkansas for good, the Store was my favorite place to be. Alone and empty in the mornings, it looked like an unopened present from a stranger. Opening the front doors was pulling the ribbon off the unexpected gift. The light would come in softly (we faced north), easing itself over the shelves of mackerel, salmon, tobacco, thread. It fell flat on the big vat of lard and by noontime during the summer the grease had softened to a thick soup. Whenever I walked into the Store in the afternoon, I sensed that it was tired. I alone could hear the slow pulse of its job half done. But just before bedtime, after numerous people had walked in and out, had argued over their bills, or joked about their neighbors, or just dropped in "to give Sister Henderson a 'Hi y'all,'" the promise of magic mornings returned to the Store and spread itself over the family in washed life waves.

X Momma opened boxes of crispy crackers and we sat around the meat block at the rear of the Store. I sliced onions, and Bailey opened two or even three cans of sardines and allowed their juice of oil and fishing boats to ooze down and around the sides. That was supper. In the evening, when we were alone like that, Uncle Willie didn't stutter or shake or give any indication that he had an "affliction." It seemed that the peace of a day's ending was an assurance that the covenant God made with children, Negroes, and the crippled was still in effect.

~

Throwing scoops of corn to the chickens and mixing sour dry mash with leftover food and oily dishwater for the hogs were among our evening chores. Bailey and I sloshed down twilight trails to the pig pens, and standing on the first fence rungs we poured down the unappealing concoctions to our grateful hogs. They mashed their tender pink snouts down into the slop, and rooted and grunted their satisfaction. We always grunted a reply only half in jest. We were also grateful that we had concluded the dirtiest of chores and had only gotten the evil-smelling swill on our shoes, stockings, feet and hands.

~

In Stamps the custom was to can everything that could possibly be preserved. During the killing season, after the first frost, all neighbors helped each other to slaughter hogs and even the quiet, big-eyed cows if they had stopped giving milk.

The missionary ladies of the Christian Methodist Episcopal Church helped Momma prepare the pork for sausage. They squeezed their fat arms elbow deep in the ground meat, mixed it with gray nose-opening sage, pepper and salt, and made tasty little samples for all obedient children who brought wood for the slick black stove. The men chopped off the larger pieces of meat and laid them in the smokehouse to begin the curing process. They opened the knuckle of the hams with their deadly-looking knives, took out a certain round harmless bone ("it could make the meat go

bad") and rubbed salt, coarse brown salt that looked like fine gravel, into the flesh, and the blood popped to the surface.

Throughout the year, until the next frost, we took our meals from the smokehouse, the little garden that lay cousin-close to the Store and from the shelves of canned foods. There were choices on the shelves that could set a hungry child's mouth to watering. Green beans, snapped always the right length, collards, cabbage, juicy red tomato preserves that came into their own on steaming buttered biscuits, and sausage, beets, berries and every fruit grown in Arkansas.

But at least twice yearly Momma would feel that as children we should have fresh meat included in our diets. We were then given money—pennies, nickels, and dimes entrusted to Bailey—and sent to town to buy liver. Since the whites had refrigerators, their butchers bought the meat from commercial slaughterhouses in Texarkana and sold it to the wealthy even in the peak of summer.

Crossing the Black area of Stamps which in childhood's narrow measure seemed a whole world, we were obliged by custom to stop and speak to every person we met, and Bailey felt constrained to spend a few minutes playing with each friend. There was a joy in going to town with money in our pockets (Bailey's pockets were as good as my own) and time on our hands. But the pleasure fled when we reached the white part of town. After we left Mr. Willie Williams' Do Drop Inn, the last stop before whitefolksville, we had to cross the pond and adventure the railroad tracks. We were explorers walking without weapons into man-eating animals' territory.

In Stamps the segregation was so complete that most Black children didn't really, absolutely know what whites looked like. Other than that they were different, to be dreaded, and in that dread was included the hostility of the powerless against the powerful, the poor against the rich, the worker against the worked for and the ragged against the well dressed.

I remember never believing that whites were really real.

COMPREHENSION

1. Why does the narrator move with her brother from California to Stamps, Arkansas?

2. Who is in charge of the Store?

3. What sorts of items are sold in the Store?

4. How do the morning customers differ from the afternoon customers?

5. Why are the customers always disappointed after the day's work?

6. What happens in Stamps after the first frost?

7. What is the situation between African Americans and whites in Stamps, Arkansas?

8. Draw a line to match the following words with their correct meanings.

   inordinate   a. wealthy

   affluent   b. predicted

   prophesied   c. out of proportion

CRITICAL THINKING

1. Explain why the Store is so important to the community of Stamps.

2. Reread the two paragraphs with the ✔ next to them. What does the narrator's self-punishment reveal about her character?

3. Look back at the paragraph with an ✗ next to it. What do you think the "covenant" is?

4. Why is the narrator so frightened about going to the white part of town?

5. How does the atmosphere of the Store compare to the atmosphere of the white part of town?

_____

_____

SKILL FOCUS: SETTING

1. How does the narrator describe the town of Stamps?

   _____

   _____

2. What are some of the details that tell you when this account takes place?

   _____

   _____

3. Write a detail about the Store from the account that appeals to each of the five senses.

   sight: _____

   sound: _____

   _____

   touch: _____

   smell: _____

   taste: _____

4. The Store in the morning and the Store in the afternoon are described very differently. What do the differences in setting tell you about life in Stamps?

   _____

   _____

5. What overall effect does the setting of the Store have on the account?

   _____

   _____

Reading-Writing Connection

On a separate sheet of paper, write a letter to a friend describing a place that would make you feel safe and comfortable. Include details that appeal to the senses to make the setting vivid.

76   LESSON 19   Setting

LESSON 20

Skill: Analyzing

BACKGROUND INFORMATION

"Our Global Economy" traces the roots of economic development in places around the world and compares the economies of several countries today. Today countries around the world are involved in trade, new industries influence global markets, and countries are merging under a unified currency system. As a result, the world economy has a very complex structure.

SKILL FOCUS: Analyzing

When you **analyze** a piece of writing, you break it down into parts, examine the parts, and determine how the parts relate to one another. The first step is to determine the author's purpose. For example, a piece of expository writing, or writing that explains, can have several purposes. Here are some purposes of expository writing.

- to explain a process, situation, or event
- to analyze a problem
- to analyze causes and effects
- to explain problems and solutions
- to compare and contrast people, places, or ideas

The next step is to determine how the writer achieves that purpose. For example, does the writer:

- use facts and statistics?
- use examples?
- use quotations?
- describe causes and effects?
- compare and contrast?
- describe problems and solutions?

▶ Read the paragraph below. Then answer the questions in the next column.

The United Kingdom is one of the top five economic powers in the world. Its economy relies heavily on its services sector. In fact, services make up two-thirds of Britain's gross domestic product, or GDP. Britain's financial and business sector is also strong, making up 20 percent of the GDP. Other sectors that contribute to the GDP include communications and construction.

1. What is the author's purpose for writing this paragraph?

_____

_____

2. How does the author achieve this purpose?

_____

_____

CONTEXT CLUES: Appositives

Sometimes there are **appositive** context clues that can help you determine the meanings of new words. An appositive word or phrase explains a word that comes before it. It is usually set off by commas, parentheses, or dashes and starts with the word *or*.

Read the following sentence and look for appositive context clues that explain the underlined word.

By the end of the twentieth century, trade among countries had become an important part of the __global__, or world, economy.

If you don't know the meaning of the word *global*, the appositive *world* can help you.

▶ Read the sentence below. Circle the appositive that explains what the underlined word means.

__Distributing__, or delivering, its resources brings in income which enables the country to produce more commodities.

In this selection, the words *commodities, capsules,* and *labor costs* are underlined. Look for appositive phrases that explain the meaning of each word.

> **Strategy Tip**
>
> As you read "Our Global Economy," analyze the information the writer provides in each section. Consider how the information is presented and how the purpose of the selection is achieved.

LESSON 20 Analyzing **77**

READING A SOCIAL STUDIES SELECTION

Our Global Economy

There is an old saying that "money makes the world go around." If this is true, then economics is what turns the wheel. Economics is the science that deals with the economy—the production, distribution, and using up of commodities, or goods that can be sold or traded. Distributing, or delivering, a country's resources locally or to other parts of the world brings in income, or money, which enables the country to produce more commodities. This allows a country or people to survive monetarily.

From Farms to Foreign Trade

The global economy of today is very different from what it was in the past. Thousands of years ago, people did not live in towns or villages. Instead they were what scientists call "hunter-gatherers." They hunted animals and they gathered plants. They moved from place to place, following the herds of animals on which they relied for food.

Then about 10,000 years ago, people discovered that they could grow crops by planting seeds from certain kinds of plants. No longer did they have to follow the herds and search for edible plants that grew wild. Instead they could remain in one place and grow a continuing supply of food.

The first farms were based on this very basic idea. People began to settle near the farms, creating small villages. Trade began between farmers and villagers, and between one farm and another.

As time passed, these small farm villages grew. Tradespeople and merchants provided **goods and services**, attracting still more people. Over the centuries, major cities arose with complex methods of trading commodities. As cities traded with other cities, the economy became regional and then national. As the economies of countries in Asia and Europe expanded, so did foreign trade, the exchange of goods and services between nations.

By the end of the twentieth century, a global economy had arisen. Countries in all parts of the world were trading with each other. In doing so, many countries became dependent on each other to maintain their own wealth and prosperity.

Measuring a Country's Wealth

In the Middle Ages, a country's wealth was measured by the goods it had that could be bought or traded. Goods were mainly natural resources, such as gold and other precious metals. The main national goal was often to have as much wealth as possible. This motivated countries to acquire more land and explore uncharted territories.

Today a country's wealth is measured in terms of its **gross domestic product** (GDP). This is the total value of goods and services produced in a country for a specific time period. The GDP is not only a measure of a country's wealth. It is also a measure of a country's economic activity.

The GDP can be used to track a country's progress and to compare its economy with other countries. The bar graph in Figure 1 shows the GDP of the United States from 2000 to 2005. The graph in Figure 2 compares the GDP of the United States with those of Japan, France, Germany, and the United Kingdom (UK).

When the GDP is divided by the country's population, the result is the GDP per person. The graph in Figure 3 shows the GDP per person in the

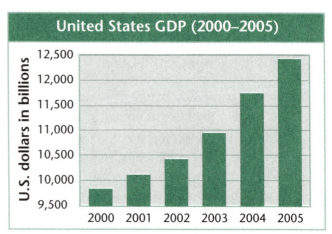

FIGURE 1. By tracking the GDP of a country, economists can analyze a country's rate of economic growth, as well as new economic trends.

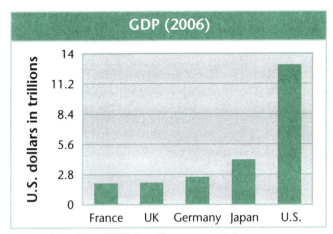

FIGURE 2. The GDP for these countries was measured for the year 2006.

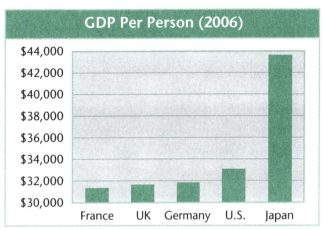

FIGURE 4. These figures compare the GDP per person in four industrialized countries in 2006.

United States between 2000 and 2005. The graph in Figure 4 in the next column compares the GDP per person of the United States with other countries.

The GDP per person can be used to analyze the **standard of living** for people in a country. For example, if the GDP increases at a greater rate than the country's population, then the standard of living is probably on the rise. If, however, the population increases at a greater rate than the GDP, the living standards are probably falling.

Country Capsules

What are the driving forces behind a country's economy? Here are some quick capsules, or brief summaries, of some nations around the world.

An analysis of the bar graphs reveals that in 2006 the United States had the highest GDP of the countries shown. In fact, the United States has the highest GDP of any country in the world. It is a highly **industrialized** country and a leader in many areas, including information technology. It exports and imports more goods than any other country.

The GDP of Japan in 2006 was second highest. Japan has a large manufacturing base, chiefly in cars and electronics, which are sold worldwide. Japan has several extremely large companies, whose products have turned their names into household words overseas. A large group of smaller to medium-sized Japanese companies is also recognized as providing innovative products for the world market.

Other countries in Asia are becoming more industrialized. China has seen a change in recent years. Many people are moving from rural regions to metropolitan areas in search of work. At the same time, industry is also moving out to the countryside, providing jobs for millions of rural residents. Korea has a form of business called the *chaebol*, or conglomerates. Conglomerates are businesses made up of many smaller companies. Some of these companies may be familiar to consumers in the United States, because they produce and market a variety of goods, from electronics to motor vehicles.

The European economy underwent an amazing change in its economic structure in the late 1990s. On January 1, 1999, 11 countries in Europe introduced a new monetary unit called the **euro**. Previously, those countries had their own **currencies**, or types of money. For example,

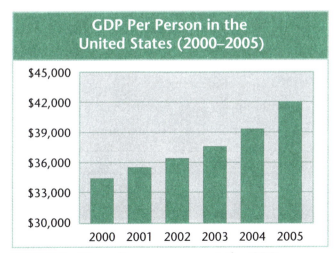

FIGURE 3. These figures represent the GDP per person in the United States during the years 2000 to 2005.

LESSON 20 Analyzing **79**

Germany had the mark and Italy had the lira. Today, Germany and Italy, along with France, Spain, Belgium, Austria, Portugal, Finland, Ireland, the Netherlands, Slovenia, and Luxembourg, have one common currency—the euro.

In the early 1990s, West Germany merged with the formerly Communist East Germany, forming one nation. The integration of these two countries has been a drain on the German economy. Labor costs—the money it takes to employ a person—became the highest in the world. That is good for the employees, but not good for industry.

France has a varied economy. Agriculture is a huge industry, the largest of any western European country. Manufacturing and tourism are also large sectors of France's economic picture.

In less industrialized nations, the economy may rely more heavily on agriculture or the services industry. A service industry is an industry in which services are provided to a consumer. Doctors and lawyers provide services. In Mexico, the service sector contributed just over two-thirds of the GDP. Although agriculture accounted for only 3.9 percent of the GDP, 18 percent of Mexico's workforce is employed in agriculture.

Brazil has an abundance of natural resources, leading to the production of a variety of agricultural products, including coffee, sugar, tobacco, and cocoa. Brazil became more industrialized during the 1960s and 1980s, providing for a more diversified economy.

Whether they are driven by natural resources, agriculture, industry, or technology, more and more countries around the world are eager to become part of the global economy.

COMPREHENSION

1. What does the abbreviation GDP stand for?

2. What advantage did farming offer people over hunting-gathering?

3. How did farms lead to bigger cities?

4. How did countries measure wealth long ago?

5. What is the science of economics?

6. Draw a line to match the following words with their correct meanings.

commodities   a. brief summaries

capsules   b. the money it takes to employ a person

labor costs   c. goods that can be sold or traded

80 LESSON 20 Analyzing

CRITICAL THINKING

1. Identify each of the following statements as a fact or opinion. Write *F* or *O* on the line.

   _____ **a.** Economics is an interesting way to study a country.

   _____ **b.** Economics involves analyzing the GDP of a country.

   _____ **c.** In 2006, the United States had the highest GDP of any country.

   _____ **d.** The United States has the world's best economy.

2. Describe how the establishment of farms led to increased trade.

   _____

   _____

3. Compare the GDP of the United States to the GDP of the United Kingdom in 2006.

   _____

   _____

4. Look at the statistics for the United States as shown in Figure 1 and Figure 3. What conclusions can you draw about the economy of the United States between 2000 and 2005?

   _____

   _____

SKILL FOCUS: ANALYZING

1. What is the author's purpose in writing this selection?

   _____

   _____

2. What details does the writer use to explain the transition from a farm economy to a global economy?

   _____

   _____

3. What is the author's purpose for writing the section titled "Measuring a Country's Wealth"?

   _____

   _____

4. How does the writer support the idea that the United States is a world leader in economics?

   _____

   _____

Reading-Writing Connection

Think of a foreign country that you might someday like to visit. Research the country's economy and write a paragraph that analyzes the economy. Tell how the economy compares with the economy of the United States. Use a chart or graph to present your information.

LESSON 20 Analyzing **81**

LESSON 21

Skill: Main Idea and Supporting Details

BACKGROUND INFORMATION

"Quicksand" takes a close-up, scientific look at the strange natural phenomenon called quicksand. At one time, people thought that quicksand was a special type of sand that, if stepped upon, would drag a person or an animal to its death. Actually any sand can become "quick" if it becomes saturated by water that cannot drain. The danger is not that quicksand will drag someone down, but that by struggling to get out, a person might lose his or her balance and drown.

SKILL FOCUS: Main Idea and Supporting Details

Authors try to write as clearly as possible so that their **main idea**—the most important point—comes across to their readers. To help readers understand the main idea, an author provides **supporting details**. Most details answer such questions as *who, what, where, when, how,* and *why.* In science writing, these details can include the following.

- facts based on experience or observation
- sensory descriptions
- specific examples
- logical reasons
- visuals such as illustrations and charts

▶ Read the paragraph below. Underline the main idea. Then fill in the Main Idea and Supporting Details Map with information from the paragraph below.

Quicksand is likely to be found in three different environments. One environment is along a riverbank. Another is near a stream. The third is around a lake shoreline.

CONTEXT CLUES: Cause and Effect

In your reading, you may come across unfamiliar words. You can often determine their meanings by using **cause-and-effect** clues from the surrounding text. Read the following sentence.

*A person can stand on the surface of that sand without becoming **engulfed** in it because the sand particles can support the person's weight.*

In the sentence above, the word *engulfed* describes the effect of the sand particles' ability to support a person's weight. You can infer that *engulfed* means "to be swallowed up by."

▶ Read the sentence below. On the lines write what you think the underlined word means. In the sentence, circle the phrase from a cause-and-effect relationship that helped you figure out the word's meaning.

***Struggling** is what usually causes a person to lose his or her footing and subsequently to drown in quicksand.*

_____

_____

In this selection, the words *saturated, lubricant,* and *suspension* are underlined. As you read, analyze the cause-and-effect relationships to figure out the words' meanings.

> ### Strategy Tip
>
> As you read "Quicksand," pay special attention to the section headings in boldfaced type. Consider how they help you identify the main ideas in the selection.

Main Idea

Supporting Details

82   LESSON 21   Main Idea and Supporting Details

READING A SCIENCE SELECTION

Quicksand

Why does quicksand provoke such curiosity in us? Why is it so mysterious, so frightening? Perhaps those feelings are the subconscious effect of old movies, in which people are sucked into quicksand pools right in the middle of a desert or jungle. A more likely answer, however, is that quicksand is a phenomenon that challenges our assumptions about the world in which we live. Quicksand, instead of being solid and dependable as the earth "should" be, betrays our trust in the firmness of the ground beneath our feet.

How is quicksand similar to or different from the rest of the world's soil, and why is it "quick"?

The Goodwin Sands on the coast of Kent in England soak up water from the changing tides, creating hidden pools of quicksand.

Everyday Sand

Soil scientists at one time believed quicksand to be a separate classification of soil, made of particles that were rounded, like tiny ball bearings. Today, however, quicksand is thought to be ordinary sand, buoyed up by **hydrostatic pressure** from below, such as water from underground springs. The sand grains can be large or small, smooth in shape or angular.

To understand quicksand, it is important to understand the characteristics of "normal" sand. In dry sand, or sand that is not too wet, the **frictional forces** between the particles are large enough to cause the sand to be relatively solid. The force of the sand grains pushing up on a **mass** equals the weight of the mass pushing down. A person can stand on the surface of that sand without becoming engulfed in it because the sand particles can support the person's weight.

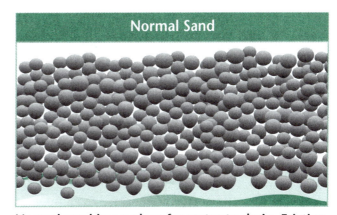

Normal sand has a place for water to drain. Friction between the grains causes the sand to be relatively solid so that the sand can support weight.

A small amount of water, in fact, will strengthen the sand's structure because it produces a force that pulls the grains together. Proof of this is the various shapes and "castles" one can make out of damp beach sand. If too much water is mixed with the sand, however, the water molecules force the grains apart. What structure there was in the sand is completely destroyed, and the sand balls turn to mush.

Putting the "Quick" in Quicksand

Water is also the key factor in making quicksand "quick." Quicksand forms when sand accumulates in hollows and holes and becomes totally saturated with water that has nowhere to drain—perhaps because a layer of clay or other dense material lies underneath the sand. In these situations, the water pressure beneath the sand is

LESSON 21 Main Idea and Supporting Details **83**

equal to—or slightly greater than—the weight of the sand particles. When the water pressure is high enough, the sand grains have little or no friction between them. The water flowing between the grains forms a kind of <u>lubricant</u>. Mud and vegetation also may be mixed into this <u>suspension</u>, producing a "soup" that can be very sticky—and potentially deadly.

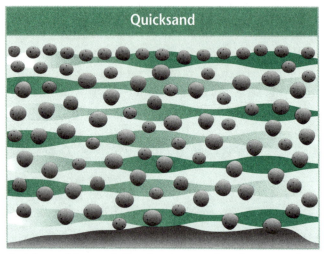

Quicksand is sand that is saturated with water that has no place to drain. The sand cannot support the weight of objects on its surface.

When this suspension is subjected to an upward flow (if you were to step into it, for example), it goes into motion and becomes "quick." The pressure between the grains of sand decreases, causing the frictional forces between them also to decrease. A cushion of water keeps each grain of sand from bumping into its neighbors. The result is that the sand offers no resistance to the weight of anything resting on its surface. The sand becomes unable to bear a load, so any load placed upon it will sink.

Finding Quicksand

Quicksand is likely to be found in three different environments. The soils that are most susceptible to forming quicksand are along rivers, streams, and lake shorelines. However, quicksand also can be formed in hilly areas with loose soil and shallow groundwater or in areas with a high probability of earthquakes. Old movies with quicksand pits in jungles may be close to the mark—but there would be little chance of finding quicksand in the desert, which is just too dry.

Getting Trapped

✗ One of the interesting characteristics of quicksand is its high **specific gravity**—that is, the ratio of its mass to its volume. A body will tend to float in quicksand because the specific gravity of quicksand is higher than the specific gravity of water. Quicksand does not "suck" things down. Actually, because the **density** of the human body is less than that of the sand-water mixture, you cannot sink below the surface (much like being in a swimming pool, where you can just float by not moving around). In fact, since quicksand is denser than water, you would float better on quicksand than you would on water. Indeed if you do not struggle in quicksand, you will just float on the surface. Struggling is what usually causes a person to lose his or her footing and subsequently drown in quicksand.

Therefore, if you are ever caught in quicksand, take this advice: Flop on your back to get the maximum surface area resting on top of the quicksand. Once you are on your back, slowly pull out one leg and then the other leg. Once you have both legs out, roll across the surface of the quicksand until you are on firm ground again.

COMPREHENSION

1. How have soil scientists classified quicksand in the past and today?

   _____
   _____
   _____

2. What happens when too much water is mixed with "normal" sand?

   _____
   _____
   _____

3. How is quicksand formed?

_____

_____

_____

_____

_____

4. List three contrasting environments where quicksand might be found.

_____

_____

_____

5. Complete each of the following sentences with one of the three words shown below.

suspension   saturated   lubricant

a. The towel was _____ with water.

b. The mechanic used a _____ on the motor to make its parts move more smoothly.

c. The olive oil in the salad dressing was held in _____.

CRITICAL THINKING

1. Identify each of the following statements as fact or opinion. Write *F* or *O* on the line.

_____ **a.** Quicksand is extremely dangerous.

_____ **b.** Quicksand might be found along a lake's shoreline.

_____ **c.** The Sahara is not likely to have quicksand.

2. Describe how you might prove that water strengthens the structure of sand.

_____

_____

3. Quicksand is also known as "running sand." Why do you think this is so?

_____

_____

4. Reread the section with an ✘ next to its heading. Do you think wild animals would be safe if they were caught in quicksand? Explain.

_____

_____

5. Explain why the fear that people have about getting trapped in quicksand is unfounded.

_____

_____

LESSON 21 Main Idea and Supporting Details **85**

SKILL FOCUS: MAIN IDEA AND SUPPORTING DETAILS

1. Review the first paragraph of the selection.
   a. What main idea is expressed in the paragraph?

   _____

   b. What detail supports that main idea?

   _____

2. Review the section titled "Everyday Sand."
   a. What is its main idea?

   _____
   _____

   b. What details support that main idea?

   _____
   _____

3. Review the section titled "Putting the 'Quick' in Quicksand."
   a. What is its main idea?

   _____
   _____

   b. What details support that main idea?

   _____
   _____

4. Give three examples of *who*, *what*, *where*, *when*, *why*, and *how* questions that are answered in the selection.

   _____
   _____

5. In this selection, how is the main idea of the final paragraph connected to the main idea of the first paragraph?

   _____
   _____

Reading-Writing Connection

Suppose you were the advertising director of WAQ (Words About Quicksand). On a separate sheet of paper, write a slogan to help people save themselves if they are caught in quicksand.

86 LESSON 21 Main Idea and Supporting Details

LESSON 22

Skill: Using a Calculator

BACKGROUND INFORMATION

"Getting the Most Out of a Calculator" describes many uses for calculators. People have used calculating devices in one form or another for thousands of years. In the twentieth century, the invention of the electronic calculator made working with large numbers quicker and easier. While calculators have decreased the need for long, tedious calculations by hand, they have not replaced the need to understand how to add, subtract, multiply, and divide.

SKILL FOCUS: Using a Calculator

In order for a **calculator** to process information, the correct combinations of numbers and functions must be entered. If you accidentally hit a wrong number or function key, the answer will be incorrect.

Here are some ways to improve your accuracy when using a calculator.

- Read both the math expression you want to calculate and the answer the calculator displays. When you read the problem, estimate the answer or look for ways to simplify the problem so you do not need a calculator.

- When you read the display, do not just copy the numbers. Check to see if the result makes sense. For example, if you are adding two whole numbers, there should not be a decimal in the answer.

▶ Using a calculator, solve each of the math equations below.

1. $536 \times 10 =$ _____

2. $53{,}597 + 39{,}201 =$ _____

3. $35{,}943 + 23{,}942 =$ _____

4. $732 \times 3 =$ _____

5. $257 + 2{,}952 =$ _____

WORD CLUES

As you read "Getting the Most Out of a Calculator," you may come upon some terms you don't recognize. The terms *order of operations*, *automatic constant*, *power*, and *exponent* are words with mathematical meanings. If you want to know more about these terms, look them up in your math textbooks.

▶ Look up the words *power* and *exponent* in a dictionary. Write the mathematical meaning of each word on the lines below.

1. power: _____

_____

2. exponent: _____

_____

Strategy Tip

In "Getting the Most Out of a Calculator," you will read examples of some of the features of a calculator. Try each example, using a calculator. If your answer does not match the answer given in the text, reread the example and try again.

READING A MATHEMATICS SELECTION

Getting the Most Out of a Calculator

Almost everyone seems to know how to use calculators to perform simple arithmetical operations—addition, subtraction, multiplication, and division. However, many students—even many adults who use calculators in their everyday lives—do not realize that a calculator can do a lot more than this. When calculators are used effectively, they become very powerful math tools.

A recent survey of high school math students asked the following questions.

- Do you know how to use a calculator to evaluate an expression with more than one operation?

- Of what use is a calculator's automatic constant feature?

- How can you tell if you have made an error in a calculator computation?

- How do you know when to use your calculator?

By the time you finish reading this selection, you will be able to answer these questions with confidence.

> **1.** Do you know how to use a calculator to evaluate an expression with more than one operation?

All calculators do not have the same features. **Scientific calculators** are calculators that use algebraic logic, which means that they automatically work according to the **order of operations**. The order of operations is a rule that states the order in which to perform the operations within an expression. This feature in a calculator allows you to key in an expression in the order in which the numbers appear.

Simpler calculators, sometimes called four-function calculators, do not follow the order of operations. Therefore, you have to enter an expression following the order of operations. Here is the order.

1. Do any work within parentheses.

2. Evaluate any **exponents**.

3. Do any multiplication or division, from left to right.

4. Do any addition or subtraction, from left to right.

For example, evaluate the following expression.

$$50 - 4 \times 7 + 12$$

Before you start punching in numbers, read the expression and find all the operations. In this case, there are three operations—subtraction, multiplication, and addition. Now, use the order of operations. Perform the multiplication first.

$$4 \times 7 = 28$$

Then rewrite the expression, replacing 4×7 with 28.

$$50 - 28 + 12$$

Now the only operations left are subtraction and addition. You perform these operations in the order in which they appear.

$$50 - 28 + 12 = 34$$

> **2.** Of what use is a calculator's automatic constant feature?

Most calculators have an **automatic constant** feature. Think about a time when you used a calculator to perform an operation on a number over and over again. You probably alternated between hitting the number key and the operation key many times. Instead of doing this, use the automatic constant feature, which allows you to get the answer more quickly by repeatedly hitting the = (equal) key.

Suppose, for example, that you are asked to evaluate 4^5 (read: "four to the fifth **power**"). You could enter this key code.

$$4 \boxtimes 4 \boxtimes 4 \boxtimes 4 \boxtimes 4 \boxminus 1{,}024$$

88 LESSON 22 Using a Calculator

The automatic constant, however, allows you to use a simpler key code.

$$4 \boxtimes \boxminus \boxminus \boxminus \boxminus \ 1{,}024$$

Notice that inputting "$4 \boxtimes \boxminus$" is the same as inputting 4×4, or 16. It is also the same as 4^2 (read: "four squared" or "four to the second power"). Pressing $\boxminus$ each additional time raises the base (in this case, 4) to the next higher power.

Scientific calculators have another way to find powers. Look for a button with $\boxed{y^x}$ or $\boxed{\wedge}$. Both of these buttons work the same way. To find the value of 8^3, enter the base, 8, then $\boxed{y^x}$ or $\boxed{\wedge}$, and then the exponent, 3.

$$8 \ \boxed{y^x} \ 3 = 512$$
$$8 \ \boxed{\wedge} \ 3 = 512$$

Calculators can vary. The power button on some calculators may look different from the power button described above. However, do not use the $\boxed{e^x}$ key, which performs a different function.

> **3.** How can you tell if you have made an error in a calculator computation?

A common mistake is punching in the wrong number or operation key. In many cases you can avoid this mistake by estimating the result before you calculate and by checking the digits of each factor.

Suppose, for example, that you need to find the product of 347 and 454.

$$347 \times 454$$

Estimate the product before you use your calculator, by rounding each factor: 347 rounds to 300; 454 rounds to 500. Multiply the rounded numbers.

$$300 \times 500 = 150{,}000$$

So, 150,000 is one estimate for the product of 347 and 454. Now use your calculator to find the product of 347 and 454.

$$347 \boxtimes 454 \boxminus 157{,}538$$

This result is close to the estimate of 150,000.

When you are adding, subtracting, or multiplying, you should also check the last digits of each factor. In the preceding example, multiply the

last digits of each factor: $7 \times 4 = 28$. The last digit of this product, 8, should be the same as the last digit of the product of 347×454.

Keep in mind that neither method defends against all errors; after all, it is you who have to choose the correct operations.

> **4.** How do you know when to use your calculator?

In many classes, on many standardized tests, and in many workplaces, you are free to use a calculator whenever you want. However, a calculator is not always the quickest, most accurate method. Before you begin a calculation, look to see if you can simplify the problem first. Read the example.

$$14{,}000 \times 3{,}000$$

Using a calculator would take eleven key strokes, and you could easily miscount the number of zeros. Instead count the zeros before you multiply. There are six zeros in the factors, so you know that there will be at least six zeros in the product.

$$14{,}000 \times 3{,}000 = \underline{\quad}{,}000{,}000$$

Then multiply the two numbers, 14 and 3. Use a calculator if you want.

$$14{,}000 \times 3{,}000 = 42{,}000{,}000$$

Here is another example. The following expression contains several fractions. To get the product, you could multiply all the numerators and then divide by all of the denominators, but you can look for a simpler way.

$$\frac{5}{11} \times \frac{6}{13} \times \frac{7}{15} \times \frac{15}{6} \times \frac{11}{7} \times \frac{13}{8}$$

Notice that there are common factors in the numerator and denominator. After you simplify the expression, it becomes $\frac{5}{8}$.

$$\frac{5}{\cancel{11}} \times \frac{\cancel{6}}{\cancel{13}} \times \frac{\cancel{7}}{\cancel{15}} \times \frac{\cancel{15}}{\cancel{6}} \times \frac{\cancel{11}}{\cancel{7}} \times \frac{\cancel{13}}{8} = \frac{5}{8}$$

When you choose to use a calculator to solve a problem, it is important to remember that a calculator only performs calculations; it cannot think. It is up to you to figure out how to solve the problem and which operations and numbers to use.

LESSON 22 Using a Calculator **89**

COMPREHENSION

1. What does the automatic constant feature on a calculator do?

   _____

   _____

2. Do all calculators have the automatic constant feature?

   _____

   _____

3. Show two ways to find the value of a power, such as 3^5, on a calculator.

   _____

   _____

4. After parentheses and exponents, what comes next in the order of operations?

   _____

   _____

CRITICAL THINKING

1. What is a scientific calculator, and how can it help to evaluate an expression with more than one operation?

   _____

   _____

2. When trying to find the product of 45 and 27, your calculator displayed 1,260. How can you quickly tell that you made a mistake in entering the numbers?

   _____

   _____

3. A student used a calculator to multiply 17,000 and 5,000. The student's answer was 8,500,000. Is the answer correct? If not, what mistake could the student have made?

   _____

   _____

SKILL FOCUS: USING A CALCULATOR

1. A local theater sold 45 tickets for $25.00 each and 115 tickets for $15.50 each.

   a. Write an expression that shows the total ticket sales.

   _____

   b. Using a pencil and paper, estimate how much money the theater made in ticket sales.

   _____

   c. How would you enter the information into a calculator that is not a scientific calculator?

   _____

   d. Find the actual total.

   _____

2. Suppose you have to solve an equation with several operations. Number the following operations in the order in which you would perform them on a simple calculator.

   _____ **a.** division _____ **b.** exponents _____ **c.** addition

3. Tell whether the following calculator sequence and display is from a scientific calculator or a simpler calculator.

   63 ⊟ 9 ⊠ 5 ⊞ 100 ⊡ 20 ⊟ 23

   _____

4. Estimate the value of each of the following expressions. Then use your calculator to find the actual value.

   a. 34,944 × 39

   Estimate: _____

   Actual product: _____

   b. 59,765 × 42

   Estimate: _____

   Actual product: _____

   c. 43,958 − 890

   Estimate: _____

   Actual difference: _____

   d. 62,387 + 215

   Estimate: _____

   Actual sum: _____

   e. 15,389 ÷ 507

   Estimate: _____

   Actual quotient: _____

   f. 71,893 − 1,914

   Estimate: _____

   Actual difference: _____

5. Imagine that you are a consumer wishing to purchase several items, but you are worried that you may not have enough money.

   a. Using a pencil and paper, estimate how much the total will be.

$7.95	$7.95	$34.95	$12.75	$12.75
$7.95	$12.75	$34.95	$12.75	$12.75
$7.95	$34.95	$34.95	$7.95	$7.95

   _____

   b. Now find the total with your calculator, using the automatic constant feature where appropriate.

   _____

   c. Write the sequence you could use on a scientific calculator to find the total.

   _____

Reading-Writing Connection

Suppose that you work at a card shop and that you have to keep track of inventory. How could you use the calculator skills you learned in this lesson to save time and work more efficiently? On a separate sheet of paper, write a paragraph in which you explain your views.

LESSON 22 Using a Calculator **91**

LESSON 23

Skill: Multiple-Meaning Words

Multiple-meaning words are those that have more than one meaning. You can identify the meaning of the word by the context of the phrase or sentence.

Here are some words that have two different meanings.

aerial	**a.** an antenna for radio or TV	**b.** occurring in the air
associate	**a.** a person one works with	**b.** to make a mental connection
bracket	**a.** a grouping	**b.** a support for a shelf
contract	**a.** a legal agreement	**b.** to grow smaller
conviction	**a.** a strong opinion	**b.** the legal decision that a person is guilty of a crime
discount	**a.** to sell for less	**b.** to doubt or disregard what has been said
foundation	**a.** an organization set up to help people or groups	**b.** a base that supports a building
issue	**a.** a question being debated	**b.** a recent edition of a publication
lobby	**a.** the waiting room at a building's entrance	**b.** to influence a government to do favors for a special group
novel	**a.** a full-length book of fiction	**b.** new and different

A. Decide how the multiple-meaning word in boldfaced type is used in each sentence. Then write *a* or *b* on the line to show which meaning from the list above fits the sentence.

1. _____ The supermarket industry will **lobby** for the repeal of certain tax laws.

2. _____ In her will, the wealthy woman set up a **foundation** to help children in need.

3. _____ When I want to remember someone's name, I try to **associate** the person's name and face in my mind.

4. _____ An **issue** in our high school is whether or not to have a dress code.

5. _____ The trial of the criminal ended with his **conviction** for robbery.

6. _____ The TV **aerial** sits on top of the set.

7. _____ The store decided to **discount** all its winter clothes at the beginning of the spring season.

8. _____ Mariko's ambition is to write a **novel** that will become a best seller.

9. _____ Be careful to install a **bracket** under each shelf.

10. _____ Whenever you make a **contract** to buy something, read it carefully before you sign it.

11. _____ The judge told the jury to **discount** what the witness said.

12. _____ While you are exercising, your muscles both expand and **contract**.

13. _____ Inside the marble **lobby** of the office building was the security guard's station.

14. _____ In his campaign speech, Julio spoke with great **conviction** about the changes he wished to make at school.

15. _____ Earning more money put the young couple in a higher tax **bracket**.

16. _____ Showing what one has learned by completing a project, instead of taking a test, is a **novel** but sound idea.

17. _____ Once the **foundation** begins to crack, the building is doomed.

18. _____ Jenna has a job as a sales **associate** at a clothing store.

19. _____ Which **issue** of the magazine are you reading?

20. _____ The photograph taken from the airplane showed an **aerial** view of the town.

Some words have entirely different meanings when used in different subject areas. Here are some examples of such words.

| area | figure | mass | force |
| tone | right | country | volume |

B. Read the two definitions for each word below. On the line provided, write the word from the list that fits the two definitions.

1. _____
   Social Studies: a region, as of land
   Mathematics: a measure of the surface of a solid

2. _____
   Music: characteristic quality of a specific instrument or voice
   Literature: the attitude of an author toward his or her subject

3. _____
   Social Studies: majority of people
   Mathematics: a body or quantity of matter of nonspecific shape

4. _____
   Mathematics: a symbol for a number
   Art: the outline or shape of something

5. _____
   Science: a quantity that produces an acceleration of a body in the direction of its application
   Social Studies: imposition of one's will against resistance

6. _____
   Music: popular music derived from folk music of the rural United States
   Social Studies: a state or nation

7. _____
   Social Studies: a just moral and legal claim
   Mathematics: angle of 90° formed by two perpendicular line segments

8. _____
   Mathematics: the size of a three-dimensional object or region of space
   Music: the loudness of sound

LESSON 23 Multiple-Meaning Words **93**

LESSON 24
Skill: Recognizing Denotation and Connotation

A **denotation** is the exact meaning of a word that you would find in a dictionary. A **connotation**, on the other hand, is the **positive** or **negative** feeling associated with a word. For example, what is the difference in connotation between *curious* and *nosy*? They both have to do with wanting to find out more, but the first word has a positive connotation, while the second has a negative one.

When you read, pay attention to the **word choice** the writer has made. The connotations of the words chosen can tell you much about the author's attitude toward his or her subject matter.

A. Label each of the following words *P* for positive connotation or *N* for negative connotation. Write the letter on the blank.

1. childish _____
2. stubborn _____
3. persistent _____
4. dignified _____
5. arrogant _____
6. propaganda _____
7. home _____

8. idealist _____
9. rebel _____
10. mob _____
11. feeble _____
12. youthful _____
13. mature _____
14. pushy _____

15. assertive _____
16. thorough _____
17. long-winded _____
18. determined _____
19. obsessed _____
20. gang _____

B. In each sentence below, underline the word in parentheses that has a negative connotation.

1. The dress was plain and (cheap, inexpensive).

2. The stranger had a (humble, shabby) appearance.

3. Everyone thought that her sense of humor was rather (peculiar, unique).

4. The teenagers liked to dress in a (sloppy, casual) way.

5. Poverty can be a major (challenge, obstacle) in a person's life.

C. In each sentence below, underline the word in parentheses that has a positive connotation.

1. The grandfather was (scrimping, saving) in order to give money to his grandchildren.

2. The team felt (confident, arrogant) about its chance to win the game.

3. He is a very (aggressive, assertive) person.

4. We've spent all weekend being (relaxed, idle).

5. The politician spent a lot of her time (scheming, planning) to get ahead in her party.

LESSON 25

Skill: Recognizing Propaganda

Often used by politicians and advertisers, **propaganda** aims at persuading an audience to agree with someone's ideas about a person, product, or cause. The information in propaganda is not always accurate. Common **propaganda techniques** include the following.

- **Loaded Words:** Using words that appeal to the emotions.
- **Faulty Cause and Effect:** Claiming that one event caused another when there is no such connection.
- **Testimonial:** Having a famous person suggest that others should do, believe, or buy something because that person claims to.
- **Transfer:** Trying to get a listener to transfer positive feelings about something such as love, nature, or family to a person, product, or cause by associating the two.
- **Bandwagon:** Urging a listener not to miss out on something that everyone else is enjoying or benefiting from.
- **Either-Or:** Trying to convince someone that there are only two choices when there may be more.
- **Mudslinging:** Using negative information about opponents or competitors that is not backed up by facts.

In the space provided, identify the propaganda technique used in each of these advertisements. Then tell briefly how you recognized each technique.

1. Want to be more popular? Wear Irresistible cologne and people will flock to you.

   _____

2. Dennis Deadeye uses only ProMaster basketballs. ProMaster is the basketball of the stars!

   _____

3. Our competitors have hidden costs in their repair contracts, but Marvel Mechanics is always honest and never overcharges.

   _____

4. Our scented deodorizer brings the fragrance of a field of wildflowers into your home.

   _____

5. If you don't vote for the new wilderness park, you don't love nature or animals.

   _____

6. People from all over the country are spending their vacations at Two Rivers Amusement Park. Shouldn't your family be there, too?

   _____

7. Leaders drive the new Bobcat sports vehicle. They love its style, its aggressiveness, its ability to put them ahead of the crowd.

   _____

LESSON 25 Recognizing Propaganda **95**

LESSON 26

Skill: Reading a Bus Schedule

Whether you are commuting to work, going shopping, or visiting a friend, traveling by bus can be an easy, inexpensive way to get around town. When you travel by bus, it usually is wise to check the **bus schedule** beforehand. Most bus schedules show when the buses run, when and where they stop, and where you can transfer to other buses. During rush hour, there may be more buses or express buses to serve the extra passengers. There also may be more time between stops to accommodate the extra traffic.

This partial bus schedule provides information about Route 103. Read from left to right along each line to find the times of the different stops. The schedule also gives additional information about service along the route.

ROUTE 103—WESTBOUND TO CENTRAL AVENUE TERMINAL

	Orchard and 12th	Pinecrest Mall[1]	Adams and Division	Division and 45th	Division and 69th	Central Ave Terminal[2]
Monday–Friday						
A.M.	7:30	7:42	7:50	7:56	8:05	8:14
	7:45	7:57	8:05	8:14	8:20	8:29
	8:00	8:12	8:20	8:26	8:35	8:44
	8:05	8:17	—	—	—	8:40
	8:10	8:22	8:30	8:38	8:49	9:00
	8:20	8:32	—	—	—	8:55
	8:30	8:42	8:50	8:56	9:05	9:14
P.M.	4:30	4:42	4:50	4:58	5:09	5:20
	5:00	5:12	5:20	5:28	5:39	5:50
	5:30	5:42	5:50	5:58	6:09	6:20
	6:00	6:12	6:20	6:26	6:35	6:44
	6:30	6:42	6:50	6:56	7:05	7:14
	7:00	7:12	7:20	7:26	7:35	7:44
	7:45	7:57	8:03	8:08	8:17	8:25
	8:30	8:42	8:48	8:53	9:02	9:10
	9:30	9:42	9:48	9:53	10:02	10:10
	10:30	—	10:45	10:50	10:59	11:07
Saturday						
A.M.	8:30	—	8:45	8:50	8:59	9:07
	10:30	10:42	10:48	10:53	11:02	11:10
P.M.	12:00	12:12	12:18	12:23	12:32	12:40
	1:00	1:12	1:18	1:23	1:32	1:40
	2:00	2:12	2:18	2:23	2:32	2:40
	6:00	6:12	6:18	6:23	6:32	6:40
	7:30	4:42	7:48	7:53	8:02	8:10
	9:00	9:12	9:18	9:23	9:32	9:40
	10:30	—	10:45	10:50	10:59	11:07
Sunday and Holidays						
A.M.	8:30	—	8:45	8:50	8:59	9:07
	10:30	10:42	10:48	10:53	11:02	11:10
P.M.	12:00	12:12	12:18	12:23	12:32	12:40
	1:30	1:42	1:48	1:53	2:02	2:10
	3:00	3:12	3:18	3:23	3:32	3:40
	4:30	4:42	4:48	4:53	5:02	5:10
	6:00	6:12	6:18	6:23	632	6:40
	7:30	—	7:45	7:50	7:59	8:07

Notes:

[1]Transfer to 60, 84, and 101.
[2]Transfer to 55, 65, 90, 94, 97, 100, and 105.

Boldfaced Type indicates express service.

All buses are lift-equipped.

Fare: $1.25; exact change (coins or token) only; free transfers good for one hour after issuance.

96 LESSON 26 Reading a Bus Schedule

A. Use the information from the bus schedule on page 96 to complete each sentence.

1. Route 103 begins at the corner of _____ and _____.

2. The route ends at _____.

3. On weekdays, bus service begins at _____ and ends at _____.

4. _____ express buses operate each weekday morning, skipping _____ stops each.

5. It takes _____ minutes to go from Orchard and 12th to Pinecrest Mall.

6. It takes several minutes longer to make the entire run on weekday mornings and late

   afternoons, probably because _____.

7. If you catch the 3:00 P.M. bus on Labor Day, you will arrive at _____ at 3:23 P.M.

8. If you take the noon 103 bus on Sunday and transfer to the 84 bus at Pinecrest Mall,

   your free transfer is good until _____.

9. On Saturday, you are meeting a friend for a 7:10 P.M. movie at a theater near the
   Central Avenue Terminal. You should catch the bus that stops at Adams and Division

   at _____ to avoid being late.

10. If you use a wheelchair, you can take any bus because _____.

B. Fill in the circle next to the correct answer to each question.

1. If you leave Orchard and 12th on the 2:00 P.M. bus on Saturday, at what time will you arrive at Division and 69th?
   - ○ 2:32 P.M.
   - ○ 2:40 P.M.
   - ○ 2:23 P.M.
   - ○ 2:45 P.M.

2. During the weekend, which stop is skipped early in the morning and late in the evening?
   - ○ Division and 69th
   - ○ Division and 45th
   - ○ Pinecrest Mall
   - ○ Central Ave. Terminal

3. On a weekday, how much faster is an express bus than a regular bus going from Orchard and 12th to Central Avenue Terminal?
   - ○ 8 minutes
   - ○ 10 minutes
   - ○ 9 minutes
   - ○ 11 minutes

4. How many bus routes including route 103 meet at the Central Avenue Terminal?
   - ○ four
   - ○ nine
   - ○ seven
   - ○ eight

5. On Monday, if you miss the 8:49 A.M. bus at Division and 69th, when can you catch the next one there?
   - ○ 9:00 A.M.
   - ○ 11:02 A.M.
   - ○ 9:05 A.M.
   - ○ 5:09 P.M.

6. What time does the last bus leave Pinecrest Mall on a Sunday?
   - ○ 6:18 P.M.
   - ○ 6:12 P.M.
   - ○ 7:30 P.M.
   - ○ 9:12 P.M.

LESSON 26 Reading a Bus Schedule **97**

unit four

Perseverance

LESSON 27

Skill: Theme

BACKGROUND INFORMATION

"The Turtle" is an excerpt from John Steinbeck's novel *The Grapes of Wrath.* This novel was first published in 1939 when it exposed the difficulties migrant workers faced during the Great Depression. "The Turtle" is an example of Steinbeck's use of "interchapters." They provided social background, presented historical information, or recorded natural occurrences. In addition to describing the turtle's progress in detail, Steinbeck also uses the turtle as a symbol of determination in the novel.

SKILL FOCUS: Theme

Most literary works have a central message, or **theme.** The theme is more than the subject of the work. It is a general statement about life, expressed or suggested by the author. The theme often reveals the author's opinion about the subject. A literary work may have more than one theme, but one major theme will usually stand out.

In a literary work, the author rarely states the theme directly. More often, the reader must infer the theme through the events that occur and the ways in which the characters speak, think, and behave. When you are trying to determine the major theme of a literary work that is implied, ask yourself: *What is the main message the author wants to convey?*

▶ Read the short excerpt below. Then complete the Idea Web by filling in clues to the theme.

And now a light truck approached, and as it came near, the driver saw the turtle and swerved to hit it. His front wheel struck the edge of the shell, flipped the turtle like a tiddly-wink, spun it like a coin, and rolled it off the highway. The truck went back to its course along the right side.

Character's Behavior	Character's Behavior

Theme: People have no respect for living creatures.

Character's Behavior

CONTEXT CLUES: Details

If you come across a word you don't know in a story, **detail** context clues in the sentence or in nearby sentences can help you figure out its meaning.

Read the sentence below. Look for details that help you understand the meaning of the underlined word.

*He came over the grass leaving a beaten trail behind him, and the hill, which was the highway **embankment**, reared up ahead of him.*

From the detail context clues, you can tell that the *embankment* is the slope of the hill that supports the highway.

▶ Read the sentence below. Circle the words that provide details to help you figure out the meaning of the underlined word.

*The grass heads were heavy with oat beards to catch on a dog's coat, and foxtails to tangle in a horse's **fetlocks**, and clover burrs to fasten in sheep's wool.*

In "The Turtle," the words *dispersed, threshed,* and *parapet* are underlined. Look for details as you read to help you figure out the words' meanings.

> **Strategy Tip**
>
> As you read "The Turtle," try to identify the writer's attitude toward his subject.

98   LESSON 27   Theme

READING A LITERATURE SELECTION

THE TURTLE

John Steinbeck

The concrete highway was edged with a mat of tangled, broken, dry grass, and the grass heads were heavy with oat beards to catch on a dog's coat, and foxtails to tangle in a horse's fetlocks, and clover burrs to fasten in sheep's wool. Sleeping life was waiting to be spread and <u>dispersed</u>, every seed armed with an appliance of dispersal, twisting darts and parachutes for the wind, little spears and balls of tiny thorns, and all waiting for animals and for the wind, for a man's trouser cuff or the hem of a woman's skirt, all passive but armed with appliances of activity, still, but each possessed of movement.

✔ The sun lay on the grass and warmed it, and in the shade under the grass the insects moved, ants and ant lions to set traps for them, grasshoppers to jump into the air and flick their yellow wings for a second, sow bugs like little armadillos, plodding restlessly on many tender feet. And over the grass at the roadside a land turtle crawled, turning aside for nothing, dragging his high-domed shell over the grass. His hard legs and yellow-nailed feet <u>threshed</u> slowly through the grass, not really walking, but boosting and dragging his shell along. The barley beards slid off his shell and the clover burrs fell on him and rolled to the ground. His horny beak was partly open, and his fierce, humorous eyes, under brows like fingernails, stared straight ahead. He came over the grass leaving a beaten trail behind him, and the hill, which was the highway embankment, reared up ahead of him. For a moment he stopped, his head held high.

He blinked and looked up and down. At last he started to climb the embankment. Front clawed feet reached forward but did not touch. The hind feet kicked his shell along, and it scraped on the grass, and on the gravel. As the embankment grew steeper and steeper, the more frantic were the efforts of the land turtle. Pushing hind legs strained and slipped, boosting the shell along, and the horny head protruded as far as the neck could stretch. Little by little the shell slid up the embankment until at last a <u>parapet</u> cut straight across its line of march, the shoulder of the road, a concrete wall four inches high. As though they worked independently the hind legs pushed the shell against the wall. The head upraised

LESSON 27 Theme

and peered over the wall to the broad smooth plain of cement. Now the hands, braced on top of the wall, strained and lifted, and the shell came slowly up and rested its front end on the wall. For a moment the turtle rested. A red ant ran into the shell, into the soft skin inside the shell, and suddenly head and legs snapped in, and the armored tail clamped in sideways. The red ant was crushed between body and legs. And one head of wild oats was clamped into the shell by a front leg. For a long moment the turtle lay still, and then the neck crept out and the old humorous frowning eyes looked about and the legs and tail came out. The back legs went to work, straining like elephant legs, and the shell tipped to an angle so that the front legs could not reach the level cement plain. But higher and higher the hind legs boosted it, until at last the center of balance was reached, the front tipped down, the front legs scratched at the pavement, and it was up. But the head of wild oats was held by its stem around the front legs.

Now the going was easy, and all the legs worked, and the shell boosted along, waggling from side to side. A sedan driven by a forty-year-old woman approached. She saw the turtle and swung to the

right, off the highway, the wheels screamed and a cloud of dust boiled up. Two wheels left for a moment and then settled. The car skidded back onto the road, and went on, but more slowly. The turtle had jerked into its shell, but now it hurried on, for the highway was burning hot.

And now a light truck approached, and as it came near, the driver saw the turtle and swerved to hit it. His front wheel struck the edge of the shell, flipped the turtle like a tiddly-wink, spun it like a coin, and rolled it off the highway. The truck went back to its course along the right side. Lying on its back, the turtle was tight in its shell for a long time. But at last its legs waved in the air, reaching for something to pull it over. Its front foot caught a piece of quartz and little by little the shell pulled over and flopped upright. The wild oat head fell out and three of the spearhead seeds stuck in the ground. And as the turtle crawled on down the embankment, its shell dragged dirt over the seeds. The turtle entered a dust road and jerked itself along, drawing a wavy shallow trench in the dust with its shell. The old humorous eyes looked ahead, and the horny beak opened a little. His yellow toenails slipped a fraction in the dust.

COMPREHENSION

1. Where is the story set?

   _____

   _____

   _____

2. What creature gets caught in the turtle's shell? What happens to it?

   _____

   _____

   _____

3. What happens after the turtle climbs over the concrete wall?

   _____

   _____

   _____

4. What does the driver of the sedan do when she sees the turtle in the road?

   _____

   _____

   _____

5. What happens after the turtle is hit?

   _____

   _____

   _____

6. Draw a line to match the following words with their correct meanings.

   threshed   **a.** scattered

   dispersed   **b.** low barrier

   parapet   **c.** tossed about or flailed

100 LESSON 27 Theme

CRITICAL THINKING

1. Reread the paragraph with the ✔ next to it. What mood, or "feeling," does it create?

2. Explain why the author describes the ant's death.

3. What does the truck driver's action reveal about him?

4. What does the turtle's reaction to being hit by the truck reveal about it?

5. How are the experiences of the turtle similar to human experiences?

6. Predict what the turtle will do next.

SKILL FOCUS: THEME

1. What is the subject of the story?

2. What do the turtle's actions reveal about its character?

3. What effect do the obstacles, such as the wall and the truck driver, have on the turtle?

4. How do you think the writer feels about the turtle and its journey?

5. What do you think is the central message, or theme, of this selection?

Reading-Writing Connection
On a separate sheet of paper, write a paragraph that explains how the theme of this selection applies to your life. Think of a difficult situation that you have faced. What obstacles did you have to overcome? How did your perseverance help you overcome those obstacles?

LESSON 27 Theme

LESSON 28

Skill: Analyzing a Primary Source

BACKGROUND INFORMATION

In his speech "I See the Promised Land," Dr. Martin Luther King, Jr. recalled the dramatic events in the struggle to end segregation in Birmingham, Alabama. In the 1960s, King led a series of protest campaigns that gained him national attention as a civil rights leader. As a result of his leadership, he received the 1964 Nobel Prize for peace. Four years later, as he supported striking African American garbage workers in Memphis, King was assassinated.

SKILL FOCUS: Analyzing a Primary Source

When studying the past, historians and writers often turn to **primary sources**, or firsthand descriptions of historical events. Among the many kinds of primary sources are letters, diaries, and speeches that were written or spoken by people who were involved in a historical event.

The following steps will help you analyze a primary source.

1. Identify the source by asking: *Who wrote it? What is it about? When was it written or spoken? When does the event described take place?*
2. Determine the writer's point of view.
3. Decide whether the source is reliable. *Does the writer give an accurate view of the event?*
4. Analyze the primary source to learn about the historical event. *What facts did you learn?*

▶ Analyze the following excerpt from "I See the Promised Land." In the Idea Web in the next column, write facts learned from King's speech.

You know what happened the other day, and the press dealt only with the window-breaking. I read the articles. They very seldom got around to mentioning the fact that one thousand sanitation workers were on strike, and that Memphis is not being fair to them, and that Mayor Loeb is in dire need of a doctor. They didn't get around to that.

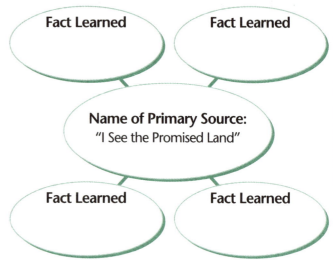

CONTEXT CLUES: Definition

If a word in a primary source is unfamiliar, you often can get a good idea of its meaning by using context clues. For example, when giving a speech, speakers often provide a **definition** of a specific word to emphasize its importance.

Look for definition context clues in the following sentence that define the underlined word.

*Never stop and forget that **collectively**, that means all of us together, collectively we are richer than all the nations in the world, with the exception of nine.*

In this example, Dr. King directly states that *collectively* means "all of us together."

▶ Read the sentences below. Circle the definition of the underlined word.

*We don't need any bricks and bottles, we don't need any **Molotov cocktails**. Those are bombs made from bottles with rags in their openings that you ignite.*

In this selection, the words *unity*, *injustice*, and *longevity* are underlined. Look for the definitions in nearby text to learn the meanings of these words.

> **Strategy Tip**
>
> Read Dr. King's speech aloud to appreciate his passion and persuasiveness as a speaker.

I See the Promised Land

Martin Luther King, Jr.

…Trouble is in the land. Confusion all around.… But I know, somehow, that only when it is dark enough, can you see the stars. And I see God working in this period of the twentieth century in a way that men, in some strange way, are responding—something is happening in our world. The masses of people are rising up. And wherever they are assembled today, whether they are in Johannesburg, South Africa; Nairobi, Kenya; Accra, Ghana; New York City; Atlanta, Georgia; Jackson, Mississippi; or Memphis, Tennessee—the cry is always the same: "We want to be free."

…We have been forced to a point where we're going to have to grapple with the problems that men have been trying to grapple with through history, but the demands didn't force them to do it. Survival demands that we grapple with them. Men, for years now, have been talking about war and peace. But now, no longer can they just talk about it. It is no longer a choice between violence and **nonviolence** in this world; it's nonviolence or nonexistence.

That is where we are today. And also in the **human rights** revolution, if something isn't done, and in a hurry, to bring the colored peoples of the world out of their long years of poverty, their long years of hurt and neglect, the whole world is doomed. Now, I'm just happy that God has allowed me to live in this period, to see what is unfolding. And I'm happy that he's allowed me to be in Memphis.

I can remember, I can remember when Negroes were just going around as Ralph has said, so often, scratching where they didn't itch, and laughing when they were not tickled. But that day is all over. We mean business now, and we are determined to gain our rightful place in God's world.

And that's all this whole thing is about. We aren't engaged in any negative protest and in any negative arguments with anybody. We are saying that we are

Martin Luther King, Jr. made many speeches about civil rights.

determined to be men. We are determined to be people. We are saying that we are God's children. And that we don't have to live like we are forced to live.

Now, what does all of this mean in this great period of history? It means that we've got to stay together. We've got to stay together and maintain <u>unity</u>. You know, whenever Pharaoh wanted to prolong the period of slavery in Egypt, he had a favorite, favorite formula for doing it. What was that? He kept the slaves fighting among themselves. But whenever the slaves get together, something happens in Pharaoh's court, and he cannot hold the slaves in slavery. When the slaves get together, that's the beginning of getting out of slavery. Now let us maintain unity.

Secondly, let us keep the issues where they are. The issue is <u>injustice</u>. The issue is the refusal of Memphis to be fair and honest in its dealings with its public servants, who happen to be sanitation workers. Now, we've got to keep attention on that. That's always the problem with a little violence. You know what happened the other day, and the press dealt only with the window-breaking. I read the articles. They very seldom got around to mentioning the fact that sanitation workers were on strike, and that Memphis is not being fair to them, and that Mayor Loeb is in dire need of a doctor. They didn't get around to that.

Now we're going to march again, and we've got to march again, in order to put the issue where it is supposed to be. And force everybody to see that there are thirteen hundred of God's children here suffering, sometimes going hungry, going through dark and dreary nights wondering how this thing is going to come out. That's the issue. And we've got to say to the nation: We know it's coming out. For when people get caught up with that which is right and they are willing to sacrifice for it, there is no stopping point short of victory.

We aren't going to let any mace stop us. We are masters in our nonviolent movement in disarming police forces; they don't know what to do. I've seen them so often. I remember in Birmingham, Alabama, when we were in that majestic struggle there we would move out of the 16th Street Baptist Church day after day; by the hundreds we would move out. And Bull Connor would tell them to send the dogs forth and they did come; but we just went before the dogs singing: "Ain't gonna let nobody turn me round." Bull Connor next would say, "Turn the fire hoses on." And as I said to you the other night, Bull Connor didn't know history. He knew a kind of physics that somehow didn't relate to the transphysics that we knew about. And that was the fact that there was a certain kind of fire that no water could put out. And we went before the fire hoses; we had known water. If we were Baptist or some other denomination, we had been immersed. If we were Methodist, and some others, we had been sprinkled, but we knew water.

That couldn't stop us. And we just went on before the dogs and we would look at them; and we'd go on before the water hoses and we would look at it, and we'd just go on singing "Over my head I see freedom in the air." And then we would be thrown in the paddy wagons, and sometimes we were stacked in there like sardines in a can. And they would throw us in, and old Bull would say, "Take them off," and they did; and we would just go in the paddy wagon singing, "We Shall Overcome." And every now and then we'd get in the jail, and we'd see the jailers looking through the windows being moved by our prayers, and being moved by our words and our songs. And there was a power there which Bull Connor couldn't adjust to; and so we ended up transforming Bull into a steer, and we won our struggle in Birmingham.

Now we've got to go on to Memphis just like that. I call upon you to be with us Monday. Now about injunctions: We have an injunction and we're going into court tomorrow morning to fight this illegal, **unconstitutional** injunction. All we say to America is "Be true to what you said on paper." If I lived in China or even Russia, or any totalitarian country, maybe I could understand the denial of certain basic First Amendment privileges, because they hadn't committed themselves to that over there. But somewhere I read of the freedom of assembly. Somewhere I read of the freedom of speech. Somewhere I read of the freedom of the press. Somewhere I read that the greatness of America is the right to protest for right. And so just as I say, we aren't going to let any injunction turn us around. We are going on.

We need all of you.... It's all right to talk about

"streets flowing with milk and honey," but God has commanded us to be concerned about the slums down here, and his children who can't eat three square meals a day. It's all right to talk about the new Jerusalem, but one day, God's preacher must talk about the new New York, the new Atlanta, the new Philadelphia, the new Los Angeles, the new Memphis, Tennessee. This is what we have to do.

Now the other thing we'll have to do is this: Always anchor our external direct action with the power of **economic withdrawal**. Now, we are poor people, individually, we are poor when you compare us with white society in America. We are poor. Never stop and forget that collectively, that means all of us together, collectively we are richer than all the nations in the world, with the exception of nine. Did you ever think about that? After you leave the United States, Soviet Russia, Great Britain, West Germany, France, and I could name the others, the Negro collectively is richer than most nations of the world. We have an annual income of more than thirty billion dollars a year, which is more than all of the exports of the United States, and more than the national budget of Canada. Did you know that? That's power right there, if we know how to pool it.

We don't have to argue with anybody. We don't have to curse and go around acting bad with our words. We don't need any bricks and bottles, we don't need any Molotov cocktails, we just need to go around to these stores, and to these massive industries in our country, and say, "God sent us by here, to say to you that you're not treating his children right. And we've come by here to ask you to make the first item on your agenda—fair treatment, where God's children are concerned. Now, if you are not prepared to do that, we do have an agenda that we must follow. And our agenda calls for withdrawing economic support from you . . . ."

But not only that, we've got to strengthen black institutions. I call upon you to take your money out of the banks downtown and deposit your money in Tri-State Bank—we want a "bank-in" movement in Memphis. So go by the savings and loan association. I'm not asking you something that we don't do ourselves at SCLC. Judge Hooks and others will tell you that we have an account here in the savings and loan association from the Southern Christian Leadership Conference. We're just telling you to follow what we're doing. Put your money there. You have six or seven black insurance companies in Memphis. Take out your insurance there. We want to have an "insurance-in."

Now these are some practical things we can do. We begin the process of building a greater economic base. And at the same time, we are putting pressure where it really hurts. I ask you to follow through here.

Now, let me say as I move to my conclusion that we've got to give ourselves to this struggle until the end. Nothing would be more tragic than to stop at this point, in Memphis. We've got to see it through. And when we have our march, you need to be there. Be concerned about your brother. You may not be on strike. But either we go up together, or we go down together. . . .

That's the question before you tonight. Not, "If I stop to help the sanitation workers, what will happen to all of the hours that I usually spend in my office every day and every week as a pastor?" The question is not, "If I stop to help this man in need, what will happen to me?" "If I do not stop to help the sanitation workers, what will happen to them?" That's the question.

Let us rise up tonight with a greater readiness. Let us stand with a greater determination. And let us move on in these powerful days, these days of challenge to make America what it ought to be. We have an opportunity to make America a better nation. And I want to thank God, once more, for allowing me to be here with you. . . .

Well, I don't know what will happen now. We've got some difficult days ahead. But it doesn't matter with me now. Because I've been to the mountaintop. And I don't mind. Like anybody, I would like to live a long life. Longevity has its place. But I'm not concerned about that now. I just want to do God's will. And He's allowed me to go up to the mountain. And I've looked over. And I've seen the promised land. I may not get there with you. But I want you to know tonight, that we, as a people, will get to the promised land. And I'm happy, tonight. I'm not worried about anything. I'm not fearing any man. Mine eyes have seen the glory of the coming of the Lord.

COMPREHENSION

1. Reread the opening paragraph.

   a. Who does Dr. King say are rising up in the world?

   _____

   b. According to Dr. King, what do they want?

   _____

2. According to Dr. King, what did Pharaoh encourage his slaves to do to prevent them from working together?

   _____

   _____

3. According to Dr. King, what is the main issue for striking sanitation workers in Memphis?

   _____

   _____

4. In addition to nonviolent protest, what other kinds of actions does Dr. King recommend to bring about positive change?

   _____

   _____

5. As Dr. King reaches the end of his speech, what does he say he has seen?

   _____

   _____

6. Complete each sentence with the correct word.

   longevity   unity   injustice

   a. People strove for _____ in order to bring about harmony to their community.

   b. The people of this region enjoy _____, living well into their nineties.

   c. Putting somebody in prison without a trial is a(n) _____.

CRITICAL THINKING

1. Identify each of the following statements by writing *fact* or *opinion* on the line.

   _____ **a.** Dr. King refers to events in Birmingham, Alabama, as a struggle for civil rights.

   _____ **b.** Dr. King's speech moved everyone.

   _____ **c.** Dr. King repeats words and phrases to emphasize his ideas about civil and human rights.

2. What do you think Dr. King means when he says that in Birmingham, "there was a certain kind of fire that no water could put out"?

   _____

   _____

   _____

3. Explain why you think Dr. King uses Birmingham as an example to inspire the striking workers in Memphis.

   _____

   _____

   _____

   _____

4. As Dr. King reaches his conclusion, why do you think he asks the people of Memphis to march with the sanitation workers?

   _____

   _____

   _____

SKILL FOCUS: ANALYZING A PRIMARY SOURCE

1. Identify the primary source you just read by answering the following questions.

   a. Who delivered this speech?

   _____

   _____

   b. What is the speech about?

   _____

   _____

2. Name three specific things Dr. King was trying to persuade his audience to do.

   _____

   _____

3. Dr. King was both a participant and an observer of the events of Birmingham and Memphis. If you were a historian writing about these events, would you consider his speech a reliable primary source? Explain.

   _____

   _____

4. What might you learn about the Civil Rights Movement from this speech that you might not learn from your history textbook?

   _____

   _____

5. How might the Memphis audience have responded to this speech?

   _____

   _____

Reading-Writing Connection

Think about an issue in your school or community that you would like to change or improve. On a separate sheet of paper, write a brief speech that states your views and tries to persuade your audience to work with you to bring about change.

LESSON 29

Skill: Reading a Diagram

BACKGROUND INFORMATION

"How a Camera Works" explores how photographic techniques were invented, then developed and refined, and finally perfected. Photography has come a long way since the camera obscura was invented in the mid-1500s. People can take photos using a digital camera and e-mail the image to their friends. Even so, modern cameras still work in basically the same way as the camera obscura.

SKILL FOCUS: Reading a Diagram

In a scientific article, a description, a theory, or an idea can be made much clearer if it is illustrated with a picture, or **diagram**. A diagram can show the parts of something, or it can show how things move or interact.

To analyze a diagram, follow these steps.

1. Read the title of the diagram, as well as the caption. Both contain important information.
2. Read the labels that identify the parts of the diagram.
3. Study how the parts of the diagram fit together.
4. If the diagram illustrates a part of the text, use the information in it to understand the text.

▶ Use the diagram below to answer the questions in the next column.

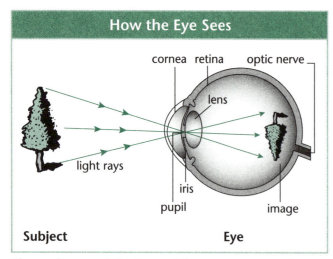

How the Eye Sees

Subject — Eye

The surface and the lens of the eye are curved, so light rays bend as they pass through.

1. What is the title of the diagram?
   _____

2. What do the labels show?
   _____
   _____

CONTEXT CLUES: Make Inferences

Scientific writings may include unfamiliar words or words that are used in new ways. Often these words are defined in the sentence in which they appear. If they are not, you may be able to **infer** their meanings by looking at the surrounding words and sentences and using what you already know.

Read the sentence below and use inference context clues to help define the underlined word.

> *Much later, artists captured* semblances *of people and scenes on large canvases using paints and brushes.*

If you didn't know the meaning of the word *semblances,* by reading the sentence carefully and using what you already know, you could infer that *semblances* are representations, images, or pictures.

▶ Read the sentence below. On the line, write what you infer the meaning of the underlined word to be. Circle the part of the sentence that helped you infer this meaning.

> *British physicist Ernest Rutherford* bombarded *a thin sheet of gold with countless alpha particles at high speed.*

_____

As you read, look for context clues to figure out the meanings of *projected*, *preserved*, and *iodine*.

Strategy Tip

In "How a Camera Works," look carefully at each diagram. Study the captions and labels. Use the information to help you understand the ideas presented in the text.

108   LESSON 29   Reading a Diagram

READING A SCIENCE SELECTION

How a Camera Works

Taking a picture is an ideal way to capture a moment in time. The image is captured on film, and it can be viewed for years to come, for others to learn from and enjoy.

People have always had a desire to record their world in visual form. Early cave paintings dating back thousands of years captured the images of animals native to that place at that time. Much later, artists captured semblances of people and scenes on large canvases using paints and brushes. Although they are considered historical documents, paintings are never entirely accurate, for they represent an artist's vision, rather than an objective viewpoint.

People wanted to be able to reproduce an exact image of a person, place, or thing. Inventors set out to achieve this goal.

The Camera Obscura

Photography can be traced back to ancient Greece. The Greek philosopher Aristotle is said to have known of the basic principle, although he could not have known that this principle would lead to the future field of photography. What was known was that if a dark room had a small hole in a wall, an image of the scene outside the room would appear on the opposite wall, upside down.

The diagram in Figure 1 helps explain this. Light travels in straight waves at a certain speed. In order to pass through the tiny hole, the light slows down. This causes the **waves of light** to bend. As they do so, the image from outside flips, so that it appears upside down on the opposite wall.

Through the centuries, people experimented with this idea. In the mid-1500s, a device known as the **camera obscura** was invented. This term means "darkened room" in Latin. Basically the camera obscura was a box with a hole in it and a surface for capturing the image that was projected through the hole. Artists often used the camera obscura as a way to draw an exact representation of something. Eventually a lens was added to sharpen the image, and later a mirror was added so that the image could be drawn right-side up. See Figure 2 below.

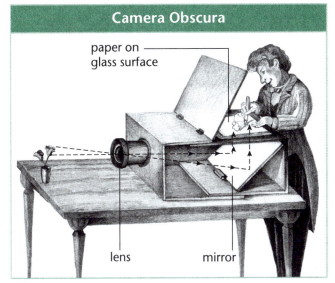

FIGURE 2. The camera obscura allowed people to capture an image on paper, as long as they were willing to draw it.

The camera obscura helped make it possible to record images accurately, but it was still necessary for someone to draw the projected image to record it. People wanted the image to be preserved without anyone having to draw it. This was the goal that drove many pioneers working in the field that would become known as photography.

Making It Stick

In the early 1800s, people began to experiment with ways to make the images "stick"—to preserve

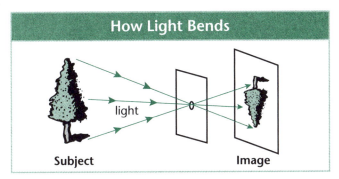

FIGURE 1. This small hole works like the lens in the human eye or the lens in a camera. It slows down the light and causes it to bend.

LESSON 29 Reading a Diagram   **109**

them automatically. Many people felt that if the right combinations of chemicals were spread over the paper, the chemicals might be able to trap the image, preserving it. In time, it was proven that they were right.

One of the first men to capture an image on paper was Joseph Niepce (Nee EPS) from France. In the early 1800s, Niepce began experimenting with silver compounds. Setting up a small camera obscura and a silver-coated sheet of paper, he was able to capture the image of a birdhouse outside his window. The colors, however, were reversed: All the dark colors were light and the light colors were dark. What Niepce had actually done was make a **negative** of the image.

Niepce did not give up. He told his brother, "With patience, anything can be done," and he kept at it. Finally in 1827, Niepce arrived at the answer. After much observation and experimentation, he set up his camera obscura and inserted a pewter plate coated with bitumen of Judea. He had observed that this particular type of asphalt changed color when it was exposed to sunlight. This could reverse the colors of his negative.

He set up his new idea in the window of his workroom for the entire day. The pewter plate did, indeed, capture a faint image of the outside world. This image, which survives today, is considered the world's first photograph.

The Daguerreotype

While Niepce was patiently experimenting with photography, another Frenchmen was also finding new ways to use the camera obscura. Louis Daguerre had created the diorama, which was thrilling audiences in Paris. Using a camera obscura, he would re-create a scene in several painted sections, then display it inside a theater, slowly revealing different sections of it.

He and Niepce became partners in 1829. Together they experimented again and again with ways to perfect the techniques of preserving a picture. After a few years, Daguerre went back to using paper coated with silver compounds instead of a pewter plate. He began adding <u>iodine</u> to the silver to make it more sensitive to light.

Finally in 1837, instead of pewter or paper, Daguerre used a copper plate coated with silver. He placed the plate in a box that had iodine vapor, where the silver mixed with the iodine to form a coat of silver iodide.

Next Daguerre set the plate inside the camera obscura, now called the *camera*. The plate needed to be exposed to light for 15 to 20 minutes for the image to stick. He next put the plate into a box with mercury vapor. The mercury vapor reacted with the silver, switching the light colors to dark and dark colors to light. (See Figure 3.) Then he spread a salt solution over the plate to preserve the image.

Daguerre had at last accomplished what he had set out to do. He named his invention after himself—the **daguerreotype**.

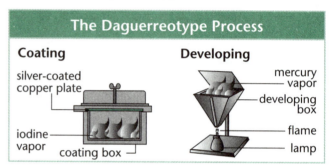

FIGURE 3. The Daguerreotype process preserved a camera's image.

From Plates to Paper

What Daguerre had not been able to do, however, was to reproduce an image on paper rather than on a plate. In England, though, a man named William Henry Fox Talbot was also experimenting with photography. He was building on the original plan by using silver-coated paper and spreading a salt solution over the paper to save the image. However, light and dark colors were still reversed. He was determined to overcome this problem.

Talbot came upon the idea of spreading wax over the original image, which made the paper around the image transparent. On top of this, he laid another sheet of paper, coated with the silver compound. Light then turned the darker portions of the original image lighter, and vice versa. Talbot had discovered the photographic technique of making **positive** prints from negative images—a process still in use today.

Getting Better and Better

Photography still had a long way to go, but the groundwork had been laid. Images still took a long time to reproduce on paper. Therefore moving objects could not usually be photographed because they appeared and disappeared too quickly to be captured. People had to sit for long periods of time in one position, without flinching, so the image would transfer exactly.

As the years passed, cameras and photography techniques were improved and refined. Today there are many different kinds of cameras, from simple box cameras with no adjustments to digital cameras with a variety of adjustable settings. Figure 4 shows how a 35mm camera records an image on film. As you can see, the concept is very similar to the camera obscura, invented more than four centuries ago.

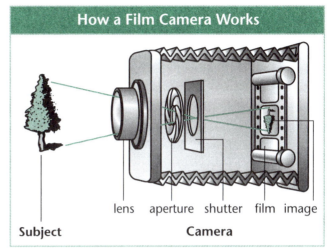

FIGURE 4. Compare this diagram with Figure 2. You will see that the basic principle of the camera obscura is the basis for film photography today.

COMPREHENSION

1. When was the camera obscura invented?
   _____
   _____

2. How did Niepce's photographic technique differ from Daguerre's?
   _____
   _____

3. Why was it difficult to capture moving objects in early photographs?
   _____
   _____
   _____

4. Number the following events in order to show the progress of discoveries in photography.

   _____ Daguerre used a copper plate.

   _____ Niepce experimented with pewter plates.

   _____ Talbot made a negative, then a positive.

   _____ Niepce experimented with paper.

5. Write the letter of the correct meaning on the line next to each word.

   _____ projected   a. saved

   _____ preserved   b. a chemical that makes silver compounds more sensitive to light

   _____ iodine   c. threw forward

CRITICAL THINKING

1. Explain why people in the 1800s might have wanted to capture images of their everyday world in either drawings or photographs.
   _____
   _____
   _____
   _____

2. Why do you think it took hundreds of years for people to build upon the principle of the camera obscura?
   _____
   _____
   _____
   _____

LESSON 29 Reading a Diagram

3. Describe how Daguerre's dioramas might be similar to movies today.

4. Explain why *camera obscura* is a good name for this early apparatus.

5. Why might Niepce and Daguerre have decided to become partners?

6. What effect did William Henry Fox Talbot's discoveries have on modern photography?

SKILL FOCUS: READING A DIAGRAM

1. Examine Figure 1. Explain what it illustrates.

2. In what way is Figure 2 similar to Figure 1?

3. What do the lines in Figure 2 indicate?

4. Figure 3 shows a process, or a sequence of steps. What process does it illustrate?

5. Along with the steps of the process, what other information does Figure 3 help you to see?

6. How is the diagram in Figure 4 comparable to the diagram in Figure 2?

Reading-Writing Connection

Choose one of the diagrams from the selection. On a separate sheet of paper, write a paragraph that explains the diagram's purpose.

LESSON 30

Skill: Word Problems

BACKGROUND INFORMATION

"Solving Word Problems" gives a five-step process to follow in order to solve word problems. When you solve a word problem in math, you are asked a question that depends on numerical information for an answer. Your challenge is to change words into familiar mathematical symbols. Many word problems can be reduced to an equation whose solution answers the question. The problem establishes a situation and provides enough information for you to solve the problem. You decide what operations to use to answer the question.

SKILL FOCUS: Word Problems

When you solve a word problem, follow these steps.

1. **Read the problem.** First be sure you understand all the words. Then think about the question asked or the information you are to supply. Also try to picture in your mind the information given.

2. **Decide how to find the answer.** Try to translate sentences into equations. Focus on the question and think of any formulas that relate to the question.

3. **Estimate the answer.** Before solving the equation, ask yourself what a reasonable answer might be. Use rounded numbers to estimate.

4. **Carry out the plan.** Solve the equation.

5. **Reread the problem.** Compare your answer to your estimate. Determine if your answer is reasonable. Finally write your answer using the appropriate units.

▶ Read the word problem below. Then answer the questions about it.

The 40-story oil platform had been in operation for only a year when it exploded with 9,500 barrels of oil on board. If 9,500 barrels is about 400,000 gallons of oil, how many gallons are in one barrel?

1. What does the problem ask you to find?

_____

2. What math operation should you use to solve the problem?

_____

3. Write an equation to solve the problem.

_____

4. Solve the equation.

_____

5. Answer the question.

_____

WORD CLUES

As you read a word problem, be alert for words that indicate a mathematical operation. For example, the words *more* and *total* often indicate addition, while the words *difference* or *remaining* often indicate subtraction. Also keep in mind that some words can be written as formulas. For example, see below.

$$\text{Percent} = \frac{\text{part}}{\text{whole}} \times 100$$

▶ Read the following word problem. Circle the word that indicates the mathematical operation that should be used.

If an oil platform had 8,400 barrels on board on Monday and 7,200 barrels on Wednesday, what is the difference in the number of barrels?

┌─ **Strategy Tip** ─┐

As you read "Solving Word Problems," follow the five steps as you solve each problem. Make sure that your answer responds to the original question and includes the correct unit.

LESSON 30   Word Problems   **113**

READING A MATHEMATICS SELECTION

Solving Word Problems

The United States produces more garbage than any place else in the world—250,000,000 tons a year! What do we do with it all? What will we do with it in the future?

Environmental concerns are the subjects of many mathematics word problems. The next time you are challenged by a word problem on this or any other subject, use the following five steps to help you solve it.

1. Read the problem.
2. Decide how to find the answer.
3. Estimate the answer.
4. Carry out the plan.
5. Reread the problem.

Read the Problem

On March 15, 2001, about 75 miles off the Brazilian coast, huge explosions shattered the air. Ten men lost their lives, and the world's largest oil rig—a floating platform 40 stories tall and valued at some $350 million—had been crippled. A week later, it sank to the bottom of the Atlantic in water that was nearly a mile deep. After three months of investigations, no one could say exactly what caused the explosion. The platform, which had 9,500 barrels of oil on board—about 400,000 gallons—had begun operating only a year earlier. It had been pumping 80,000 gallons of oil per day. The total Brazilian oil output was about 1,600,000 gallons per day. What percent of the total Brazilian oil output was the oil platform pumping?

Reread the problem. Be sure that you understand the situation. Are there any words that you do not know? If so, look in a dictionary for their meanings. Now read the question again and skim back over the problem to see if there is enough information to answer the question or if there is any extra information—information that is not needed to answer the question. Say the question aloud to yourself. *What percent of the total Brazilian oil output was the oil platform pumping?*

Decide How to Find the Answer

Focus on the question. You are looking for a percent, which means "a part of 100 in a whole." Remember the formula for percent.

$$P = \frac{\text{part}}{\text{whole}} \times 100$$

Now find the part and the whole. In this problem, the total Brazilian output is the whole and the part is the amount pumped by the platform. Find this information in the problem.

- *The platform pumped 80,000 gallons per day.*
- *The total Brazilian oil output was 1,600,000 gallons of oil per day.*

Notice that the problem contains some unnecessary information. For example, the facts "40 stories tall," "valued at $350 million," and "9,500 barrels of oil on board—about 400,000 gallons" are not needed to answer the question.

Now restate the question in terms of the important facts: *What percent of 1,600,000 is 80,000?* Fill in the values in the percent formula.

$$P = \frac{80,000}{1,600,000} \times 100$$

Estimate the Answer

You can **estimate** the answer by simplifying the fraction to $\frac{8}{160}$. Then round each number to estimate the value of the fraction: 8 rounds to 10, 160 rounds to 150.

$$P = \frac{10}{150} \times 100 = .07 \times 100 = 7\%$$

So, 80,000 is about 7% of 1,600,000.

Carry Out the Plan

$$P = \frac{80,000}{1,600,000} \times 100$$

Simplify the fraction and divide.

$$P = .05 \times 100$$

80,000 is 5% of 1,600,000.

114 LESSON 30 Word Problems

Reread the Problem

Compare your answer to your estimate to determine if your answer is reasonable. Since the answer, 5%, is close to the estimate, the answer is reasonable. Write your answer as a sentence that responds to the original question. *The oil platform was pumping 5% of the total Brazilian oil output.*

Use the five steps to solve the following word problem.

Read: *In some parts of the world, millions of tons of each year's grain supply are grown by depleting the groundwater. Water tables are dropping 1.6 meters a year beneath a large part of irrigated farmland in northern China. They are dropping 20 centimeters a year across two-thirds of India's Punjab, the nation's "breadbasket." How many times faster are the water tables dropping in northern China than in the Punjab?*

Make sure that you know the meanings of all the words in the problem. If you do not know the meanings of the words *depleting, water tables,* and *irrigated,* look them up in a dictionary. Then restate the question for yourself. *Compare the rate the water tables are dropping in northern China to the rate they are dropping in India's Punjab.*

Decide: You are asked to compare two **rates**. Rates are usually compared in ratios or multiples. Find the ratio of the greater to the smaller.

$$\frac{\text{rate in northern China}}{\text{rate in the Punjab}}$$

Find those values in the problem.

- *Water tables are dropping 1.6 meters a year in northern China.*
- *They are dropping 20 centimeters a year in the Punjab.*

The facts "millions of tons of grain" and "two-thirds of India's Punjab" are not necessary to the solution of this problem.

The rates are given for the same unit of time, a year, but use different units of length, centimeters and meters. To find the answer, express both amounts in the same units; rewrite 1.6 meters as an **equivalent** number of centimeters.

$$1 \text{ m} = 100 \text{ cm, so}$$
$$1.6 \text{ m} = 160 \text{ cm}$$

Put these values into the ratio above.

$$\frac{\text{rate in northern China}}{\text{rate in the Punjab}} = \frac{160}{20}$$

Estimate: One meter is much more than one centimeter, so you can expect the ratio to be high.

Carry Out: $\dfrac{160}{20} = \dfrac{8}{1} = 8$

Reread: Your answer, 8, is a high ratio. It means that every time the water table in the Punjab drops 1 centimeter, 1 meter, or 1 inch, the water table in northern China drops 8 centimeters, 8 meters, or 8 inches. *In northern China, the water tables are dropping 8 times faster than in India's Punjab.*

COMPREHENSION

1. What is the second step in solving a word problem?

   _____

2. Describe one way you can estimate an answer.

   _____

3. Identify the last step in solving a word problem.

   _____

LESSON 30 Word Problems **115**

CRITICAL THINKING

1. In solving a word problem, you find that a local pizzeria makes 98,000 pizzas a day. What would you suspect about your answer?

   _____

2. Every day George drinks 2 cups of milk, 2 pints of water, and a quart of juice. A problem asks you to find how many cups of liquid George consumes a day. Before performing any operations, what should you do?

   _____

3. A geologist's chart lists all of the earthquakes that have occurred on the West Coast in the past 10 years. What operation would she have to perform to find out the average number of earthquakes per year?

   _____

SKILL FOCUS: WORD PROBLEMS

Solve each word problem by following the five steps.

1. **Read:** A department store is charging $129.99 for a dress. This price is 150% of what the department store paid to purchase it. How much does the dress cost the department store?

   Decide: _____

   Estimate: _____

   Carry Out: _____

   Reread: _____

2. **Read:** Patrick weighs 20 pounds more than Chris. Their combined weight is 348 pounds. How much does Chris weigh?

   Decide: _____

   Estimate: _____

   _____

   Carry Out: _____

   Reread: _____

Reading-Writing Connection

On a separate sheet of paper, create a word problem using a recent newspaper article that includes numerical information. Then use the five steps to solve the problem.

LESSON 31

Skill: Transitional Words and Phrases

Certain words and phrases provide links, or transitions, between ideas conveyed in writing. For example, the word *because* shows a cause-and-effect relationship between ideas. **Transitional words and phrases** can be used both in a paragraph and between paragraphs to help the reader move smoothly from one idea to the next.

Here are some types of transitions with their example words and phrases.

Time: first, next, when, after, before, then, soon, at last
Cause and Effect: because, therefore, for this reason, as a result
Comparison and Contrast: like, but, unlike, although, however, on the other hand
Examples: like, for example, such as, that is, namely
Additions: also, another, furthermore, moreover, in addition

Read the following passage. Fill in the blanks with transitional words or phrases that help make the meaning of the sentences clearer.

The Development of the First Automobiles

The first automobiles ran on steam engines. A French army officer invented a three-wheeled steam tractor for moving cannons in 1769. _____, the tractor had to stop every 10 or 15 minutes to build up steam before moving again. _____, steam carriages that could carry 20 passengers and travel up to 15 miles an hour appeared in England in the 1830s. _____ the carriages were useful, they were noisy, dirtied the air with smoke, scattered hot ashes, and frightened people and horses. Laws were passed against them in England. _____, further development of the steam automobile occurred in America during the late nineteenth and early twentieth centuries. _____, more than 100 American companies made steam automobiles from 1900 to the 1920s. _____, steam cars had too many problems. They had to stop too often to build up steam. _____, they were dangerous because of open fires and steam that could scald people.

_____, electric cars were invented in the late 1890s and early 1900s. Electric cars were popular at first _____ they ran quietly and were safe and clean. _____, their batteries had to be recharged every 50 miles. _____, the electric car eventually became unpopular. The gasoline-powered car was developed at the same time as the electric and steam versions, _____ it relied on an internal combustion engine. In 1896, American engineers Ford, King, Olds, and Winton introduced gasoline cars to the American public, and _____ this became the most widely used type of car.

LESSON 32
Skill: Improving Reading Rate

> Good readers vary their **reading rates**, depending on the difficulty of the material they are reading. For example, they might read a challenging science, social studies, or mathematics selection more slowly and carefully than a romance novel. Sometimes it is necessary to reread sentences or paragraphs that contain complex ideas. Good readers also stop to read diagrams, maps, and charts, which require increased attention and slower reading.

Use the following selection to check your reading rate. Use a watch or a clock with a second hand to time yourself. Start right on a minute and write the starting time when you begin reading. Write your ending time when you finish reading.

Museums Under the Waves

Starting Time _____

When a Swedish ship that sank in 1628 was recovered from the harbor of Stockholm in Sweden, historians and scientists were thrilled by the opportunity to explore this relic of the past. The ship's construction revealed much about how ships were built and operated during the seventeenth century. Objects, or artifacts, made by human beings, provided a picture of daily life almost 400 years ago.

Underwater archaeology—the study of wrecked ships and airplanes, and of human settlements that have sunk beneath seas and other bodies of water—is really a product of the last 50 years. The rapid growth of this science has occurred because of the invention of lighter and better underwater diving equipment, such as scuba gear, sonar, and magnetic instruments that find objects underwater, and small submarines piloted by remote control that can carry explorers and cameras across the ocean floor.

Magnometers are instruments used by divers to locate large iron objects, such as ship anchors, up to 30 feet away. Sonar instruments use sound waves to locate underwater shipwrecks, planes, and artifacts. They are set up on the ocean floor to extend their beams over a range of several miles. The sound waves bounce off the surface of objects and are recorded on the instrument. Cameras that are water-tight and pressure-resistant are stationed underwater to take pictures without anyone operating them. The dark ocean waters are illuminated by the bright, quick flash of strobe lights. These lights are synchronized with the camera, so that pictures can be taken continually. A camera and strobe light can be hung on a line off the edge of a boat and take hundreds of pictures as the boat moves along, searching for wrecks and artifacts.

Using these instruments, underwater archaeologists have made some exciting finds. Sonar was used to find the wreck of the *Monitor*, an iron-plated Union ship that fought an important

Scientists use remote-controlled vehicles like this to detect and collect underwater objects for research.

118 LESSON 32 Improving Reading Rate

Civil War battle against the Confederate *Merrimac*. The *Monitor* sank near Cape Hatteras, North Carolina, in 1862. It was discovered over a hundred years later, and 2,000 pictures were taken of the wreck by underwater cameras. Underwater archaeologists have also discovered 5,000-year-old boats in the Mediterranean Sea, ships from the Spanish Armada of 1588 that sank near the coasts of England and Ireland, and 300-year-old Spanish ships traveling home from the New World with treasures of gold. In 1985, sonar, strobe lights, and underwater cameras were used to search Loch Ness, a large lake in Scotland where a fabled sea monster is rumored to live. Explorers found wrecked fishing boats and a plane from World War II, but no sea monster.

Underwater archaeology can provide us with many links to the past. In ancient ports all over the world are sunken ships that span 6,000 years. There are also sunken settlements in seas and lakes that can give us important clues to life in ancient times. Underwater archaeologists want to study these objects to add to the world's knowledge of history, but they have to fight two enemies. One enemy is treasure hunters who dive for ancient artifacts that they can sell to collectors. Once sold, these objects are scattered all over the world and are lost to scientists and historians who wish to study them. The second enemy is dredging machines that are used to repair harbors and ports. These machines destroy wrecks and their artifacts or bury them deeper under sand and mud. By educating the public about the importance of underwater "museums" of the past, archaeologists are hoping to get support for laws to protect underwater treasures from theft and destruction.

This diver is exploring a shipwreck off the coast of Egypt in the Red Sea.

Ending Time _____

To find the total time it took you to read the selection, do the following. (1) Subtract your starting time from the ending time. (2) Divide the number of words in the selection by the difference expressed in seconds.

If it took you 3 minutes and 20 seconds ($3 \times 60 + 20 = 200$ seconds) to read the selection, you would have read 3 words per second ($600 \div 200 = 3$). (3) To find the number of words per minute (WPM), multiply your rate per second by 60. Your answer would be 180 WPM.

Words in selection: 600

	Hr.	Min.	Sec.
Ending Time:	_____	_____	_____
Starting Time:	_____	_____	00
Total Time:	_____	_____	_____

No. words: 600 = _____ words per second

No. seconds: _____

_____ × 60 = _____ WPM

To check your understanding of the selection, circle the letter of the correct answer to each question.

1. Why are shipwrecks from the past important?
   a. They provide information on how to build ships today.
   b. Museums will pay a lot for them.
   c. Shipwrecks from the past are not important.
   d. They provide clues to life in the past.

2. Why has underwater archaeology developed chiefly in the past 50 years?
   a. Better equipment has made underwater exploration easier.
   b. Many ships were lost in the past 50 years.
   c. Governments began allocating money for exploration 50 years ago.
   d. Underwater archeology does not cost a lot of money.

3. How does sonar work?
   a. It uses sound waves to locate objects.
   b. It uses magnetism to locate objects.
   c. It uses underwater cameras to locate objects.
   d. It uses light waves to locate objects.

4. Which of these would a magnometer *not* be able to detect?
   a. an anchor
   b. ceramic pottery
   c. iron-plated ships
   d. all of the above

5. What were scientists hoping to find in a large lake in Scotland in 1985?
   a. the Confederate *Merrimac*
   b. the Loch Ness monster
   c. Spanish ships loaded with gold
   d. 5,000-year-old ships

6. What are the two greatest obstacles that underwater archaeology faces today?
   a. lack of government funding for exploration and few trained archaeologists
   b. few wrecks left to discover and lack of equipment
   c. treasure hunters and dredging machines
   d. poor equipment and water pollution

LESSON 33

Skill: Distinguishing Fact From Opinion

As you read books, newspapers, or magazines, you should be able to distinguish facts from opinions. A statement of **fact** is information that can be proven to be true or false. A statement of **opinion** is a personal belief. People's opinions on a topic or idea may differ.

As you read the following selection, think about which statements are facts and which are opinions.

Are Sport Utility Vehicles Worth Their High Price?

A sport utility vehicle (SUV) is a utility vehicle weighing 8,500 pounds or less. Sport utility vehicles are popular because they are loaded with a combination of qualities—many standard features of passenger cars and special features for driving on and off paved roads. SUVs offer ruggedness, engine power, roominess, and comfort. Many are equipped with 4-wheel drive to give the extra traction needed for driving in difficult conditions, such as on snow, mud, or sand.

Is a sport utility vehicle too much vehicle for too much money? On the high-end scale, a luxury-priced SUV is over $82,000! Other makes and models come in more typically at $45,000. For these prices, some critics complain, SUVs should not have a ride like horse-drawn wagons because of their outdated, inferior suspension systems.

Prospective customers need to realistically evaluate their transportation needs. While the multipurpose SUVs are not passenger cars, most owners use SUVs in much the same way—for both everyday commuting and shopping and for light recreation.

Because sport utility vehicles are more top-heavy than passenger cars, the SUVs handle and maneuver differently. They are not designed like passenger cars to round corners at high speeds. Reckless SUV drivers cause their vehicles to roll over at a much higher rate than do drivers of passenger vehicles.

Sport utility vehicles may only be a passing trend. After all, another choice—be it a luxury sports car or a sturdy station wagon—may give more value for the dollar. In the final analysis, this old adage works best: "Let the buyer beware!"

One critical advantage of the SUV over the passenger car, however, is its larger size and greater weight. When these two types of vehicles collide in a traffic accident, the SUV will most often be less damaged. One significant disadvantage is that SUVs are subject to U.S. standards for trucks, not cars, and so are not required to have safety features such as airbags and impact-absorbing bumpers.

Read the following statements, which are based on the selection above. On the line before each statement, write *F* if it is a fact or *O* if it is an opinion.

_____ 1. Four-wheel drive gives extra traction for driving in difficult conditions.

_____ 2. A sport utility vehicle is too much vehicle for too much money.

_____ 3. A sport utility vehicle is larger and heavier than a passenger car.

_____ 4. Sport utility vehicles are only a passing trend.

_____ 5. SUVs are subject to the same U.S. standards as trucks.

LESSON 34

Skill: Completing an Employment Application

> Most of the businesses for which you might want to work will require you to complete an **employment application**. Employment applications vary widely, but most of them ask for details about these areas:
>
> • **personal information**, such as your Social Security number and home address
>
> • **educational information**, which summarizes the schoolwork you have done
>
> • **employment history**, which tells when and where you have worked before
>
> • **skills and availability**, which explain your strengths and identify when you can work

Employers use this information to get a quick picture of who you are and how you might fit into their workplace. Often they will use the application to decide whether or not to interview you for a job.

It is important to have this information ready before you go to a business and ask for an employment application. Some businesses will require you to complete the application while you are there.

A. Use the employment application on page 123 to answer the questions that follow. On the line after each sentence, write whether the statement is *true* or *false*.

1. The applicant's middle name is William. _____

2. He lives in the city of Forest Hills, New York. _____

3. He is not currently employed because he has just completed service in the Army. _____

4. He hopes to start a new part-time job at a rate of $8.50 an hour. _____

5. He can work for five days each week. _____

6. If there is no answer at his home phone, he probably can be reached at (718) 555-7486. _____

7. As a juvenile, he was convicted of shoplifting. _____

8. In the past, he has worked at a supermarket and a homeless shelter. _____

B. Complete this statement from **William Davis**, using facts from his employment application on page 123.

"My name is William Davis. I've decided to become a part-time student, so I'm applying for a job as a

_____ here. I can work some hours every weekday except _____; I can

work a full day on Saturdays, too. I can't work on Sundays, because I _____

_____. I worked for a little more than a year as a stock clerk at _____.

122 LESSON 34 Completing an Employment Application

Employment Application

Personal Information

Date of Application __6 / 9 / 08__

Name (last)	(First)	(Middlle)	Social Security No.
Davis	William	Joseph	555-55-5556

Home Address	City	State	Zip
1434 North Liberty Street	Forest Hills	NY	11375

Home Telephone	Alternate Telephone
(718) 555-3002	(718) 555-7486

Position Applying For: __cashier__

Date Available: __6/21/08__ Rate of Pay Expected: __$8.50/hr__

☐ Full-time ☑ Part-time ☐ Temporary ☐ Summer

Days and Hours Available		Day	Mon	Tues	Wed	Thur	Fri	Sat	Sun
	From	5:00	1:00	–	1:00	5:00	8:00	–	
	To	9:00	9:00	–	9:00	9:00	6:00	–	

Are you 18 years of age or older? ☑ Yes ☐ No

Can you submit proof of your legal right to work in the United States? ☑ Yes ☐ No

Have you ever been convicted of a crime (other than a minor traffic violation)? ☐ Yes ☑ No If yes, explain.

Education

Circle the highest level of education completed:

Elementary	High School	College	Graduate School	Other
5 6 7 8	9 10 11 12	13 ⑭ 15 16		

Are you currently a student? ☑ Yes ☐ No

Employment History

List entire employment history, starting with your present or most recent employer. Explain any time during this period that you were unemployed.

From: 9/07 To: 6/08	Name	City College	Job Title/Duties	Reason for Leaving
	Address	34 Kennedy Boulevard, NY, NY	Student: not working because of heavy course load	I now plan to work part-time and go to school part time
	Phone	(212) 555-4300		
	Supervisor	NA	Starting Pay NA	Ending Pay NA

From: 7/06 To: 9/07	Name	ABC Supermarket	Job Title/Duties	Reason for Leaving
	Address	880 Jackson Avenue, NY, NY	Stock clerk: loading shelves, helping with inventory, pricing	I wanted to take extra college courses and could not work the hours requested.
	Phone	(212) 555-0121		
	Supervisor	Denise Brightman	Starting Pay $6.75/hr.	Ending Pay $7.75/hr.

Are you or have you been involved in volunteer work? ☑ Yes ☐ No If yes, explain.

In high school I spent part of each summer helping with repairs and cooking at Community Haven, a homeless shelter. I am also a volunteer soccer coach at a kids' sports program on Sunday afternoons.

What do you see as your greatest strengths as a worker?

I am dependable and will complete any task that my job requires. I am willing to work hard, and I am eager to learn new skills or how to do my current job even better.

May we contact your present employer? ☐ Yes ☐ No ☑ Not currently employed

APPLICANT'S SIGNATURE:	DATE SIGNED:
William Davis	6/9/08

LESSON 34 Completing an Employment Application **123**

unit five
Transitions

LESSON 35
Skill: Figures of Speech

BACKGROUND INFORMATION
"The Road Not Taken," "Mother to Son," and "Grandfather" are three poems that explore the journey of life, from its "starting place" to an "end of the road." Throughout the centuries, writers have tried to find a way to define life through poetry. Poetry often makes use of figures of speech and symbols to make points. Changes in our lives are compared to twists and turns in a path.

SKILL FOCUS: Figures of Speech
Figures of speech are not meant to be taken literally, or word for word. They encourage people to think about things in new and different ways. Although they can appear in all types of writing, figures of speech are especially common in poetry. Here are three of the most common types of figures of speech.

- **Simile** A simile is a comparison using the word *like* or *as*. For example, "snow covered the landscape *like* a soft white blanket."
- **Metaphor** A metaphor is a comparison that does *not* use the word *like* or *as*, such as "a white blanket of snow."
- **Personification** Personification occurs when the author gives nonhuman things human traits. For example, "The friendly sun smiled down on us."

▶ As you read the following poem, look for examples of simile, metaphor, and personification. List them on the chart.

> I view life as an ocean voyage,
>   a journey out to sea.
> With waves that roll along quite smooth,
>   a sky that is cloud-free.
> Until one day dark clouds frown down,
>   the sea begins to rise.
> And then my ocean voyage is a
>   tidal wave in disguise.

Figure of Speech	Example
Simile	
Metaphor	
Personification	

CONTEXT CLUES: Dictionary Definitions
When you see an unfamiliar word while reading poetry, look for context clues. You may need to refer to a **dictionary** for the exact meaning.

Read the following poem and look for context clues to help explain the underlined word.

> *You have earthen eyes*
> *made* <u>fertile</u> *with older days:*
> *watery days without end, seemingly,*

If you study the line that comes before and after this line in the poem, you can conclude that *fertile* has some connection with farming and the growth of plants.

▶ Read the following lines of poetry. Use a dictionary to look up the meaning of the underlined word. Then, in your own words, write a definition for the word as it is used in the sentence.

> *You sit* <u>cushioned</u> *from the world*
> *In that chair;*
> *You rest, and I watch.*

_____

_____

In this selection, the words *diverged*, *trodden*, and *laden* are underlined. Look for clues in the figurative language to determine their meanings.

Strategy Tip

As you read the poems, consider how each poet uses language to help you think about the journey of life.

124   LESSON 35   Figures of Speech

READING A LITERATURE SELECTION

The Road Not Taken
Robert Frost

Two roads <u>diverged</u> in a yellow wood,
And sorry I could not travel both
And be one traveler, long I stood
And looked down one as far as I could
To where it bent in the undergrowth;

Then took the other, just as fair,
And having perhaps the better claim,
Because it was grassy and wanted wear;
Though as for that, the passing there
Had worn them really about the same.

And both that morning equally lay
In leaves no step had <u>trodden</u> black.
Oh! I kept the first for another day!
Yet knowing how way leads on to way,
I doubted if I should ever come back.

I shall be telling this with a sigh
Somewhere ages and ages hence:
Two roads diverged in a wood, and I—
I took the one less traveled by,
And that has made all the difference.

Grandfather
James Lim

You sit cushioned from the world
in that chair;
you rest, and I watch.
The stillness of the room
settles lightly on the floor,
settles lightly like dust—
it streams
down to the earth,
is <u>laden</u> with sunlight.
You are old
like roots are old.
You have earthen eyes
made fertile with older days:
watery days without end, seemingly,
and days
with a stillness in the air
like a fog, thick and lonely.

You waited, always, for mountains,
but now you rest. The room is silent,
and you are old,
your roots are old,
Tell me a story
before the sun sets.

Mother to Son
Langston Hughes

Well, son, I'll tell you,
Life for me ain't been no crystal stair.
It's had tacks in it,
And splinters,
And boards torn up,
And places with no carpet on the floor—
Bare.
But all the time
I'se been a-climbin' on,
and reachin' landin's,
And turnin' corners.
And sometimes goin' in the dark
Where there ain't been no light.
So, boy, don't you turn back.
Don't you set down on the steps
'Cause you finds it kinder hard.
Don't you fall now—
For I'se still goin', honey,
I'se still climbin',
And life for me ain't been no crystal stair.

Langston Hughes (1902–1967)

LESSON 35 Figures of Speech **125**

COMPREHENSION

1. Where does "The Road Not Taken" occur?

2. Which path does the traveler choose to follow, and how does he describe that path?

3. In "Mother to Son," what does the mother say that life has not been for her?

4. According to his mother, how can the son keep from turning back, sitting down, or falling?

5. Describe the setting in which the speaker of "Grandfather" watches the elderly man.

6. What does the speaker want his grandfather to do, and when?

7. Complete each sentence by filling in the correct word from below.

   diverged   laden   trodden

   a. The single path _____ and became two paths.
   b. The donkey was _____ with heavy sacks of corn.
   c. The dusty road was _____ by many travelers on foot.

CRITICAL THINKING

1. In "The Road Not Taken," explain why the speaker feels a conflict within himself.

2. Explain the theme, or central message, of "The Road Not Taken."

3. Look at the lines of "Grandfather," marked with an ✗. What do you think the speaker means when he says "before the sun sets"?

4. Describe how the speaker wants herself and her son to be alike.

5. In "Mother to Son," what has kept the stairway from being easy to climb? Name as many details as you can find in the poem.

126   LESSON 35   Figures of Speech

SKILL FOCUS: FIGURES OF SPEECH

1. Several metaphors appear in "The Road Not Taken."

   a. What is the "yellow wood"?

   _____

   _____

   b. What is the "undergrowth" into which one road bends?

   _____

   _____

2. "The Road Not Taken" is built on an extended metaphor.

   a. What do you think the "two roads" represent? Explain.

   _____

   _____

   b. Describe how this metaphor supports the entire poem.

   _____

   _____

3. Reread the passage in "Mother to Son" with the ✔ next to it, paying attention to the figures of speech in those lines. What do tacks, splinters, torn-up boards, and bare patches of floor have in common with life?

   _____

   _____

4. Explain the similes from "Grandfather" by completing these sentences.

   a. The stillness in his room falls gently, the way _____ does.

   b. It is a thick stillness, as thick as _____.

   c. Grandfather is as old as _____ are.

5. What human trait does the poet give the fog in "Grandfather"? What effect does this personification have?

   _____

   _____

Reading-Writing Connection

We all face decisions and changes as we go through life. Think about some change or decision that you have faced that would probably have a lasting impact on your life. On a separate sheet of paper, write a poem or a paragraph describing the experience.

LESSON 35 Figures of Speech **127**

LESSON 36
Skill: Cause and Effect

BACKGROUND INFORMATION
"After Independence" is about the effects of the American Revolution—effects not only on the United States, but also on countries around the world. Sometimes an event that takes place in another country may appear unimportant to us. However, it can have an impact on your life. For example, a stock market crash in Asia can cause problems in the American stock market that could result in the loss of jobs for people you know.

SKILL FOCUS: Cause and Effect
Any event has at least one **cause**, or reason for happening. This event can also have an **effect**, or a result. When you read about events, understanding causes and effects can help you understand them better.

To analyze cause and effect, follow these steps.

1. Determine the event or situation being described.
2. Look for reasons, or causes, for the event or situation.
3. Look for results, or effects, of the event or situation.
4. Keep in mind that an effect can become a cause for something else, resulting in a chain of causes and effects.

▶ Read the paragraph below. Write the causes and effects in the chart. Notice that some effects become causes, which lead to other effects.

When thousands of British Loyalists fled the country, state governments seized their abandoned estates and sold them as small farms. This policy greatly increased the number of landowners, which in turn increased the number of people who were able to vote.

CONTEXT CLUES: Synonyms
When you come across an unfamiliar word in your reading, you can often figure out its meaning by using synonyms as context clues. **Synonyms** are words that have the same or similar meanings.

Read the following sentences and look for synonym context clues that help explain the meaning of the underlined word.

*In 1777, the state constitution of Vermont **forbade** slavery. In the years that followed, other states also prohibited slavery.*

If you don't know the meaning of the word *forbade*, the word *prohibited* in the second sentence can help you. The words *forbade* and *prohibited* are synonyms, or words with the same or similar meanings.

▶ Read the sentences below. Circle the word that is a synonym for the underlined word.

*The **founding** of the United States of America was only one result of the American Revolution. Establishing a new nation, however, did become the most important result.*

In this selection, the words *forging*, *rejection*, and *repercussions* are underlined. Look for synonyms to help figure out the meanings of these words.

Strategy Tip
As you read "After Independence," think about how the events of the American Revolution are linked together by cause and effect. Ask yourself: *Why was the American Revolution so important to so many nations around the world?*

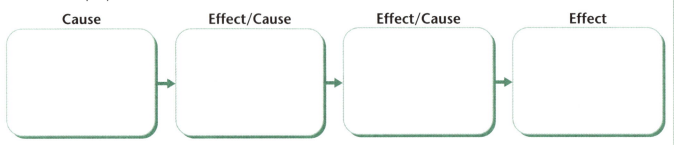

Cause → Effect/Cause → Effect/Cause → Effect

READING A SOCIAL STUDIES SELECTION

After Independence

From the first shots fired in 1775 to the surrender of General Cornwallis to George Washington in 1781, American colonists fought to break free of British rule and to establish a new nation. The founding of the United States of America was not the only result of the Revolutionary War, however. Like a ripple in a pond, the effects of America's great experiment in democracy were far-reaching and complex.

New Challenges for a New Nation

Although they won the war, the American colonies did not return to "business as usual." The colonies had been 13 separate entities, each governing itself with varying degrees of interference from Great Britain. The Declaration of Independence, however, had established a bond—a "United Colonies," even a "United States of America."

With independence, the colonies had to consider their federal ties as well as their futures as states. While national representatives were <u>forging</u> the documents that would govern the nation as a whole—first the Articles of Confederation and then the Constitution (KHAN stə TOO shən)—each state wrote—its own constitution. Every state constitution included a bill of rights, which generally listed the old "rights of Englishmen," including the right to trial by jury, and added the new freedoms of speech, press, and religion. The states also chose governors, either by representative assembly or by direct vote. They reduced property qualifications so that even small farmers and tradespeople could vote.

The end of the war also brought other advances in **democracy**. To emphasize their <u>rejection</u> of European monarchies, Americans refused to accept all titles of nobility. When thousands of British Loyalists fled the country, state governments seized the abandoned estates. Despite the urging of Congress that they pay the owners, the state governments sold them as small farms. This policy greatly increased the number of landowners, which

in turn increased the number of people who were able to vote. Voting gave the small farmers more power. In some states small farmers even gained control of the government.

In the North, the Revolution affected the status of some African Americans. During the war, African Americans, both free and enslaved, joined the armed forces. As a reward, several states granted freedom to soldiers who had been enslaved. In 1777, the state constitution of Vermont forbade slavery, and in 1783 Massachusetts also abolished slavery. One by one, the other northern states followed these examples. Furthermore, an increased demand for workers after the Revolution enabled many northern African Americans to improve their standard of living. Societies working for the **abolition** of slavery grew in the North. Even in the South there was a movement to free enslaved African Americans. However, southern abolitionists soon were defeated by the emergence of cotton as the most important crop in the South. Cotton required a large body of inexpensive labor in order to be profitable. The abolitionists could not overcome the economic pressure that the system imposed.

The slavery issue would become an ever-greater problem in the years ahead, but more immediate problems surfaced after the Revolution. For one thing, the United States still faced challenges from Britain and Spain. British forces continued to occupy several forts in the Great Lakes, and British trade policies attempted to bar American merchants from "British" markets. Spain, which still held Florida and lands west of the Mississippi River, closed the river to American shipping. It wanted to curb what it saw as American expansionism (ek SPAN shən i zəm). The ill will produced by these situations was not easily resolved.

The war had also been costly. The Confederation Congress faced debts not only to foreign governments that had lent aid but also to American

LESSON 36 Cause and Effect **129**

The combination of the U.S. flag and a map of the world shows that events in the United States have causes and effects throughout the world.

people. The soldiers had not yet been paid for their military service. American civilians who had lent money to the war effort were not paid. Attempts to raise the funds by imposing taxes met a great deal of opposition and had little success. Resulting difficulties included hardships in beginning federal projects (such as building new roads) and the creation of a national image that many foreign governments refused to take seriously. Indeed, another century would pass before the United States would firmly establish itself as a world power.

An Impact in Other Lands

Despite the challenges that the new nation was facing, it remained true that the United States was the first to proclaim the democratic principles set forth in the Declaration of Independence. In strong, even startling language, this document stated that all people are created equal, that all people have rights that cannot be taken away, that the government should be run by the people, and that the people have the right to overthrow an unjust government. In Europe, these democratic ideals fostered a new way of thinking about government and society.

In Great Britain, the loss of the war enabled **Parliament** (PAHR lə ment) to reestablish its leadership of the British government. As a result, during the next century, royal power was further reduced, and the right to vote was extended. Once dominated by the House of Lords, Parliament saw its power gradually transferred to the House of Commons.

Democratic ideas also spread to France, stirring the French people to revolt against their **absolute monarchy** in 1789. French armies then spread revolutionary ideas throughout Western Europe. Eventually, most of the countries of Western Europe became democracies or revised their monarchies to include more democratic ideas.

During the early nineteenth century, many people in colonial Latin America followed the example of the United States. They revolted against the rule of Spain and Portugal—and they won their independence. Most Latin American countries became republics, modeling their governments on that of the United States.

Though the American Revolution was fought more than 200 years ago, its repercussions are still being felt around the world. Few people could have guessed that the American Revolution would have such far-reaching consequences.

COMPREHENSION

1. After the Revolution, how did the colonies' thoughts about government change?

   _____

   _____

   _____

2. What did all the state constitutions have in common?

   _____

   _____

   _____

3. What happened to the British Loyalists' estates after their owners fled?

   _____

   _____

   _____

4. What new ideas did the Declaration of Independence include?

   _____

   _____

   _____

5. What happened to the British government after the American Revolution?

   _____

   _____

   _____

6. Write the letter of the correct meaning on the line next to each word.

   ___ rejection   **a.** giving shape to; making

   ___ forging   **b.** the act of refusing to accept or recognize

   ___ repercussions   **c.** effects

CRITICAL THINKING

1. Explain why the national government had little success in raising money by taxation.

   _____

   _____

2. Explain why it was important to increase the number of landowners in the United States.

   _____

   _____

3. Why did American expansionism cause problems with Britain and Spain?

   _____

   _____

4. Describe how your life might change if you were an African American living in the South after the Revolution.

   _____

   _____

LESSON 36   Cause and Effect   **131**

5. In your opinion, which idea expressed in the Declaration of Independence had the greatest impact on foreign governments? Explain your answer.

_____

_____

SKILL FOCUS: CAUSE AND EFFECT

1. What was the primary effect of the American Revolutionary War?

_____

_____

2. What caused the defeat of abolitionism in the South?

_____

_____

3. What effect did the war debt have on the national government?

_____

_____

4. Fill in this chart listing three effects of the American Revolution on other countries.

Cause	Effect
the loss of the Revolutionary War by Great Britain	
spread of democratic ideals to France	
spread of democratic ideals to Latin America	

Reading-Writing Connection

Although the American Revolution took place more than 200 years ago, it has had a continuing impact on our lives. Write a paragraph on a separate sheet of paper about how the Revolution affects some aspect of life in the United States today.

LESSON 37
Skill: Steps in a Process

BACKGROUND INFORMATION
"From Star to Supernova" is about the steps that a star goes through in its life and how scientists have solved some of the mysteries of space. By studying rays of light, scientists have determined what stars are made of. This has led to the discovery of different types of stars and the different stages of a star's life. As new theories and techniques emerge, scientists observe stars and analyze them in new ways.

SKILL FOCUS: Steps in a Process
By understanding the **steps in a process** such as a life cycle, you can better understand the process. A life cycle has a very definite order in which things happen. For example, people are born, grow into children, develop into teenagers, and then become adults. Adults eventually grow old and die. To identify steps in a process, ask yourself these questions.

- What process is being described?
- What is the first step in the process?
- What is the final outcome of the process?

Transitional words provide clues to the sequence of steps in a process. Some transitional words are *first*, *then*, *next*, and *finally*.

▸ Read the paragraph below. Then complete the Flowchart with the missing steps in the process.

A comet is a lump of rock, ice, and dust that travels through space. As the comet nears the sun, the ice begins to melt. Then it turns into a vapor, or gas. Next the dust from the comet is set free. This released gas and dust form a cloud. The cloud reflects the sun's light, which is what we see on Earth.

CONTEXT CLUES: Appositive Phrases
In science writing, the meaning of a new word is often made clear by a phrase that follows it. This is called an **appositive phrase**. It is set apart by commas, dashes, or parentheses, and starts with the word *or*.

Read the sentence below. Look for an appositive phrase that helps explain the underlined word.

*Like the sun, all stars **emit**, or give off, light.*

If you are not sure of the meaning of the word *emit*, the appositive phrase *or give off* can help you.

▸ Read the sentence below. Circle the appositive phrase that helps you understand the meaning of the underlined word.

*Photographic equipment seemed to be especially sensitive to the ultraviolet light emitted by stars, light that the naked eye was not able to **discern**, or notice.*

In this selection, the words *dense*, *inherent*, and *luminosity* are underlined. As you read, look for appositive phrases to learn their meanings.

> **Strategy Tip**
>
> As you read "From Star to Supernova," think about the different steps in the process that stars go through.

Why We See Comets

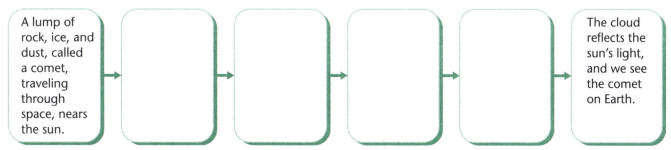

LESSON 37 Steps in a Process **133**

> READING A SCIENCE SELECTION

From Star to Supernova

We see stars on nights when the sky is clear of clouds. We also see a star by day. The sun that warms our planet and around which our planet moves is just one of billions of stars in the universe. Scientists believe that it is probably a medium-sized star, called a yellow star.

Like the sun, all stars emit, or give off, light. Light is a form of radiation. Scientists have found ways to study this radiation not only to determine a star's life cycle, but also the different types of stars.

The Birth of a Star

To understand the birth of a star, it helps first to learn what stars are made of. Like all objects, stars are made up of elements. What gives any object its qualities is its combination of elements. (Water, for example, is made up of the elements hydrogen and oxygen.) Most stars consist mainly of hydrogen and a small amount of helium, both of which are gases. Hydrogen is the fuel that produces the sun's energy and makes it shine.

Hydrogen and helium usually form into a star inside a nebula—a huge cloud of swirling gas and dust in space. As the gas and dust particles zoom around, gravity begins to pull large clumps of gas and dust together. Each clump grows and grows, until it eventually collapses because it has become too heavy. The center then becomes extremely hot and more dense, or crowded together. The intense heat begins to radiate toward the outer surface. See Figure 1 below.

When the inside of the nebula reaches a temperature of 18,000,000 degrees Fahrenheit (10,000,000 degrees Celsius), a **thermonuclear fusion reaction** begins. The atoms of the hydrogen nuclei combine and turn into helium nuclei. During this reaction, an enormous amount of energy is released. This causes the outward pressure of the hot gases to balance the weight of the star, causing the initial collapse to stop. The thermonuclear fusion continues inside the star's center core. The star now gives off its own light, which will last for millions and millions of years.

Scientists believe that our sun began life through this same process, some 5 billion years ago. They believe it took the sun 30 million years to form, and that it will shine for 5 billion years more.

The Death of a Star

Stars often change over their lifetimes. For example, the sun, which is considered a middle-aged star, has a surface temperature of about 10,000

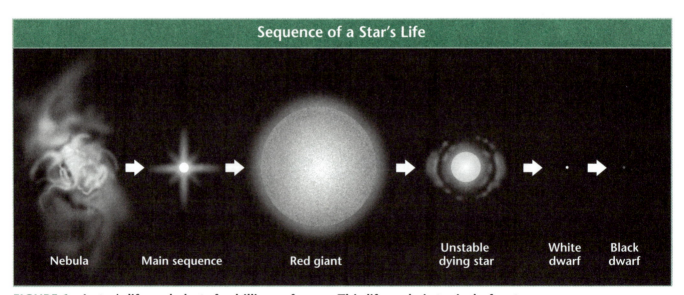

FIGURE 1. A star's life cycle lasts for billions of years. This life cycle is typical of a star.

134 LESSON 37 Steps in a Process

degrees Fahrenheit (5,537 degrees Celsius). A younger star is typically hotter, with a surface temperature of about 12,000 degrees Fahrenheit (6,648 degrees Celsius).

After burning for billions of years, a star eventually dies. A star's death begins when its hydrogen fuel has burned up. When this happens, the star begins to expand, and its surface cools and glows red. The star's red color and larger size give the star its new name—red giant.

As the star continues to expand, it eventually becomes unstable. It then emits a gas that surrounds itself, called a planetary nebula.

During the final act of the star's life, the star collapses upon itself. The star becomes very small, about the size of Earth. The star is now called a white dwarf. Finally the star's light goes out completely, and it is called a black dwarf.

Supernovas

Not all stars are the same size as the sun. Large stars, called supergiants, experience many more contractions and expansions than a yellow star, like the sun. Their nuclear reactions create many more elements, too. Along with hydrogen and helium, supergiants have such elements as carbon, nitrogen, and oxygen.

When the nuclear reaction creates iron, the supergiant collapses, sometimes in an impressive explosion called a supernova. The light emitted by the supernova can be millions of times brighter than the light emitted by the supergiant.

When the dust settles from the supernova explosion, the once giant star may have left behind a dense core, called a neutron star. Eventually that neutron star may collapse into itself, creating a black hole.

The force of a supernova is intense. It throws its materials far into space. Scientists believe that today we see the remains of a supernova explosion that occurred in the year 1054. Astronomers call these remains the Crab Nebula. New stars are born inside nebulas, so the life cycle of a star will begin again.

Studying the Stars

Scientists are able to determine information about stars by studying the light they emit. The study

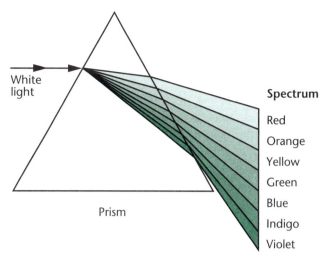

FIGURE 2. A glass prism separates a beam of light into its individual colors, or the spectrum.

of light—also called **spectroscopy**—began in the 1600s, when Sir Isaac Newton, an English scientist, discovered the **spectrum**. By shining a beam of light through a prism, Newton discovered that white light was made up of colors, or the spectrum. See Figure 2 above. Although it was an amazing discovery, not many people understood its significance.

In 1814, a German glass and lens maker named Joseph von Fraunhofer experimented with Newton's spectrum. He passed a beam of light not only through a prism, but also through a telescope. The spectrum appeared, along with seemingly countless strong and weak vertical lines. These lines fascinated Fraunhofer. He believed they were an <u>inherent</u>, or naturally existing, part of light from the sun, or **solar light**.

Fraunhofer began observing the light emitted from hundreds of stars. Mapping out the spectrum, or more specifically the **stellar spectrum**, of each star, he observed that each had its own pattern of lines. He mapped the lines of about 600 stars.

Fraunhofer took his observations one step further. Fraunhofer began viewing the light of flames. He discovered that this light also had vertical lines, and he questioned if there could be a relationship between the light emitted from the sun and the light emitted from fire.

Astrophysics

In 1859, two German scientists found the answer to Fraunhofer's question. Gustav Kirchoff and Robert Bunsen thought it could be possible to identify chemicals according to the colors they displayed when they burned. Bunsen had created a new burner (today known as the **Bunsen burner**). The flame from the burner was so pure that it created spectrums with very clear, distinct lines. Kirchoff and Bunsen discovered that any chemical element, when burned as a gas, created its own set of lines. In this way, they could identify the elements of light waves from space. The field known today as **astrophysics** had been born.

Star Categories

Astronomers now had a way of learning a great deal about the stars. As they observed and analyzed the light rays emitted from the various stars in the sky, they determined that, although all the stars seem to be different, the stars could be grouped into four main categories.

In 1868, a priest in Italy named Father Angelo Secchi, made the classifications based on observations he made from the Roman College Observatory. Type I stars were white and blue, with strong hydrogen lines. Type II stars were yellow or orange. They had many spectral lines. Type III stars were orange to red. They had many spectral lines grouped together. Type IV stars were very red, and their lines showed carbon.

Secchi's classification was not too far off the mark. As scientists moved into the twentieth century, more powerful telescopes enabled them to make more precise classifications. The invention of photography also helped in stellar research. Photographs are created by light, and photographic equipment seemed to be especially sensitive to the **ultraviolet light** emitted by stars, light that the naked eye was not able to notice.

Two scientists in the early 1900s came up with a diagram to classify the stars. The classification also led to the idea of how stars developed over their lifetimes. Ejnar Hertzsprung of Denmark and Norris Russell of the United States created the **H-R diagram**. See Figure 3 below.

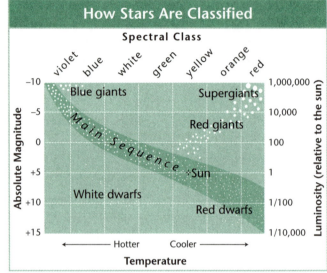

FIGURE 3. The H-R diagram is a way of classifying stars.

Hertzsprung and Russell based their classification on many star characteristics, such as their luminosity, or brightness; their temperature; their **absolute magnitude** (a measurement for how much light a star gives off), and their spectral class. Most stars seem to fall in a curved diagonal line, which is called the main sequence. Our sun falls within the main sequence. Stars plotted outside the main sequence are more rare and more special, such as white dwarfs and red giants. Figure 4 shows the classification of stars according to their spectral class and temperature.

Hertzsprung and Russell also believed that a star's path along the main sequence was a key to understanding a star's development. Although they were partially correct, it would take nuclear physics to explain several misconceptions with the H-R diagram. Still, the H-R diagram is a good guide to following the life cycle of a star.

Spectral Class							
Class	O	B	A	F	G	K	M
Temperature	above 19,300° F	above 19,300° F	13,000° to 19,300° F	10,300° to 13,000° F	8,500° to 10,300° F	5,800° to 8,500° F	below 5,800° F
Color	violet	blue	white	green	yellow	orange	red

FIGURE 4. The hottest stars are the Class O, Class B, and Class A stars, or the blue and white stars.

COMPREHENSION

1. What two elements are most stars made of?

   _____

2. How does the helium become part of a star?

   _____

   _____

3. Why does a star begin to die?

   _____

   _____

4. What is the difference between a star like the sun and a supergiant?

   _____

   _____

5. Draw a line to match the following words with their correct meanings.

   inherent   **a.** brightness

   luminosity   **b.** crowded together

   dense   **c.** a naturally existing part of

CRITICAL THINKING

1. Explain why the death of a supergiant star is also related to the birth of a new star.

   _____

   _____

   _____

   _____

   _____

2. Look at Figure 4. Compare the stars and their colors to Secchi's original classification system.

   _____

   _____

   _____

   _____

   _____

SKILL FOCUS: STEPS IN A PROCESS

Write a number before each step to show the correct order in which a supernova is formed.

_____ **a.** Nuclear reactions within the supergiant create iron.

_____ **b.** This collapse can cause a large explosion, which is a supernova.

_____ **c.** The supergiant then collapses.

_____ **d.** Nuclear reactions within a supergiant create carbon.

Reading-Writing Connection

Think of a process you have observed, step by step. It can be watching food cook, watching a storm roll in, or watching the tides on a beach. Write a paragraph describing the observation. Use transitional words in your writing.

LESSON 38

Skill: Understanding Logic

BACKGROUND INFORMATION

In "Reading Conditional Statements," you will explore logic. Logic is the language of arguments, used in legal cases, debates, and mathematical proofs. The ancient Greeks were the first to develop a formal system to prove whether a statement is true or false. However, the logic of the Greeks was expressed in everyday language rather than mathematical symbols. In the seventeenth century, the German mathematician Gottfried Willhelm Leibniz first proposed the use of a symbolic language in logic.

SKILL FOCUS: Understanding Logic

As in algebra and other fields of math, symbols are more compact and easier to understand than words. In mathematical **logic**, letters are used to represent a statement. Symbols get rid of the ambiguity of everyday language and the confusion of the terms *true* and *false*.

In mathematical logic, you don't argue whether a single statement is true or false. Instead, you consider both cases. You consider *when* the statement is true (T) and *when* the statement is false (F).

Logic uses many of the same words as everyday words, but their meanings are more precise. For example, read the following statements.

- She is better than he.

- Wednesday is the day after Sunday.

- Please do your homework.

In mathematical logic, only the second sentence is a logical statement. It is the only sentence that can be assigned a value of true or false without subjective opinion. The truth value of the second statement is false.

▶ Read the three statements below. Circle the statement that has a truth value. Then answer the questions in the next column.

- *Football is the best sport on the planet.*

- *Football games occur mostly in the fall.*

- *You should go to a football game.*

1. Why is the statement you circled a logical statement?

_____

_____

2. What is the truth value of the statement you circled?

_____

_____

3. Why are the other statements not logical statements?

_____

_____

WORD CLUES

In logic, you will encounter the words *conditional*, *converse*, *inverse*, and *contrapositive*. If you don't understand the meanings of these words, think of related words that may be more familiar to you. For example, for *conditional*, think about the *conditions* of a contract: *If* you do this, *then* I will do that. For words that have the prefixes *con-*, *in-*, and *contra-*, separate the prefix of each word from its root or base word and see if you can figure out the meaning. Consult your math textbook to verify the exact meanings of mathematical terms.

> **Strategy Tip**
>
> In "Reading Conditional Statements," you will read certain logical statements. When statements seem similar, try to focus on the differences among them.

138 LESSON 38 Understanding Logic

● ─(**READING A MATHEMATICS SELECTION**)─ ●

Reading Conditional Statements

The language of mathematical logic is made up of only a few different types of symbols. The basic unit of logic is the statement, a complete sentence that states a fact. Read the following sentences.

Statements:

- There are 12 months in a year.
- $5 + 8 = 13$
- Paris is not in France.

Not Statements:

- Apples are better than oranges.
- $7 + 8$

Each statement has a value called its **truth value**. The value is either true (T) or false (F).

Statements can be joined together to make compound statements with **connectives**, such as *and*, *or*, and *not*. The simplest connective, *not*, forms the opposite, or the **negation** (ni GAY shən), of a statement and has the opposite truth value.

- There are not 12 months in a year.
- $5 + 8 \neq 13$
- Paris is (not not) in France.

One of the most important compound statements in logical arguments is the conditional, usually in the form of "if … then …" In math, many theorems are stated as conditionals. For example, "If two parallel lines are cut by a transversal, then alternate interior angles are congruent." However, you can study the conditional with simpler verbal statements. Read the following two statements.

- You live in Oregon.
- You live in the United States.

These two statements can be joined to form a conditional statement that has a separate meaning. The statement after the "if" is called the **hypothesis** (hy PAH thə səs). The statement after the "then" is called the conclusion. The following statements are all examples of conditionals.

- If you live in Oregon, then you live in the United States.

- If a number is even, then it is divisible by 2.
- If Max is not a cat, then he is a dog.
- If $a > b$, then $a \neq b$.

There are three statements that are related to the conditional: **converse**, **inverse**, and **contrapositive** (KAHN tre PAH ze tiv). The basic statements stay the same, but their function within the conditional changes. The first statement, "If you live in Oregon, then you live in the United States," is true (T). Notice how the meaning and the truth value change in each version of the original statement.

> **Converse:** The converse of a statement reverses the hypothesis and conclusion.

Conditional: If you live in Oregon, then you live in the United States.

Converse: If you live in the United States, then you live in Oregon.

In this case, the converse is false (F).

> **Inverse:** The inverse of a conditional statement uses the negations of the hypothesis and the conclusion.

Conditional: If you live in Oregon, then you live in the United States.

Inverse: If you do not live in Oregon, then you do not live in the United States.

In this case, the inverse is false (F).

> **Contrapositive:** The contrapositive both negates the hypothesis and conclusion and reverses them.

Conditional: If you live in Oregon, then you live in the United States.

Contrapositive: If you do not live in the United States, then you do not live in Oregon.

This contrapositive is true (T).

LESSON 38 Understanding Logic **139**

A conditional and its contrapositive always have the same meaning and truth value. The converse always has the same value as the inverse, but the value may be the same as or different from the original statement. Study the chart below to see how the meaning of a conditional statement changes as you form the converse, inverse, and contrapositive.

Conditional	Converse	Inverse	Contrapositive
If you live in Oregon, then you live in the United States. (T)	If you live in the United States then you live in Oregon. (F)	If you do not live in Oregon, then you do not live in the United States. (F)	If you do not live in the United States, then you do not live in Oregon. (T)
If a number is even, then it is divisible by 2. (T)	If a number is divisible by 2, then it is even. (T)	If a number is not even, then it is not divisible by 2. (T)	If a number is not divisible by 2, then it is not even. (T)
If Max is not a cat, then he is a dog. (F)	If Max is a dog, then he is not a cat. (T)	If Max is a cat, then he is not a dog. (T)	If Max is not a dog then he is a cat. (F)
If $a > b$, then $a \neq b$. (T)	If $a \neq b$, then $a > b$. (F)	If $a \not> b$, then $a = b$. (F)	If $a = b$, then $a \not> b$. (T)

COMPREHENSION

1. What is a logical statement?

   _____

2. Can a logical statement be false?

   _____

3. What are the two parts that make up a conditional statement?

   _____

4. What is the relationship between a conditional statement and its contrapositive?

   _____

CRITICAL THINKING

1. For each statement below, write whether it is *true*, *false*, or *not a logical statement*.

   a. Dayton is the capital of South Dakota. _____

   b. Wow, that's great soup! _____

   c. An orange is a fruit. _____

2. In each pair of the following statements, the first statement is the original conditional. Write whether the second statement is its *converse*, *inverse*, or *contrapositive*.

   a. Conditional: If the temperature of the water is not 100°C, then it is not boiling.

   _____ If the water is not boiling, then its temperature is not 100°C.

   b. Conditional: If it is not cold, then it is not snowing.

   _____ If it is snowing, then it is cold.

   c. Conditional: If an animal has feathers, then it is a bird.

   _____ If an animal does not have feathers, then it is not a bird.

SKILL FOCUS: UNDERSTANDING LOGIC

1. Write the inverse, converse, and contrapositive of each of the conditional statements. Then write whether each statement is true (*T*) or false (*F*).

   a. Conditional: If today is Monday, then yesterday was Sunday. _____

      Converse: _____ _____

      Inverse: _____ _____

      Contrapositive: _____ _____

   b. Conditional: If an angle is acute, then its measure is 30°. _____

      Converse: _____ _____

      Inverse: _____ _____

      Contrapositive: _____ _____

   c. Conditional: If $a = 3$, then $a + 5 = 10$. _____

      Converse: _____ _____

      Inverse: _____ _____

      Contrapositive: _____ _____

2. Write a conditional statement in words. Then write its converse, inverse, and contrapositive. Give the truth value of each statement.

   Conditional: _____ _____

   Converse: _____ _____

   Inverse: _____ _____

   Contrapositive: _____ _____

3. Write a conditional statement in mathematical symbols. Then write its converse, inverse, and contrapositive. Give the truth value of each statement.

   Conditional: _____ _____

   Converse: _____ _____

   Inverse: _____ _____

   Contrapositive: _____ _____

Reading-Writing Connection

On a separate sheet of paper, write the converse, inverse, and contrapositive of the following conditional statement: "If you study hard, then you will get good grades." Then determine the truth value of each statement.

LESSON 38 Understanding Logic **141**

LESSON 39
Skill: Reading Dialect

A **dialect** is a variety of language spoken in a particular region or by a particular group of people. Dialects differ in pronunciation, vocabulary, and sometimes grammar.

In the United States, there are distinct dialects in the Northeast, the Midwest, and the South. In literature, writers use dialect to give the flavor of a time and place. In the following excerpt from *The Adventures of Tom Sawyer* by Mark Twain, the author captures Missouri language styles of the mid-nineteenth century. The three boys—Tom Sawyer, Huck Finn, and Joe Harper—have run away from home and pretend to live as pirates, but now Joe is homesick.

A. Read the following excerpt. Then answer the questions that follow.

> "Oh, no, Joe, you'll feel better <u>by-and-by</u>," said Tom. "Just think of the fishing that's here."
>
> "I <u>don't care for</u> fishing. I want to go home."
>
> "But, Joe, <u>there ain't such another swimming-place</u> anywhere."
>
> "Swimming's no good; I don't seem to care for it, somehow, when there ain't anybody <u>to say I shan't go in</u>. I mean to go home."
>
> "Who cares?" said Tom…. "Go 'long home and get laughed at. Oh, you're a nice pirate. <u>Huck and me ain't</u> cry-babies. We'll stay, won't we, Huck? Let him go if he wants to. <u>I reckon</u> we can get along without him, per'aps."

1. For each of the six underlined groups of words, write a "translation" into modern standard American English in the space provided.

   a. by-and-by: _____

   b. don't care for: _____

   c. there ain't such another swimming-place: _____

   d. to say I shan't go in: _____

   e. Huck and me ain't: _____

   f. I reckon: _____

2. Twain uses apostrophes to show special pronunciations of some dialect words. What are the standard spellings of *'long* and *per'aps*?

   _____

3. On the lines below, explain what the boys' dialect reveals about them—their interests, concerns, and the place where they live.

   _____

   _____

142 LESSON 39 Reading Dialect

B. Read the following poem. Then answer the questions that follow.

The following is a poem in a Scottish dialect. It was written in the late eighteenth century by the Scottish poet Robert Burns.

O my Luve's like a red, red rose
    That's <u>newly sprung</u> in June!
O my Luve's like the melodie
    That's sweetly play'd in tune!

As <u>fair art thou, my bonnie lass,</u>
    So deep in luve am I;
And I will luve thee still, my dear,
    <u>Till a' the seas gang dry</u>—

Till a' the seas gang dry, my dear,
    And the rocks melt wi' the sun;
I will luve thee still, my dear,
    While the sands o' life shall run.

<u>And fare thee weel, my only Luve!</u>
    And fare thee weel awhile!
And I will come again, my Luve,
    Tho' it were ten thousand mile.

1. On the lines below, write a "translation" of each of the four underlined phrases or sentences into modern standard English.

    a. newly sprung: _____

    b. fair art thou, my bonnie lass: _____

    c. Till a' the seas gang dry: _____

    d. And fare thee weel, my only Luve!: _____

2. From the way the words are written, how does the speaker usually pronounce the words *love* and *well*?

    _____

    _____

3. Describe how the use of dialect adds to the effect of the poem. Consider the musical quality of the words, the rhythm, and what the dialect reveals about the speaker.

    _____

    _____

LESSON 39   Reading Dialect   **143**

LESSON 40

Skill: Analogies

An **analogy** is a comparison that shows that the relationship between a pair of words is similar to the relationship between another pair of words.

To complete an analogy by choosing the second pair of words, follow these steps.

1. Determine the relationship between the first pair of words.

2. Choose a second pair of words that establishes the same relationship. If more than one pair of words appear to have similar relationships, choose the pair that has the relationship closest to the relationship with the first pair.

Below are some relationships that can be expressed in analogies.

Type of Relationship	Example
type to trait	weightlifter : muscular
worker to product	farmer : crop
worker to workplace	teacher : classroom
worker to tool	conductor : baton
product to material	igloo : snow
item to purpose	oven : bake
temporal relation	yesterday : tomorrow
group to part	pride : lion

Complete each of the following analogies by circling the letter of the correct word pair. Then on the line provided, identify the type of relationship expressed in each analogy.

1. GENERAL : ARMY ::
   - **a.** soldier : sailor
   - **b.** pilot : plane
   - **c.** admiral : navy
   - **d.** sergeant : corporal

   Type: _____

2. DANCER : GRACEFUL ::
   - **a.** swimmer : wet
   - **b.** speaker : loud
   - **c.** runner : clumsy
   - **d.** acrobat : nimble

   Type: _____

3. BAKER : BREAD ::
   - **a.** consumer : money
   - **b.** trucker : truck
   - **c.** tailor : suit
   - **d.** doctor : patient

   Type: _____

4. SCULPTOR : CHISEL ::
   - **a.** singer : song
   - **b.** speaker : speech
   - **c.** painter : canvas
   - **d.** knitter : needles

   Type: _____

5. SUBSEQUENT : PRIOR ::
   - **a.** present : current
   - **b.** eventual : eternal
   - **c.** after : before
   - **d.** novel : recent

   Type: _____

6. CLOWN : AMUSING ::
   - **a.** runner : fast
   - **b.** farmer : crop
   - **c.** actor : funny
   - **d.** zookeeper : friendly

   Type: _____

7. SWEATER : WOOL ::
   a. vest : buttons   **c.** pants : cuffs
   b. ring : gold   **d.** shoe : sole

   Type: _____

8. POLITICIAN : SPEECH ::
   a. skater : skates   **c.** dancer : ballet
   b. pianist : recital   **d.** historian : history

   Type: _____

9. PENCIL : SKETCH ::
   a. chalk : crayons   **c.** brush : paint
   b. writer : artist   **d.** paint : canvas

   Type: _____

10. PRIDE : LION ::
    a. herd : horse   **c.** ferocious : tiger
    b. driver : car   **d.** director : play

    Type: _____

11. NANNY : NURSERY ::
    a. boxer : gloves   **c.** sleeper : bedroom
    b. cook : kitchen   **d.** principal : students

    Type: _____

12. SCIENTIST : LABORATORY ::
    a. lion tamer : lion
    b. football player : touchdown
    c. conductor : station
    d. police officer : station house

    Type: _____

13. BREAD : FLOUR ::
    a. honey : bee   **c.** soup : appetizer
    b. candy : sugar   **d.** rolls : biscuits

    Type: _____

14. SUNRISE : SUNSET ::
    a. dawn : noon   **c.** midnight : midday
    b. yesterday : today   **d.** morning : evening

    Type: _____

15. TRACTOR : PLOW ::
    a. car : transport   **c.** reaper : sow
    b. train : tracks   **d.** crop : harvest

    Type: _____

16. SCHOOL : FISH ::
    a. designer : house   **c.** flock : bird
    b. colorful : colors   **d.** rehearse : play

    Type: _____

17. CAST : ACTOR ::
    a. orchestra : musician
    b. cowardly : lion
    c. artist : sculpture
    d. circus : tent

    Type: _____

18. MICROBIOLOGIST : MICROSCOPE ::
    a. surgeon : scalpel   **c.** swimmer : pool
    b. teacher : desk   **d.** veterinarian : dog

    Type: _____

LESSON 40   Analogies   **145**

LESSON 41

Skill: Reading a Road Map

Whether you travel for business or for fun, you can use a **road map** as a guide. A road map shows interstate highways, federal highways, and state routes. Each type of roadway is marked differently so that you can tell the types apart. Most road maps also mark campgrounds, airports, rest areas, exit numbers on some roadways, and distances between certain towns.

The **legend** included with a road map explains the symbols and methods of marking roadways. It also has a **scale**, marked in miles and kilometers, by which you can estimate the distance between two points.

Study the road map of the Chicago area, and answer the questions on page 147.

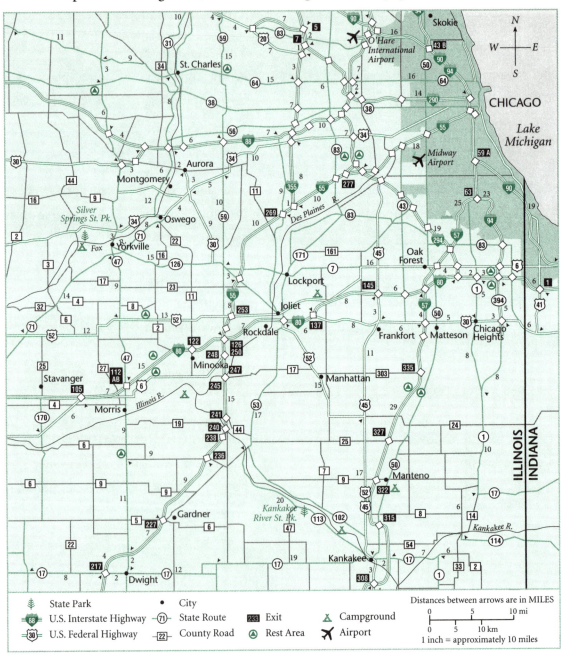

146 LESSON 41 Reading a Road Map

A. On the line after each sentence, write whether the statement is *true* or *false*.

1. Two airports service the Chicago metropolitan area.   _____

2. The town of Manhattan, Illinois, is located along Highway 45.   _____

3. Kankakee, Gardner, and Matteson are all to the south of Chicago.   _____

4. To get to Minooka from Chicago, you must get off Interstate 80 at Exit 122.   _____

5. There is a campground about 20 miles to the southwest of Aurora.   _____

6. Rest areas are located only along interstate highways.   _____

7. It is about a 15-mile drive from Frankfort to Chicago Heights.   _____

8. The map shows part of the course of the Kaskaskia River.   _____

9. If you are driving north toward Chicago and you pass Chicago Heights, you are traveling on State Route 1.   _____

10. If you want to go from Joliet to Yorkville, you can drive west on Interstate 88 and then north on State Route 47.   _____

B. Use information from the road map to complete each sentence.

1. Chicago is located _____ of Aurora and _____ of Chicago Heights.

2. This map shows the state line between Illinois and _____.

3. Rockdale and Lockport are just outside the city of _____.

4. Silver Springs State Park is located between Highway _____ and State Route _____.

5. To arrive in Gardner, get off Interstate 55 at Exit _____.

6. It is about a _____ -mile drive from Frankfort to Kankakee.

7. If you are traveling north on Interstate 57, you can find rest areas just before Exit _____.

8. The distance between Yorkville and Oswego is about _____ kilometers.

9. Suppose you live in Chicago Heights. If you want to visit the campground near Manteno,

   you would drive _____ on Highway 30 until it crosses _____ and

   then go _____ on Interstate 57 to Exit _____.

10. Write directions for your friends who plan to drive from Oak Forest to Dwight. Include route numbers they should follow.

   _____

   _____

   _____

LESSON 41   Reading a Road Map   **147**

unit six
Perspectives

LESSON 42

Skill: Mood and Tone

BACKGROUND INFORMATION
In "The House on the Border," Turkish author Aziz Nesin satirizes both law enforcement and human foolishness. Nesin had a genius for observing and describing the ridiculous in any situation. His works, in which he exposes intolerance, absurdity, cruelty, and stupidity in a changing society, have been translated into 20 foreign languages.

SKILL FOCUS: Mood and Tone
Part of the enjoyment in reading a story comes from entering the author's world. Part of this world is the author's own voice. It is the sense you get as you read the story, a sense of how the author feels about the topic. This sense, or "feeling," is called the story's **mood** or **tone**.

The mood or tone is the author's attitude toward or feelings about the subject. For example, an author may express regret over a missed opportunity or encouragement toward a friend or defiance against an injustice. An author may adopt a formal, informal, playful, satirical, or ironic tone.

▶ Read the descriptions in the boxes. They describe the same thing in different ways. Then choose from the following tones: *eerie, sarcastic,* or *optimistic.* Write the correct tone below each description.

CONTEXT CLUES: Details
Using **details** in the nearby text can provide the meaning of an unknown word. These are called detail context clues. As you read the following sentences, look for detail context clues.

*Imitating a **basso profundo** to the best of my ability, "Who are you?" I asked. It was a deep-chested growl.*

The detail *deep-chested* implies a sound that has a low pitch. *Basso profundo* is a low male singing voice.

▶ Read the sentences below. Circle the words that provide details that help you to figure out the meaning of the underlined word.

What if the thief should die of hunger? Or heart failure? After all, he was <u>trussed</u> up like a chicken. What if the ropes would impede the circulation of his blood?

In this selection, look for details for the underlined words *irresistible, nocturnal,* and *collaborate* to help understand their meanings.

Strategy Tip
As you read "The House on the Border," think about how the story's mood or tone is revealed.

It was a beautiful house. A house in which dreams could be fulfilled, a family could be raised. The sun shone golden over its roof, lending it a warm glow. With this as our new home, the future could be nothing but bright.	So this is what they called a house, and I suppose it was, if you consider four walls with holes and a sagging roof a house. It was, if a house to you has no doors or windows.	The house loomed up before us, a monster on the hill, its door a wide open mouth, its windows eyes that glared down at us. Our hair stood on end as the house sat silently glaring at us.
_____	_____	_____

148   LESSON 42   Mood and Tone

READING A LITERATURE SELECTION

The House on the Border

Aziz Nesin

Translated by Gönul Süveren

We had moved into the house the day before. It was a nice place. That morning when I walked out, our next-door neighbor, an old man, was watching the street with avid curiosity and called us from his window.

"You shouldn't have rented that place," he cackled.

I stared at him coldly.

"Is this a new way of greeting neighbors?" I growled. "What do you mean we shouldn't have moved in there?"

He was not fazed.

"Thieves break into that house often," he announced with relish. "It's my neighborly duty to warn you."

As if the thieves couldn't break into his house too! Why should robbers favor only ours?

Rather annoyed, I entered the grocery store at the corner to buy cigarettes.

"There are such characters around," I mumbled.

"What's the matter?" asked the grocer.

"Some old goat told me that thieves usually rob the house we just moved into," I complained.

The grocer nodded. "Well, the old goat was right. You shouldn't have rented that house. It's robbed frequently."

I was furious. Without answering him, I walked out of the store. The whole day was ruined, naturally. I fumed till evening. That night a couple from our block visited us. They were nice people. We talked about this and that till midnight. When they were about to leave, the husband turned and looked at us strangely.

"It's a beautiful house," he said, "but thieves never leave it alone."

Since they were already out of the house, I couldn't ask him: "Why is this house supposed to be <u>irresistible</u> to thieves? Why shouldn't they honor your home too?"

Seeing my ferocious scowl, my wife started to laugh.

"Dearest," she said, "don't you understand? God knows, they have thousands of tricks for scaring tenants away. This must be the newest one. They will drive us out, and, since the rent is low, they will either move in themselves or bring in one of their relatives."

It was possible. But I couldn't sleep a wink that night. It was as if I had a date with the thief. I waited for him breathlessly, whispering to myself: "He will be here any moment."

I must have dozed off. I jumped up at a slight noise and grabbed the gun I had hidden under my pillow.

LESSON 42 Mood and Tone

"Don't move or I'll shoot," I yelled into the darkness.

As I already said, we had moved in the day before. Now, confronted with a <u>nocturnal</u> visitor, I forgot where the light switch was. Groping in the dark, I got entangled in every conceivable object and bumped into the walls in search of a switch. As if this was not enough, some darned thing coiled around my shapely ankles, and with a resounding crash, I found myself on the floor. "The dirty—," I muttered under my breath. "He tripped me." Unfortunately, during my solo flight to the floor, the gun had fallen from my hand and bounced away.

The darkness was suddenly filled with a horrible laughter: "Heh! Heh! Heh!"

"Are we shooting a domestic horror movie?" I shouted. "If you are a man, show your face, you... you villain!"

"I suppose you were looking for the switch," a voice said in the darkness. "It's amazing how all the new tenants make the same mistake."

"Do you know what I'm going to do to you?"

"No," said the man in the darkness. "I don't know. Now, may I turn on the lights and help you?"

I heard the click of the switch, and the room was flooded with light. Apparently, when I had crashed down, I had rolled under the table. As for my wife, she was securely lodged under the bed.

There in the middle of the room stood a man larger than life—twice my size, I mean.

I knew that if I emerged from my hiding place, I couldn't scare him. I decided he wouldn't be able to size me up if I stayed there.

Imitating a basso profundo to the best of my ability, "Who are you?" I asked. It was a deep-chested growl.

"I'm the thief," he answered calmly.

"Oh, yeah?" I said. "If you think I'm a fool, you're mistaken. You're not a thief. You're trying to scare us away and move in here. Look at me, look closely. Do I look like an idiot?"

He didn't answer my question. "You'll see whether I'm a thief or not," he said instead.

You'd have thought it was his own father's house. He started to rummage through the drawers, picking out what items he fancied and talking to us all the while. I have to admit that he was quite friendly.

"So you turned this into a bedroom.... The family before you used it as a study. The ones before them too..."

"Now look," I said. "You're robbing me. I'll report you to the police."

Without stopping, "Please do," he replied. "Go to the precinct. And don't forget to give them my best regards."

"But you'll run away while I'm gone."

"I won't."

"You will! You will clean up the whole house and steal away." It was a dilemma. "I have an idea," I said. "First I'll tie you up, then I'll go to the police."

"Help!" shrieked my wife suddenly.

Were all the neighbors waiting on our doorstep, I wonder? As if on cue, they stampeded into the house, chattering excitedly. But did they look at us or offer sympathy? No. They were full of curiosity and in good spirits.

"Another robbery," they said.

"What, again?"

"Who is it this time?"

"Let's see."

Some of them were downright friendly with the thief. They even asked him how he was, while he calmly went on packing our things.

"Help!" I croaked. "Help! I must bind him up. I'll go to the precinct."

One of the neighbors shook his head.

"It won't do you any good," he said. "But I never stop people from doing what they want.... Go ahead."

What kind of a neighborhood was this anyway?

Suddenly emboldened, my wife brought me the clothesline. The thief didn't resist while I tied him up securely. We carried him into another room and locked the door.

We ran to the police. My wife considered herself the spokesperson of the family and told the story to the chief. He asked for our address.

"Aha," said the chief. "That house."

"Yes," I answered, "that house."

"We have nothing to do with that house," he informed us. "It's not in our jurisdiction."

"What are we going to do now? Did we tie that poor fellow up for nothing?"

"If you lived in the house next door, we could have done something," the chief said. Then, as if addressing a couple of morons, he added, "You would have been in our jurisdiction."

"That house was not vacant," my wife explained patiently. "So we moved into this one."

We learned that our house was right on the border between areas under the jurisdiction of two precincts.

"The other precinct should look into the matter," said the chief.

The other precinct was quite far away. By the time we reached it, the sun was already high in the sky. We told our story again, and again they asked our address.

"That house," said one of the cops.

"That house," I said.

"If you lived next door, we would have done something. Your house is not within our jurisdiction."

"Poor man," murmured my wife. "We tied him up."

"Tell me," I cried out impatiently. "Tell me one thing. Under whose jurisdiction are we? Who is supposed to look after us?"

✖ "The state gendarmerie," said the cop. "Your house is under their jurisdiction. The police have nothing to do with it."

We left the cops.

"Let's go home first," suggested my wife. "I'm worried about the thief. He might die, you know."

She was right, of course. What if the thief should die of hunger? Or heart failure? After all, he was trussed up like a chicken. What if the ropes would impede the circulation of his blood? What if...

We went home. The thief was where we had left him.

"How are you?" I asked anxiously.

"Fine, fine," he answered. "But I'm hungry."

My wife ran to the kitchen. Alas, we had spinach, but—would you believe it—it was the only dish the thief detested. My wife dashed to the butcher, bought some steaks, and fed the thief.

This time we went to the gendarmerie. After listening to our story, the commandant asked for our address.

"Aha," he said. "That house."

Apparently, we had rented a famous place.

The commandant shook his head. "This is not a case for the gendarmerie. You should call the police."

"Now look," I cried. "We went to the police. They sent us here. Now you say we must call the cops. Is this a runaround? Isn't there anybody to look into the case?"

The commandant pulled out a map.

"I hope you know how to read a map," he said. "Here, it gives the height. See? One hundred and forty feet. This is the water tower—116 feet—and here is the hill. Now, this area is under the jurisdiction of the gendarmerie. If your house were built further up, say about two yards toward the northwest, you would have been in our area."

"All this for two lousy yards," I said. "Do something, man! What would happen if you helped us now?"

The commandant pursed his lips. "What would happen?" he repeated. Then he nodded his head sagely. "Only we know what would happen.... Only we know." Again he put his finger on a spot on the map. "Look, this is your house. Right on the line that separates our area from the police's. See? Of course, a part of your garden is under our jurisdiction, but the robbery didn't take place there, did it?"

There was nothing we could do but go to the police again.

"Let's first see how the thief is doing," my wife suggested. "God help us if something should happen to him."

So we went home.

I almost clasped the thief to my bosom. "How are you?" I panted.

"Water! Quick!" he cried out. "I'm thirsty!"

After drinking the water, he looked at us sternly.

"Listen," he said. "Don't say that I didn't warn you. You have no right to hold me here. You are restricting the freedom of a citizen. I have a good mind to sue you."

"But what can we do?" I cried. "We don't know who is supposed to look after us. Apparently, we are in the middle of nowhere. Why they built this house right on the border line is beyond me."

LESSON 42 Mood and Tone   **151**

"Didn't I tell you? . . . Now, let me go. Otherwise I'll drag you through the courts for restricting my freedom."

"Give me time," I begged. "Give me till tonight. I want to go to the police again."

"By all means," he replied affably. "Go and see anyone you wish. But it's futile. I've been aware of the situation for a long time now. They have to decide whether to include your house in one of the areas or change the borders. Till then…"

Again, we went to the precinct. This time the chief brought out a map, too.

"Look," he sighed, "this area is under the jurisdiction of the gendarmerie. Your garden and a small part of the house are within their area. Only a fraction of the house is under our jurisdiction."

"The bedroom is in your area," I pointed out. "And the robbery took place there."

He looked at me owlishly. "Quite. First this must be definitely established. Then there is another problem: The thief didn't fly in through the window, did he? He crossed the garden and then entered your house. Right? And the garden is under the jurisdiction of the gendarmerie. Yours is not a new problem. It is already under discussion. First they have to reach a decision; then they have to inform us of their decision concerning the area your house is supposed to be in. Then we can act accordingly."

We returned home. Our elderly next-door neighbor was at the window, as usual.

"So they broke into the house again," he cackled.

"Yes," I nodded.

"No one stays there long," he said cheerfully. "That's why the rent is low. Neither the owner nor the tenants could live there. The owner decided to pull down the house and rebuild it two yards further up. But then he found you fools—I mean he found you and rented the place."

His wife was looking at us sadly. "It's not your fault," she informed us. "It's the owner's. When they build a house they think of water, gas, electricity, and the view. But do they think of the jurisdiction? No! What sort of a fool would build a house right on the border?"

✔ I couldn't answer that question even if I wanted to.

Since we had paid the whole year's rent in advance, to move away was out of the question. So we went home and untied the thief. Then we settled down comfortably in the study and discussed the world situation for a while. The thief dined with us that evening.

"So long," he said after the meal. "I'll be back tonight."

Now we have five or six resident thieves. All our neighbors are familiar with them. We <u>collaborate</u> with the thieves too. That is to say, we help them to defend our home against other, unfriendly thieves, who are, after all, strangers to us.

I don't know what will happen eventually. Either all eight of us, my wife and I and the six thieves, will spend the remainder of the year here, or they will include the house in one of the areas, thus enabling me to complain to the authorities. But we are now used to our friends, the thieves. And to report them would be rather embarrassing—after all, they share the household expenses now.

COMPREHENSION

1. Who warns the storyteller and his wife that they should not have rented the house?

   _____

   _____

2. When does the thief break into the house?

   _____

   _____

152   LESSON 42   Mood and Tone

3. How is the gendarmerie's response to the storyteller's complaint like the response of the police?

_____

_____

4. In the end, why does the storyteller decide to keep the thief around?

_____

_____

5. Answer each question by writing *yes* or *no* on the line provided.

a. Bats are <u>nocturnal</u> animals. Do they hunt for food during the day? _____

b. If someone is <u>irresistible</u>, would you want to stay away from the person? _____

c. If everyone on the team wants to <u>collaborate</u> on the project, is it likely to succeed? _____

CRITICAL THINKING

1. Identify each of the following statements by writing *fact* or *opinion* on the line.

_____ **a.** Neighbors' warnings about thieves were meant to drive the couple away.

_____ **b.** The storyteller should not have rented the house.

_____ **c.** The house was not in the gendarmerie's jurisdiction.

2. Describe the storyteller's emotional state after he hears the warnings.

_____

_____

_____

3. The thief doesn't act as we might expect.

a. Why are his first words to the storyteller surprising?

_____

_____

_____

b. How well does the thief know the police? Explain.

_____

_____

_____

4. What clues suggest that the couple's attitude toward the thief is beginning to change?

_____

_____

_____

_____

5. Explain why the elderly next-door neighbor is so cheerful about the couple's problem.

_____

_____

_____

_____

6. Think about the title of this story. How does it reflect what happens in this story?

_____

_____

_____

_____

LESSON 42 Mood and Tone **153**

SKILL FOCUS: MOOD AND TONE

1. The first clues we have about this story's mood or tone appear in its early conversations.

   a. Think about what the next-door neighbor first tells the storyteller and the way he talks. What is unusual about his manner of speaking?
   _____
   _____

   b. How does the grocer's manner of speaking underscore the oddness?
   _____
   _____

2. The first sound the readers hear from the thief is laughter.

   a. Why do you think he is laughing?
   _____
   _____

   b. What is laughable about the scene of the storyteller's first encounter with the thief? List as many details as you can.
   _____
   _____

3. Reread the passage with the ✘ next to it. Based on this conversation, why do you look forward to the couple's visit to the state gendarmerie?
   _____
   _____

4. How does the couple's increasing concern toward the thief add to the story's tone?
   _____
   _____

5. Reread the passage with the ✔ next to it. How does the storyteller's silence add to the story's tone?
   _____
   _____

Reading-Writing Connection

Think about a funny or unusual event that you experienced or witnessed recently. On a separate sheet of paper, write a short letter to a friend describing the event, highlighting its humorous aspect.

154 **LESSON 42** Mood and Tone

LESSON 43

Skill: Making Inferences

BACKGROUND INFORMATION

"The 'Other China'" explores the relationship between China and Taiwan, both past and present. Over the years, Taiwan has been ruled by the Chinese, the Dutch, the Spanish, the French, and the Japanese. After World War II, Taiwan was returned to China, but in 1949, as mainland China fell under Communist rule, the Nationalist government of China fled to Taiwan, establishing the "other China."

SKILL FOCUS: Making Inferences

An **inference** is an educated guess based on evidence given by the writer, but not directly stated by the writer. The evidence can include facts, statistics, descriptions, illustrations, and graphic aids. When you "read between the lines" in a written work, you are inferring.

When you make inferences, follow these steps.

1. Read the selection carefully.

2. Look for evidence that hints at what is left unsaid.

3. Use your own knowledge and experience to make an educated guess.

4. Weigh the evidence carefully to determine if it supports your inference.

▶ Read the paragraph below. Then fill in the Inference Chart with an inference about what the author means by "the West."

For centuries, Taiwan has been familiar to the West as Formosa. *That name comes from sixteenth-century Portuguese mariners who, when they first saw the island from their ship, named it "Ilha Formosa" (beautiful island). The Portuguese also named the Pescadores (Fishermen's Isles; known also as Penghu Islands).*

CONTEXT CLUES: Comparison and Contrast

When you find an unfamiliar word in your reading, you may find words to compare and contrast with the word. Look for context clues that compare or contrast with the underlined word in the following sentences.

*At first, the Nationalist government was little more than a **dictatorship**. After the death of Nationalist leader Chiang Kai-shek, however, a slow shift to democracy began.*

If you don't know the meaning of the word *dictatorship*, a more familiar word, *democracy*, in the next sentence can help you. You can infer that a dictatorship is a form of government that is in contrast with, or different from, a democracy.

▶ Read the sentence below. Circle the word that compares or contrasts with the underlined word. Then compare or contrast the underlined word with the word you circled.

*The Nationalists reformed Taiwan's system of land ownership by taking land from wealthy families and distributing it to **peasants**.*

_____

_____

In this selection, the words *severed, protectorate,* and *annexed* are underlined. Find words in the surrounding text that compare or contrast the meanings of the words.

Strategy Tip

As you read "The 'Other China,'" consider what the writer might *not* be telling you directly about the relations of the two Chinas with each other and with the United States.

What I Read		What I Already Know		Inference
	+		**=**	

LESSON 43 Making Inferences **155**

READING A SOCIAL STUDIES SELECTION

The "Other China"

One hundred miles off the coast of the **Communist** People's Republic of China, or "mainland" China, lies the island of Taiwan. In 1949, **Nationalist** forces fleeing the Communist revolution moved their government to Taiwan's capital, Taipei. They quickly established control over the entire island. Armed forces from the United States kept the island from being invaded by the Chinese Communists.

Since then, there have been "two" Chinas. When the United States formally recognized the People's Republic of China on January 1, 1979, as "China," it <u>severed</u> diplomatic ties with the "China" of Taiwan. Although the People's Republic of China governs the mainland, the government on Taiwan—the Republic of China—claims legal authority over all of China.

Like mainland China, Taiwan has been through many changes. At first, the Nationalist government was little more than a dictatorship. After the death of Nationalist leader Chiang Kai-shek in 1975, however, a slow shift to democracy began. In 1987, martial law was lifted in Taiwan after 38 years; and in 1991, the 43-year period of emergency rule ended. Taiwan held its first direct presidential election on March 23, 1996. The ruling Nationalist Party has faced increasing challenges from opposing parties. Today Taiwan is a lively democracy, where people are free to speak their minds.

History of Taiwan

Taiwan has a rich, colorful history. It became a <u>protectorate</u> (prə TEK tə rət) of the Chinese Empire in 1206, the year in which the powerful Mongol conqueror Genghis Khan founded the Yuan **dynasty**. In 1684, the island became a **prefecture** (PREE fek chər), or county, of the coastal mainland province of Fukien. Then in 1886, during the Ching dynasty (also known as the Manchu dynasty, and China's last reigning house), Taiwan was proclaimed a separate province of China.

For centuries, Taiwan has been familiar to the West as *Formosa*. That name comes from sixteenth-century Portuguese mariners who, when they first saw the island from their ship, named it "Ilha Formosa" (beautiful island). The Portuguese also named the Pescadore Islands, or the Fishermen's Isles (known also as the Penghu Islands). This archipelago (ahr kə PEL ə goh) is located in the Taiwan Strait and forms one of the 16 counties of Taiwan province.

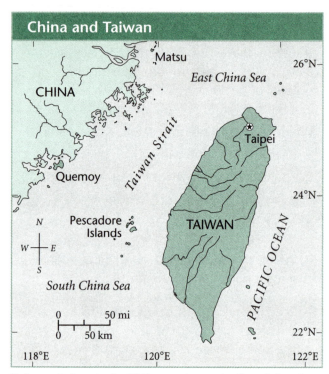

Taiwan is located off the east coast of mainland China.

The Portuguese were not the last Europeans to come to the island. The Dutch invaded Taiwan in 1624 and remained as colonists for 37 years. The Spanish invaded and occupied northernmost Taiwan in 1626, but the Dutch drove them out in 1642. The Dutch themselves were dislodged in 1661 by invading forces from the mainland, led by Cheng Cheng-kung, or Koxinga. Koxinga hoped to make Taiwan his base in the fight to overthrow the Ching dynasty and restore the Ming dynasty to power.

In 1884, the French occupied northernmost Taiwan following a dispute with China over the Yunnan-Indochina border. In March 1885, they also occupied the Pescadores; three months later, however, they withdrew from both the Pescadores and Taiwan under the terms of a treaty with China.

Following a dispute over Korea, the Japanese went to war with China in 1894. By the Treaty of Shimonoseki, concluded the following year, Taiwan and the Pescadores were ceded to Japan. Under another provision, Korea, over which China had exercised **suzerainty** (SOO zə rən tee), or feudal lordship, gained its independence briefly, but subsequently it was <u>annexed</u> by Japan. Taiwan and the Pescadores came under Chinese rule again in 1945, as part of the settlements that ended World War II.

Prosperous Economy

✔ One of the most striking features of Taiwan is its successful **free enterprise economy**. Taiwan's annual economic output topped $29,000 per person in 2006—four times higher than in mainland China. China's total output, however, is far larger, since China has a vastly larger population than Taiwan.

Many of Taiwan's people work in factories built since the 1950s. A rapid buildup of industry has made Taiwan one of the world's top ten exporting nations. Its industries produce goods ranging from computers and chemicals to automobiles. Taiwan's other top exports are textiles, clothing, electronics, processed foods, and chemicals.

The Nationalists reformed Taiwan's system of land ownership by taking land from wealthy families and distributing it to peasants. This reform helped to boost farm production. Today nine out of ten Taiwanese farmers own their own land.

Taiwan's Status

If you had visited the United Nations in the 1950s and 1960s, you would have seen a delegate from Taiwan sitting in China's seat. At the time, strong backing from the United States, a close military ally, helped Taiwan hold its seat. When China bombarded the two small islands of Quemoy and Matsu under the control of the Nationalists in 1958, U.S. leaders promised to go to war, if necessary, to protect Taiwan. Tensions later cooled, and Beijing said that it would not use force to take over Taiwan. Nevertheless, occasional flurries of military activity on one side or the other kept soldiers on the alert.

Much has changed since then, however. In the 1970s, U.S. President Richard Nixon adopted a friendlier stance toward mainland China. He wanted China's help in ending the Vietnam War. In 1971, the United Nations voted to let the Communist government in Beijing have China's seat. As the decade ended, the United States opened diplomatic relations with Beijing—which meant downgrading U.S. relations with Taiwan.

In recent years, Taiwanese leaders have softened their hard-line stance against the mainland government. Taiwanese businesses have found eager customers in China. Each year, a million or more Taiwanese citizens visit China as tourists. What they find often surprises them. Said one visitor from Taiwan, "When we go back to China, it's another culture. I'm a foreigner in that country."

Declaration of Independence?

Despite years of separation from mainland China, Taiwan has never made an official claim for independence. To do so would mean abandoning the idea—supported by both sides—that Taiwan is still part of China. The Beijing government has said that it would not accept Taiwan's independence. With democratic growth in Taiwan, however, some Taiwanese have set up political parties that are **pro-independence.**

What other future might Taiwan have? Mainland China has proposed a "one country, two systems" plan. Under that arrangement, Taiwan would recognize the authority of the government in Beijing, but Beijing would guarantee Taiwan its separate economic and political ways. Most Taiwanese cherish their "unofficial" independence and their way of life and thus do not support that proposal.

LESSON 43 Making Inferences **157**

COMPREHENSION

1. What happened in Taiwan in 1949?

   _____

   _____

2. Explain the effect on Taiwan of the United States' formal recognition of the People's Republic of China in 1979.

   _____

   _____

3. Compare the government of Taiwan and the government of mainland China.

   _____

   _____

4. In order, what countries have controlled Taiwan?

   _____

   _____

5. Identify some of Taiwan's top exports.

   _____

   _____

6. How does Taiwan's economic output compare with mainland China's?

   _____

   _____

7. Draw a line to match the following words with their correct meanings.

   protectorate   **a.** became part of a larger state or country

   severed   **b.** a weak state protected by a stronger state

   annexed   **c.** broke off

CRITICAL THINKING

1. Identify each of the following statements by writing *fact* or *opinion* on the line.

   _____ **a.** The Portuguese mariners called Taiwan "beautiful island."

   _____ **b.** The Taiwanese have better lives than the mainland Chinese.

   _____ **c.** Taiwan is a democracy.

2. Look at the map on page 156. Explain why Taiwan was important to so many countries.

   _____

   _____

3. Describe how the redistribution of wealth in Taiwan helped the economy.

   _____

   _____

4. How would you describe the relationship between mainland China and Taiwan today?

   _____

   _____

5. Why do you think Taiwan wants to remain part of China?

   _____

   _____

6. Predict what mainland China would do if Taiwan officially declared its independence.

   _____

   _____

158 LESSON 43 Making Inferences

SKILL FOCUS: MAKING INFERENCES

1. Why do you think the United States supported Taiwan in the 1950s and 1960s? Use your knowledge of the period to make an educated guess.

   _____

   _____

2. Why do you think the United States extended its diplomatic support to the People's Republic of China in the 1970s?

   _____

   _____

3. What do you think Taiwanese visitors find so surprising on their visits to mainland China?

   _____

   _____

4. Reread the paragraph marked with a ✔. What can you infer about the difference in the standard of living in Taiwan and mainland China?

   _____

   _____

5. What can you infer about the Taiwanese attitude toward the government in Beijing? Give evidence to support your inference.

   _____

   _____

6. Find Quemoy and Matsu on the map on page 156. How do you think the Taiwanese felt when mainland China bombarded the islands?

   _____

   _____

Reading-Writing Connection

On a separate sheet of paper, write a paragraph in which you explain what an inference is. Be sure to use an example of any inference you made while reading "The 'Other China.'"

LESSON 43 Making Inferences

LESSON 44

Skill: Organizing Data

BACKGROUND INFORMATION

In "Specialists of the Canine World," notice how dogs are organized by breed. In the Bronze Age—about 4500 B.C.—there were only about five different types, or breeds, of dogs. Around 350 B.C., Aristotle listed a number of specific breeds known to the Greeks, including dogs used especially for guarding or for hunting various animals. During the Renaissance, dogs were also bred to serve as companions. The first dog show was held in 1859. Today hundreds of breeds of dogs appear at dog shows throughout the world.

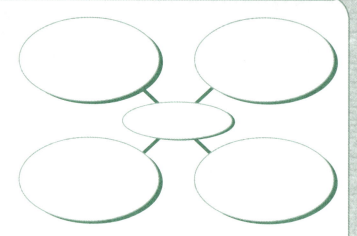

SKILL FOCUS: Organizing Data

When you are faced with a large amount of data, you need to organize it in a way that makes it manageable. One method of organizing data is **categorizing**, in which you place items in a group according to shared characteristics.

When categorizing items, follow these steps.

1. List the items you want to categorize.
2. Determine the traits that some items share.
3. Organize the items on your list into separate groups according to shared characteristics.

▶ Read the paragraph below. Write a category in the center circle of the Idea Web at the top of the next column. Write the items that belong to that category in the surrounding circles.

Some animals make perfect pets. Others are better as animals in the wild. Dogs and cats, for example, can usually survive on their own in the wild, but they get along with people and make good household animals. Wolves and mountain lions, on the other hand, do not make good pets. They are wild and usually cannot be tamed. Gerbils and hamsters can make good pets. Other members of the rodent family, such as squirrels and chipmunks, usually survive better in the wild.

CONTEXT CLUES: Examples

Sometimes in scientific writing, the surrounding text provides **examples** that enable you to figure out a word's meaning. As you read the following sentence, look for example context clues that help you know what the underlined word means.

*Working dogs earn their keep by guarding livestock from wolves, coyotes, and other **predators**.*

Wolves and coyotes are examples of predators from whom livestock must be protected. You can infer that *predators* are animals that threaten other animals.

▶ Read the sentence below. Circle the part of the sentence that provides an example for the meaning of the underlined word.

*From very early on, the dog was given a variety of **functions**, such as helping people to hunt, guarding their camps, and keeping their living quarters clean by eating bones, food scraps, and waste materials.*

In this selection, the words *frigid*, *vermin*, and *miniature* are underlined. As you read, look for examples within the text to learn their meanings.

Strategy Tip

As you read "Specialists of the Canine World," consider how the large amount of information about dogs is organized.

READING A SCIENCE SELECTION

Specialists of the Canine World

The domestic dog evolved from the wolf around 10,000 years ago and was put to use by humans to help them hunt, guard their camps, and keep their living quarters clean by eating bones, food scraps, and waste materials. Many different **breeds** of dog have been developed by humans to serve them in more and more precise ways. Today, there are roughly 400 separate breeds of dogs around the world, although most only serve as companions.

In the United States, 141 different breeds are officially recognized by the American Kennel Club (AKC), the nation's largest **purebred** dog registry.

The American Kennel Club assigns every dog breed to one of seven groups, based on the kind of work the breed was originally developed to perform. The following are the seven different groups.

Sporting Group

The dogs in this group were bred to go into woods and fields with hunters in search of game birds such as ducks and pheasants. Sporting dogs excel at finding game, holding steady while the game is shot, and then retrieving the game from either land or water. The most important qualities of a good sporting dog are that it be obedient and wait for instructions from the hunter and that it have what is called a "soft mouth," meaning that it will pick up and hold the bird gently so that the meat is not ruined for the table.

Sporting breeds are further classified according to one of three different hunting styles. Pointing breeds, such as the Irish and English setters, cover large distances and "point" when they locate a bird in the field. Retrievers, including the labrador and golden, specialize in bringing back many shot birds by remembering where they saw them fall. Spaniels, including the cocker and English springer, are smaller dogs whose job is to find a bird in heavy grass and "flush" it up into the air for the hunter to shoot.

Hounds Group

Hounds hunt game that has fur rather than feathers. Also hounds were bred to kill the game themselves rather than to wait for the hunter to shoot it. For this reason, hounds tend to be more independent and less obedient than sporting dogs.

Some hounds hunt by using their noses. Dogs that hunt this way are called scent hounds. Beagles, basset hounds, and dachshunds are popular scent hounds that were bred to hunt small game such as rabbits. Larger scent hounds are the foxhound and the coonhound. A well-known large scent hound used to find both lost children and escaped prisoners is the bloodhound. Scent hounds have a distinctive bark called a bay.

An English springer spaniel is paraded at the Annual Westminster Kennel Club Dog Show held in New York City.

LESSON 44 Organizing Data **161**

Working Group

Breeds in the working group are among the largest and most powerful of all dogs. Doberman pinschers, rottweilers, and Great Danes are used to guard people and property. Bernese mountain dogs and giant schnauzers pull carts. The Saint Bernard is famous for rescuing travelers lost in blizzards or buried under avalanches, while the Newfoundland excels in rescuing people—from the water. Some working dogs earn their keep by guarding livestock from wolves, coyotes, and other predators.

A subdivision of the working group is the sled dog, made up of the Siberian husky, the Alaskan malamute, and the Samoyed. These so-called nordic or spitz breeds, with their thick, bushy coats and tails that curl over their backs, were bred to pull sleds over snow and ice in <u>frigid</u> regions of the world.

Terrier Group

The name *terrier* comes from *terre*, the French word for "earth." The terrier breeds were bred to help farmers rid their lands of badgers, rats, muskrats, foxes, and other <u>vermin</u> that live in underground dens. Terriers as a group are feisty, noisy, and courageous. They need great courage to follow an animal underground, where the animal can and will turn and fight fiercely to defend its home and its young.

Terriers are classified as long-legged or short-legged. Among the long-legged terriers are the Airedale, the fox terrier, and the miniature schnauzer. Short-legged terriers include the West Highland white ("Westie") and the Scottish terrier ("Scottie"). Most terriers have wiry coats and thick, coarse hair on their heads and faces to protect them during close combat underground.

Herding Group

Dogs that are bred to help humans move their herds and flocks from one pasture to another belong to the herding group. They have strong instincts to work with livestock and are trained to respond from great distances to the farmer or rancher's whistle. A good herding dog can do the work of many humans on horseback.

Some herding breeds are called drovers. They drive cattle forward by nipping at their heels and keeping them moving in the right direction. Collies, Welsh corgis, and Old English sheepdogs are well-known cattle drovers. Breeds that work with sheep must keep the flock together without getting too close and frightening them. Sheep-herding breeds include the German shepherd, the Shetland sheepdog, and the border collie.

Non-Sporting Group

Breeds of dogs that just don't fit in any of the other groups are classified as non-sporting dogs. This does not mean that they were not originally bred to be useful. Many were, although over time their "jobs" went out of existence. The Dalmatian, for instance, was used to run alongside and protect horse-drawn coaches. The poodle was a water retriever, and the bulldog was used to torment bulls in a "sport" called bullbaiting.

Toy Group

The trait that toy breeds have in common is their tiny size. The largest toy, the pug, weighs about 15 pounds. The only "work" the toy breeds do is serve as lively and loving companions to their owners. Nevertheless, because they tend to be very alert and bark a lot, toys make excellent watchdogs. Because of their small size, they are especially well suited to living in small apartments.

Some toy breeds are the compact version of larger types of dogs found in other groups. The toy poodle is the same dog as the poodle, only smaller. The toy spaniels are <u>miniature</u> spaniels, although it is doubtful that one has ever flushed a bird. The Yorkshire terrier has been bred down from a larger hunting terrier, the Pomeranian from larger spitz breeds. Other toy breeds actually have been around longer than their larger counterparts. The miniature pinscher, for instance, is a much older breed than the Doberman.

Even though most dogs do not perform the tasks for which they were bred, some breed characteristics have adapted dogs to modern life. The soft mouths and gentle natures of the retrievers, for example, make them ideal family dogs. Scent hounds like beagles and dachshunds are small enough for apartment dwellers, as are the many short-legged terriers. Whatever their original purpose, dogs of every group still play a role in the lives of humans.

COMPREHENSION

1. Approximately how many breeds of dogs are there?

   _____

   _____

2. What is the difference between a pointer and a spaniel?

   _____

   _____

3. Why are hounds more independent and less obedient than sporting dogs?

   _____

   _____

4. What is the main difference between the Scottish terrier and the fox terrier?

   _____

   _____

5. What job did the Dalmatian once perform?

   _____

   _____

6. Complete each sentence by filling in the correct word from below.

   vermin   frigid   miniature

   a. Jan bought a _____ Liberty Bell at a gift store in Philadelphia.

   b. The farmer tried to get rid of the _____ that was destroying his crop.

   c. This room is becoming _____; please turn off the air conditioner!

CRITICAL THINKING

1. Why might a home be better protected by a Doberman pinscher than a Pomeranian?

   _____

   _____

2. Why wouldn't Saint Bernards, rottweilers, and Bernese mountain dogs be suitable pets for apartment dwellers?

   _____

   _____

3. Why do you think huskies, malamutes, and Samoyeds are found mainly in the North?

   _____

   _____

4. Explain why so many breeds of dog are now used only for companionship.

   _____

   _____

5. Describe traits in a dog that are most useful in helping people who are in danger. Give an example of a dog that "specializes" in each trait.

   _____

   _____

6. Evaluate which dogs are most likely to be found working at the jobs for which they were bred.

   _____

   _____

LESSON 44   Organizing Data   **163**

SKILL FOCUS: ORGANIZING DATA

1. List the seven major groups to which the American Kennel Club assigns every dog breed. Then next to each group, list the names of three breeds that belong to it.

   a. _____

   b. _____

   c. _____

   d. _____

   e. _____

   f. _____

   g. _____

2. What basis does the American Kennel Club use to group the breeds of dogs?
   _____

3. What traits do the dogs in the working group have in common?
   _____

4. What hunting styles are included in the sporting group?
   _____

5. What do dogs of the terrier group have in common?
   _____

6. What is the common trait of toy breeds?
   _____

7. What traits should a good apartment-dwelling dog have?
   _____

Reading-Writing Connection
On a separate sheet of paper, write a description of the traits that would characterize your perfect dog. Then determine which of the breeds discussed in the selection comes closest to your ideal dog.

164   LESSON 44   Organizing Data

LESSON 45

Skill: Understanding Theorems

BACKGROUND INFORMATION

In "Step by Step: The Binomial Theorem" (THEE ə rom), you will learn step by step how this algebraic theorem for expanded notation was developed. Theorems, along with postulates (PAHS chə ləts), are the building blocks of mathematics. Postulates, sometimes called axioms, are statements that are assumed to be true without proof, while theorems are statements that are proven using postulates and previously proven theorems.

SKILL FOCUS: Understanding Theorems

When you first learned math, you explored how numbers could be added, subtracted, multiplied, and divided. You learned how to solve simple equations, such as $4 \times 6 = 24$, or $96 - 40 = 56$. In algebra, you were introduced to variables, or unknowns. These unknowns appear as symbols or letters. For example, in the equation $x + 4 = 10$, the unknown is x. To figure out the answer, you apply the same math operations and numbers to both sides of the equation, until you isolate the unknown x.

$$x + 4 - 4 = 10 - 4$$
$$x + 0 = 6$$
$$x = 6$$

Using the number 6 in the equation, you see that it is true, so you have found the answer.

$$6 + 4 = 10$$

Algebra becomes a bit more complex when you have several variables and operations. For example, in the expression $x(5 + b)$, you have two operations (multiplication and addition) and two variables (x and b). The expression can be rewritten as the following.

$$x(5 + b) = 5x + bx$$

In algebra, a mathematical idea can be expressed as a formula. Numbers can be substituted for variables in the formula to find an answer. These formulas are the basis for **theorems**—explanations of mathematical concepts that have been proven to be true.

▶ Look at the math expressions below. Write the math operations that are used, and then write the expression in a different way.

1. $a(3 - 1)$

   Operations: _____

   Expression: _____

2. $x(y + 20)$

   Operations: _____

   Expression: _____

3. $x(x + y)$

   Operations: _____

   Expression: _____

WORD CLUES

When reading in math, it helps to look up unfamiliar words in your math textbook for very specific meanings. For example, in algebra, the word *term* can refer to an expression: $a + b$ can be a term. The word *variable* outside of math is an adjective that means "changing." A variable in math means "a letter that can have a different value."

Strategy Tip

"Step by Step: The Binomial Theorem" explores the binomial theorem and expanded notation. To understand the explanations, you will have to refer to the algebraic expressions used as examples. If necessary, go back and reread a section before moving on.

LESSON 45 Understanding Theorems **165**

(READING A MATHEMATICS SELECTION)

Step by Step: The Binomial Theorem

A **binomial** is a mathematical expression consisting of two terms connected by a plus or minus sign. A **theorem** is a proposition, or statement, that can be proven as true. A binomial theorem specifies the **expanded notation** of a binomial that is multiplied by itself. Expanded notation is a method of writing numbers or mathematical expressions in expanded form. The number or expression is simply rewritten in a form that identifies each term of the solution. For example, the number 592 can be rewritten as $(5 \times 100) + (9 \times 10) + (2 \times 1)$ because the 5 is in the hundreds place, the 9 is in the tens place, and the 2 is in the ones place.

The expression $a + b$ is a binomial expression because it has two terms—a and b—joined by a plus sign. The expression $(a + b)^n$ means that the binomial $a + b$ is multiplied by itself n number of times. If n is a large number, expanding the expression, or multiplying it by itself n times, can be a time-consuming task that requires a great deal of space. Mathematicians felt that there had to be a formula or theorem that would show the expansion of the binomial without having to go through the time-consuming steps of figuring it out.

In Simplest Terms

In order to figure out the formula, it helps to find a pattern. To do so, you could substitute n with different numbers in a logical fashion.

$$(a + b)^0 = 1$$
$$(a + b)^1 = 1a + 1b$$

In these two equations, the raised numbers 0 and 1 are exponents. Exponents tell how many times an expression must be multiplied by itself. Anything raised to the power of 0 is equal to 1. Anything raised to the power of 1 equals itself. The following shows why anything raised to the power of 1 is equal to itself.

$$(a + b)^1 = 1a + 1b = a + b$$

Note that in $(a + b)^1$, the raised number 1 is an exponent. In $1a + 1b$, however, the number 1 is not

raised: It is a **coefficient**. The coefficient is the number before the variable. It represents a multiplication expression: $1a$ equals 1 times a, or $1a = 1 \times a$. Anything multiplied by 1 equals itself.

$$(1 \times a) + (1 \times b) = (1a + 1b) = a + b$$

One Step Further

The expression $(a + b)^2$ means that the binomial $(a + b)$ is multiplied by itself; it is a factor two times.

$$(a + b)^2 = (a + b) \times (a + b) = (a + b)(a + b)$$

When multiplying two binomials, such as $(a + b)$ times $(a + b)$, you must multiply *each term* of the first binomial by *each term* of the second binomial, and then simplify by adding similar terms.

Step by step, you would do the following.

1. Multiply the first term of the first binomial (a) by the first term of the second binomial (a), resulting in a^2.

2. Multiply the first term of the first binomial (a) by the second term of the second binomial (b), resulting in ab.

3. Multiply the second term of the first binomial (b) by the first term of the second binomial (a), resulting in ba.

4. Multiply the second term of the first binomial (b) by the second term of the second binomial (b), resulting in b^2.

The answer would be $a^2 + ab + ba + b^2$. Since ab equals ba (a times b is equal to b times a), you can combine terms to simplify, leaving a final answer of $a^2 + 2ab + b^2$.

Therefore, in its expanded form, the expression $(a + b)^2$ is written as the following.

$$a^2 + 2ab + b^2$$

Placing a 1 in front of the a and in front of the b does not change their value. In the expression $1a^2 + 2ab + 1b^2$, the numbers 1 and 2 that appear before the variables are coefficients.

166   **LESSON 45**   Understanding Theorems

The Time-Consuming Task

The task of multiplying a binomial many times by itself can become time-consuming. Take the following examples.

$$(a + b)^3 = (a + b)(a + b)(a + b)$$
$$= a^3 + 3a^2b + 3ab^2 + b^3$$
$$(a + b)^4 = (a + b)(a + b)(a + b)(a + b)$$
$$= a^4 + 4a^3b + 6a^2b^2 + 4ab^3 + b^4$$

As you can see, as the exponents get larger, the expressions get longer and longer. These expressions—expressions with more than two terms—are called **polynomials**.

The question then arose: Was there a pattern that could explain the expansion of binomials, without having to go through the time-consuming task of multiplying them out?

Pascal's Triangle

Blaise Pascal (1623–1662) was a French mathematician. He explored many aspects of math, including probability and calculus. One of his most well-known discoveries was the pattern of coefficients in expanded notation. His system became known as **Pascal's triangle**.

To recognize Pascal's pattern, we can line up the expressions, from a 0 exponent to a 4 exponent.

$$(a + b)^0 = 1$$
$$(a + b)^1 = 1a + 1b$$
$$(a + b)^2 = 1a^2 + 2ab + 1b^2$$
$$(a + b)^3 = 1a^3 + 3a^2b + 3ab^2 + 1b^3$$
$$(a + b)^4 = 1a^4 + 4a^3b + 6a^2b^2 + 4ab^3 + 1b^4$$

Now arrange only the coefficients in a pyramid or triangular form. (Remember, the coefficient is the number before the variable.)

$$
\begin{array}{c}
1 \\
1 \quad 1 \\
1 \quad 2 \quad 1 \\
1 \quad 3 \quad 3 \quad 1 \\
1 \quad 4 \quad 6 \quad 4 \quad 1
\end{array}
$$

By setting up the numbers in this way, Pascal saw a way to figure out what the coefficients should be in each new row added to the bottom of the triangle.

Pascal discovered that each number in a row was equal to the sum of the two numbers above it in the previous row. For example, the middle number in row three is 2, which is also the sum of $1 + 1$ (the two numbers above it in the previous row). Similarly, the second number in row four is 3, which is also the sum of $1 + 2$ (the two numbers above it in the previous row.) Therefore the second number in the new bottom row should be below the 1 and 4, and should be equal to the sum of 1 and 4, which is 5. The third number should be the sum of 4 and 6. The fourth, fifth, and sixth numbers should be the sum of the numbers 6 and 4, 4 and 1, and 1 and 0, respectively.

The first and last numbers are always 1, so the sixth row of Pascal's triangle should be as follows.

$$1 \quad 5 \quad 10 \quad 10 \quad 5 \quad 1$$

Here it is as part of Pascal's triangle.

$$
\begin{array}{c}
1 \\
1 \quad 1 \\
1 \quad 2 \quad 1 \\
1 \quad 3 \quad 3 \quad 1 \\
1 \quad 4 \quad 6 \quad 4 \quad 1 \\
1 \quad 5 \quad 10 \quad 10 \quad 5 \quad 1
\end{array}
$$

Using the coefficients from Pascal's triangle, then, $(a + b)^5 = a^5 + 5a^4b + 10a^3b^2 + 10a^2b^3 + 5ab^4 + b^5$. (Note that the exponents also follow a pattern: They begin with the exponent that appears in the original polynomial, and they decrease by ones until they reach 2, and then increase by ones until they again reach the exponent that appears in the original polynomial.)

Even More Efficient

Sir Isaac Newton felt that, although Pascal's triangle worked, it was still too tedious. Newton, who was born in England in 1642, was a mathematician and philosopher. He is considered one of the most important scientists of all time. Among his greatest discoveries are the law of gravity, the development of calculus, and the discovery that white light is actually made up of the colors of the rainbow, or the spectrum.

Newton believed there had to be a formula for figuring out the coefficients without having to write out an entire Pascal triangle. For example, what if you wanted the expanded form of $(a + b)^{20}$? Should

LESSON 45 Understanding Theorems **167**

you have to sit down and write out all 21 rows of the triangle?

The Final Step

Newton decided there had to be a better way. The binomial theorem is the formula he devised. It appears below. Notice that the dots leading up to b^n indicate that additional terms would be included as needed until the variable a has an exponent with a value of 0 and b has an exponent with a value of n.

$$(a + b)^n = a^n + na^{n-1}b^1 + \frac{n(n-1)}{1(2)} a^{n-2}b^2$$
$$+ \cdots + b^n$$

For example, if the original polynomial was $(a + b)^4$, the binomial theorem would contain the following terms.

$$(a + b)^n = a^n + na^{n-1}b + \frac{n(n-1)}{1(2)} a^{n-2}b^2$$
$$+ \frac{n(n-1)(n-2)}{1(2)(3)} a^{n-3}b^3 + b^n$$

Notice that each denominator is the previous denominator multiplied by the next consecutive integer.

By substituting 4 for the value of n, we can solve the formula as below.

$$(a + b)^4 = a^4 + 4a^{(4-1)}b + \frac{4(4-1)}{1(2)} a^{(4-2)}b^2$$
$$+ \frac{4(4-1)(4-2)}{1(2)(3)} a^{(4-3)} b^3 + b^4$$
$$= a^4 + 4a^3b + \frac{4(3)}{2} a^2b^2$$
$$+ \frac{4(3)(2)}{1(6)} ab^3 + b^4$$
$$= a^4 + 4a^3b + \frac{12}{2} a^2b^2 + \frac{24}{6} ab^3 + b^4$$
$$= a^4 + 4a^3b + 6a^2b^2 + 4ab^3 + b^4$$
$$(a + b)^4 = a^4 + 4a^3b + 6a^2b^2 + 4ab^3 + b^4$$

You will recall that when no coefficient is shown, it is understood to be 1. Therefore the coefficient is 1 for the first term a^4 and for the last term b^4 in the answer above. If you look at Pascal's triangle and compare the coefficients, you'll recognize the same pattern of numbers: 1 4 6 4 1.

Newton's formula for the binomial theorem is important because by using it, you can figure out not only the coefficients, but also the exponents.

COMPREHENSION

1. In the following equation, which word identifies the number 2? $2x = 6$ Circle the correct answer.

   a. variable   **c.** exponent

   b. coefficient   **d.** term

2. In the following equation, which word identifies the letter n? $(a + b)^n$ Circle the correct answer.

   a. coefficient   **c.** exponent

   b. binomial   **d.** polynomial

3. What is the difference between a binomial expression and a polynomial expression?

   _____

   _____

4. Which of the following is an example of expanded notation? Circle the correct answer.

   a. $x + y = y + x$

   b. $2(x + y) = (x + y)^2$

   c. $(a + b) = (a + b) = 2(a + b)$

   d. $(a + b)^2 = a^2 + 2ab + b^2$

5. Write an example of each of the following.

   a. Binomial: _____

   _____

   b. Polynomial: _____

   _____

168   **LESSON 45**   Understanding Theorems

CRITICAL THINKING

1. How do you expand the term 4^5?

2. How do you expand the term y^3?

3. How do you expand the term $(2 + b)^2$?

4. How do you expand the term $(a + b)^2$?

SKILL FOCUS: UNDERSTANDING THEOREMS

1. Pascal's triangle is shown below for the coefficients up to $(a + b)^5$. What would the next row of coefficients be? Write them in the Pascal's triangle below.

    1
    1 1
    1 2 1
    1 3 3 1
    1 4 6 4 1
    1 5 10 10 5 1

    _____

2. What formula did Newton use to figure out the value of the exponents?

3. With an exponent of 6, what would the exponents be in the expanded notation?

4. Combine the coefficients from Pascal's triangle with the exponents from Newton's formula. Write the expanded notation for $(a + b)^6$.

5. State the expanded notation for $(a + b)^7$. Follow these steps.

    a. First determine the coefficients, using Pascal's triangle. Write the coefficients here.

    b. Next determine the exponents, using Newton's formula. Write the exponents here.

    c. Now write the expanded notation for $(a + b)^7$, using the numbers you calculated in steps a and b.

Reading-Writing Connection

Write a paragraph explaining which you feel more comfortable using—Pascal's triangle or Newton's formula. Be sure to support your opinion with an example of when you would use it.

LESSON 45 Understanding Theorems

LESSON 46

Skill: Comparing and Contrasting

When you read, the strategy of **comparing and contrasting** helps you better understand and organize information. For example, you can use this strategy to understand the similarities and differences between two historical figures, two scientific theories, or two characters in a novel or play. Noticing how two people, objects, or ideas are alike and different helps focus your attention on important facts about them. To help you "see" the similarities and differences, you can draw a Venn Diagram and write each fact in the appropriate section of the overlapping circles.

Read the following selection that describes hurricanes and tornadoes. Then complete the Venn Diagram on the page 171 to show how the two types of storms are alike and different.

Hurricanes and Tornadoes

A hurricane is a storm that forms over oceans in the tropics. It begins with a low-pressure area that creates winds that grow increasingly violent. These winds move at high speeds in a circle around the low-pressure center, which is called "the eye" of the storm. Hurricane winds can move at 74 to more than 155 miles (119 to more than 250 kilometers) per hour, although most hurricanes are at the low end of the range. In the Northern Hemisphere, the winds circle in a counterclockwise direction. In the Southern Hemisphere, they blow clockwise.

Inside the eye of the storm, the winds are still, but the sea is turbulent. The eye can cover 20 miles (32 kilometers), while the entire hurricane is often 300 miles (483 kilometers) in diameter. From the edge of the eye outward, heavy rains pour down and gale winds whip up the sea. Huge waves billow up. The winds also push water violently ahead, creating a storm tide along the shore. If a high tide meets the storm tide, the rapid rush of water can cause devastation on shore. The violent winds and heavy rains of the hurricane follow up the storm tide with more destruction of lives and property. Then as the hurricane moves across the land, its winds begin to slow down. The storm subsides into heavy rainfall, and the destruction ceases.

A tornado is also a violent wind storm, but it is much more concentrated in its damage. Most tornadoes are only 300 yards (275 meters) across. However, the winds can reach speeds of 300 or more miles (483 kilometers) per hour. In the Northern Hemisphere, the wind moves around the center of the storm in a counterclockwise direction. In the Southern Hemisphere, the winds move clockwise. Tornadoes occur most often on land, but they can also form at sea. Those tornadoes are known as "waterspouts." Although tornadoes form all over the world, they are most common in the Midwest and West, particularly in Kansas, Iowa, Texas, and Oklahoma.

A tornado often forms on a hot, moist, spring afternoon. A cloud becomes heavy and dark and begins to whirl and twist. Rain, hail, and lightning follow. A narrow column of whirling air that resembles a funnel reaches down from the cloud and touches the ground. On contact, great destruction occurs. Trees and buildings are blown down. People, animals, and objects fly through the air. Sometimes buildings explode because of the severe drop in air pressure. However, this violent destruction only lasts a very short time. The tornado can only destroy when it touches the ground, and this contact lasts for only 30 seconds. Unlike hurricanes, which can cover 300 miles (483 kilometers), tornadoes normally cover less than 16 miles (26 kilometers) before they are spent.

170 LESSON 46 Comparing and Contrasting

Below is a Venn Diagram that will help you compare and contrast two types of storms—hurricanes and tornadoes. In the overlapping section of the two circles, write how hurricanes and tornadoes are alike. In the remaining sections of the circles, write how they are different. The first item in each section is done for you.

DIFFERENT   **ALIKE**   **DIFFERENT**

Hurricane   Tornado

Forms over oceans in the tropics

Storms with heavy rain and high-speed winds

Can form over land or ocean; most common in Midwest and West

LESSON 46   Comparing and Contrasting   **171**

LESSON 47

Skill: Fallacies in Reasoning

Fallacies are mistakes in **reasoning**, or sound and logical thinking. Writers often use reasoning to prove that their arguments are right. When you are reading persuasive writing, such as advertisements, editorials, political speeches reported in the newspaper, or any arguments supporting a particular point of view, you must be careful to note whether the arguments are logical.

Watch out for these common types of fallacies in reasoning.

A. Too little evidence: Does the writer make a generalization based on too few instances? An example would be a letter to the editor from a person who sees teenagers acting in a rowdy way on a few occasions and then concludes that *all* teenagers are like that.

B. Wrong premise: What assumption does the writer use as the basis of his or her arguments? Below is the classic three-step way to reach a logical conclusion.

1. *Premise:* All fish that smell bad are unsafe to eat.

2. *Fact:* This fish smells bad.

3. *Logical Conclusion:* Therefore, this fish is unsafe to eat.

However, if the premise is wrong, the conclusion will be wrong, too. Read this example.

1. *False Premise:* All opera singers are temperamental.

2. *Fact:* Carla Cooper is an opera singer.

3. *Wrong Conclusion:* Therefore, Carla Cooper is temperamental.

C. Faulty cause-and-effect relationship: A very common mistake people make is to think that just because one thing happened after another, the first event is the cause of the second event. For example, a person might break a mirror. The next day, he falls and hurts his knee. He may believe that the broken mirror caused his fall.

Decide which of the above types of fallacies in reasoning was used in each of the following arguments. In the space provided, write *A*, *B*, or *C* to indicate the type of faulty logic used.

1. I've met some rich kids and they were very stuck-up. All rich kids are stuck-up. _____

2. Statistics show that a larger number of red cars are involved in accidents than cars of any other color. Therefore, it must be true that the red color causes cars to have accidents. _____

3. All ripe apples are sweet. This green apple is ripe. Therefore, it must be sweet. _____

4. My colds usually go away quickly after I eat garlic. Therefore, garlic cures colds. _____

5. There must be someone sick in the Hernandez family. I saw a car with a doctor's license plate parked in front of their house today. _____

6. Television makes people violent. Gerry watches a lot of television. Gerry must be a violent person. _____

7. Tanya Terrific, a supermodel, and Peter Pugnacious, a football star, were seen together at several parties. Therefore, they must be having a romance. _____

172 LESSON 47 Fallacies in Reasoning

LESSON 48

Skill: Etymology

One of the main features found in many dictionary entries is the origin and development of the entry word, or its **etymology**. This word history includes the earliest use of the word and any changes in form and meaning. It usually appears enclosed in brackets [ ] before or after the definition.

Tracing the pre-English source, etymologies indicate what language the word came from or whether the origin is unknown. To conserve space, lexicographers—makers of dictionaries—usually use **abbreviations** and **symbols** to indicate the language origin. These are usually explained at the beginning of the dictionary. Many words derive from Old English (**OE**) and Middle English (**ME**), which are earlier forms of English. Other words pass from one language to another, for example, from Latin (**L**), to Italian (**It**), to English. Other examples include **OHG** (Old High German), **Sp** (Spanish), **MF** (Middle French), and **Jp** (Japanese).

The etymology also gives the spelling and meaning of the word in that language. The English word may have the same meaning as or a different meaning from the word in the original language.

---

din • gy (din′ je) *adj.* **din • gi •er; -est** [origin unknown] (1736) **1** dirty; not bright or clean **2** shabby; dismal — **din • gi •ly** (–jə le) *adv.* — **din • gi • ness** (–je nəs) *n.*

ju • do (jud′ o) *n.* [Jp *judo* fr. *ju* weakness, gentleness + *do* art] (1889) a form of jujitsu that uses quick movement and leverage to throw an opponent — **judo • ist** (–o-əst, –əwəst)

ju • nior (jun′ y[ər]) *adj.* [L compar. of *juvenis* young — more at YOUNG] **1a** younger — written *jr.* after the name of a son with the same given name as his father: opposed to SENIOR **b** (1): youthful (2): designed for young people and esp. adolescents **c** of more recent date and therefore inferior or subordinate (<a ~ lien) **2** lower in rank (<– partners) **3** relating to the class of juniors at a high school or college (<the ~ prom)

mag • net (mag′ nət) *n.* [ME *magnete*, fr. MF, fr. L *magneti-*, *magnes*, fr. Gk *magnes* (*lithos*), stone of Magnesia, ancient city of Asia Minor] **1** a certain kind of material that has the property of attracting iron and producing a magnetic field external to itself; *specif:* a mass of iron, steel or alloy that has this property artifically imparted **2** a person or thing that attracts

me • sa (ma′ sa) *n.* [Sp lit. table, fr. L *mensa*] (1759) a flat-topped natural elevation usu. larger than a butte and smaller than a plateau; *also:* a broad terrace with steep side

were • wolf (wir′ -wulf, wəar′, -wer) *n. pl.* **were • wolves** (—wulvz) [ME, fr. OE *werwulf*, (akin to OHG *werwolf* werewolf), fr. *wer* man + *wulf* wolf — more at VIRILE, WOLF] a person changed into a wolf or capable of assuming a wolf's form

---

Use the sample dictionary entries shown above to answer the following questions.

1. What is the language of origin for *werewolf*? _____

2. What is the date of the first recorded use of *mesa* in English? _____

3. Which entry word derives from the name of an ancient place? _____

4. From what language does *judo* come? _____

5. Which word is a comparison of the Latin word for *young*? _____

6. What is the origin of the word *dingy*? _____

LESSON 48 Etymology **173**

LESSON 49

Skill: Comparing Car Ads

When you become responsible for your own transportation, you have many choices to make. One of those choices may be whether to purchase a new car, purchase a used car, or lease a car. Each of these choices requires a major financial commitment, so you need to consider the decision carefully.

Reading **car ads** in newspapers and magazines is a good place to start. Decide what general kind of car you want—how big it must be, how recently made, and so on. Think about the features (for example, dual air bags, cruise control, and CD/MP3 player) that you think the car must have. Find out about various cars' safety and repair records. Most of all, take stock of your finances to figure out what kind of monthly payment you can afford. (Remember, for example, that if you "lease to buy" a car, you will still have a balance to pay at the end of the lease payments.)

Compare these two car advertisements to see which choice will give you the most car for your money.

'07 Festival

PURCHASE FOR
$14,400
JUST $2,000 DOWN
was $17,250

TAKE A LOOK!
Power windows and locks
Air conditioning
Rear defroster
AM/FM/CD/MP3

32,167 miles
Very clean—
Stop in today!

'09 Nebula

Lease only **$189** /MONTH
NO MONEY DOWN!
63-month closed-end lease
Total payment $11,907
Option to buy at end of lease period

More Power Than the Blaster!
More Room Than the Classic!

Dual air bags
Power window/
locks/mirror
Air conditioning
AM/FM radio
Cruise control

Don't pass this up! Come in for a test drive!

174   LESSON 49   Comparing Car Ads

A. Use facts from the ads on page 174 to complete this chart.

	Car #1	Car #2
Name of Car		
Year of Make		
Kind of Transaction		
Amount of Down Payment		
Total Payment		
Own at End of Payment?		
Features:		
dual air bags		
air conditioning		
rear defroster		
power windows/locks		
power mirrors		
cruise control		
MP3 player		

B. Compare the ads as you complete each sentence.

1. The ad that compares its car to competitors is _____.

2. The _____ is two years older than the _____.

3. The Festival has already been driven _____ miles.

4. In terms of features, the Festival has a _____ and a

   _____; the Nebula does not.

5. The features that both cars have are _____ and _____

   and _____.

6. You might be more interested in the Nebula, however, if you wanted the options of

   _____, _____, and _____.

7. The total amount of the lease is calculated by multiplying _____

   by _____.

8. If you had been interested in the Festival before this ad appeared, you might have had

   to pay _____ more than the sale price shown here for it.

9. If you had only $500.00 for a down payment, you might be attracted to the

   _____ because _____.

10. If you were considering these two cars and payment plans, which would you
    choose, and why?

    _____

    _____

LESSON 49 Comparing Car Ads

CONTEXT CLUE WORDS

The following words are treated as context clue words in the lessons indicated. Each lesson provides instruction in a particular context clue type and includes an activity that requires you to use context clues to find word meanings. Context clue words appear in the literature, social studies, and science selections and are underlined or footnoted.

Word	Lesson
affluent	19
annexed	43
astride	11
capsules	20
cells	3
collaborate	42
commodities	20
competition	12
cytoplasm	3
dense	37
dispersed	27
diverged	35
forging	36
frigid	44
furthering	2
inherent	37
injustice	28
inordinate	19
intensity	1
iodine	29
irresistible	42
labor costs	20
laden	35
longevity	28
lubricant	21
luminosity	37
miniature	44
mitosis	3
nocturnal	42
oasis	10
oppressively	10
parapet	27
postures	1
predation	12
preserved	29
producers	12
projected	29
prophesied	19
protectorate	43
rejection	36
repercussions	36
resumed	10
reverence	1
saturated	21
secure	2
severed	43
stable	11
studded	2
suspension	21
terrain	11
threshed	27
trodden	35
unity	28
vermin	44

CONCEPT WORDS

In lessons that feature social studies, science, or mathematics selections, words that are unique to the content and whose meanings are important in the selection are treated as concept words. These words appear in boldface type and are often followed by a phonetic respelling and a definition.

Word	Lesson
abolition	36
absolute magnitude	37
absolute monarchy	36
anaphase	3
astrophysics	37
automatic constant	22
binomial	45
bisects	13
breeds	44
Bunsen burner	37
camera obscura	29
chromosomes	3
climate zones	11
coefficient	45
commensalism	12
Communist	43
congruent	13
connectives	38
consumers	12
contrapositive	38
converse	38
creoles	2
currencies	20
daguerreotype	29
daughter cells	3
decomposer	12
democracy	36
density	21
dependencies	2
desert climate	11
DNA	3
dynasty	43
economic withdrawal	28
ecosystem	12
energy pyramid	12
equations	4
equivalent	30
estimate	30
euro	20
expanded notation	45
exponents	22
expressions	4
factionalism	2
food chain	12
food web	12
formulas	4
free enterprise economy	43
frictional forces	21
genetic code	3
goods and services	20
gross domestic product	20
H-R diagram	37
human rights	28
hydrostatic pressure	21
hypothesis	38
industrialized	20
interphase	3
inverse	38
laws of heredity	3
mass	21
Mediterranean climate	11
mestizos	2
metaphase	3
monarchy	2
mulattoes	2
mutualism	12
Nationalist	43
negation	38
negative	29
nonviolence	28
nucleotides	3
order of operations	22
Pascal's triangle	45
parent cells	3
Parliament	36
perpendicular	13
polynomials	45
positive	29
power	22
prefecture	43
pro-independence	43
prophase	3
purebred	44
rates	30
republic	2
scientific calculators	22
solar light	37
specific gravity	21
spectroscopy	37
spectrum	37
standard of living	20
stellar spectrum	37
steppe climate	11
suzerainty	43
symbols	4
telophase	3
theorem	45
thermonuclear fusion reaction	37
tropical rain forest climate	11
tropical wet-and-dry climate	11
truth value	38
ultraviolet light	37
unconstitutional	28
variables	4
vertical climate	11
waves of light	29

176 Concept Words